greenwash

greenwash

BIG BRANDS AND CARBON SCAMS

GUY PEARSE

Black Inc.

Published by Black Inc.,
an imprint of Schwartz Media Pty Ltd
37–39 Langridge Street
Collingwood Vic 3066 Australia
email: enquiries@blackincbooks.com
http://www.blackincbooks.com

National Library of Australia Cataloguing-in-Publication entry

Pearse, Guy.
Greenwash : big brands and carbon scams / Guy Pearse.
ISBN: 9781863955751 (pbk.)
Includes index.
International business enterprises--Environmental aspects.
Industrial management--Environmental aspects. Environmental management.
Social responsibility of business. Deception.
658.408

Cover and book design by Peter Long
Typesetting by Duncan Blachford
Index by Geraldine Suter

Printed in Australia by Griffin Press an Accredited ISO AS/ NZS 14001:2004
Environmental Management System printer.

The paper this book is printed on is certified against the Forest Stewardship Council®
Standards. Griffin Press holds FSC chain of custody certification SGS-COC-005088.
FSC promotes environmentally responsible, socially beneficial and economically viable
management of the world's forests.

contents

For Wendy, Patrick and Harvey

introduction

Having spent most of my life trying to avoid advertising wherever possible, four years ago I decided to start collecting one particular type: that claiming certain products and the brands behind them are helping in the fight against climate change. But why? Why spend years immersed in green slogans, warm and fuzzy images of nature, and fine print?

In short, I wanted to discover whether the 'climate-friendly' revolution being advertised is real. Many consumers believe that the best way to contribute to the fight against climate change is through their wallets. Businesses around the world have seized the opportunity to cater to green-minded consumers – they recognise the value in being seen as more climate-friendly than the competition. Almost every major global brand has embarked on a campaign designed to persuade us that it is cutting its carbon footprint. Thus marketing, rather than politics, seems a more relevant window onto the issue of climate change for most people. We all know the brands, we've seen the advertisements, and many of us have made green purchases as a result of them. Many of us believe, or at least hope, that if enough of us choose similarly, it will have a big impact. Some of us like the idea of rewarding a company with our business for going green. But is the climate-friendly revolution really underway?

A great deal hinges on the answer – for governments, investors, environmental organisations, advertising agencies, people trying to do their bit through their purchases – and of course for the climate itself. As the world looks set to accommodate an extra 3 billion people this century, it's a question we need answered. And yet it is rarely even asked – the answer is generally assumed to be 'yes'.

So, are the world's biggest and greenest-looking brands actually reducing the carbon footprint of their products? Or is the proliferation of climate-friendly advertising mostly 'green-wash', a torrent of corporate spin that sounds impressive but conceals mostly business as usual? To find out the truth I've watched over 3000 TV commercials and collected around 4000 online, billboard, newspaper and magazine ads. To investigate the claims made in the advertising I've digested close to 750 company annual reports and sustainability reports. Immersing myself in this much corporate PR has felt as greasy as I imagine Morgan Spurlock felt after consuming McDonald's at every meal for a month for *Supersize Me*. At other times I've felt like Bear Grylls must when he squeezes the drinking water of last resort from an elephant dropping – forward progress means gritting one's teeth and pressing on. On the other hand, collecting this much material meant watching some very creative and funny ads, so there was a bit of fun involved too.

In *Greenwash*, I'll compare the climate-friendly campaigns and claims by the world's biggest brands with what they're actu-ally doing and with the carbon footprint of what they're selling. Whatever you spend your money on – cars, coffee, flights, pets, sport or even sex – you'll be in for some surprises as climate-friendly marketing goes on trial. Some of the most respected reputations will be exposed as the least warranted, and some of the less well regarded will emerge as worthy of our praise. Nothing is sacred and no-one is safe: not the Toyota Prius, not the World Wildlife Fund, not Richard Branson, not Oprah, not even Earth Hour.

We'll look beyond the carbon footprint of the individual products. After all, every ad for a product also advertises a brand. We'll also look beyond the carbon footprint of a brand's factories and corporate offices to consider all the emissions bound up in what it sells, since the emissions created to produce the raw materials and transport them to and from the factories are just as real. In most cases they are also many times greater than what is generated by the brand's own operations. So, we can't really know whether the total carbon footprint is falling unless we factor in supply chain emissions and those generated when people use the product. If we ignore these, as many 'green' brands want us to, 90 per cent of the carbon footprint of a brand's products might well disappear into an emissions equivalent of the Bermuda Triangle.

There is of course a great deal more to being 'green' as a company than dealing with greenhouse gas emissions alone. I don't for a moment seek to downplay the importance of other environmental challenges. Nor is the aim here to demonise big business or overlook the positive steps that many companies are making. I don't underestimate the challenge that companies face as they try to make large cuts in their carbon footprints, while remaining profitable and competitive. That said, big brands have an obligation to level with the public, both about the scale of the challenge they face and about the extent of their progress and ambition. If the overall carbon footprint of the products being sold by a company is still rising, and if the company's plans seem unlikely to change that, then it's disingenuous for a brand to pretend that it's climate-friendly.

The amount of corporate greenwash out there is vast. Think of this book as a walk along a beach strewn with the advertising industry's greenest flotsam and jetsam. This is just one of many beaches, though, so many greenwashing companies, brands, products and services are not covered here. Even so, we'll emerge with a clear answer on whether companies are really becoming climate-friendly or mostly greenwashing, and whether the revolution being advertised is real. We'll also see past the seductive branding and spin to confront the uncomfortable truths that lie behind them. Consumers will come away from *Greenwash* better equipped to pick the truly climate-friendly businesses, and help others (not least our political leaders) to be less susceptible to greenwashers and their techniques. The way I see it, the more people who learn the tricks of the greenwashing trade, the less effective these tricks will be.

banks

'Stroke him', says the online HSBC ad. 'Go on. He won't bite.' You move your cursor over the image of the polar bear. The virtual bear then rolls around as if being tickled by your intervention. 'Want to play a part in his future? Help us protect his world today' by clicking again, says the ad, and sends you to a site with tips on what you can do to cut your carbon footprint. There are also links to show you that the bank is doing much more than its fair share to rein in climate change. But now the bear has gone; the ticklish fun is over. He has served his purpose, and the bank has you where it wants you.

We're told that way back in 2005, HSBC was the first major bank to become carbon-neutral. Apparently it's now reducing its energy consumption and business travel, buying 'green' electricity where available and offsetting any remaining carbon dioxide emissions. Since 2006 HSBC has had a 'Carbon Finance Strategy' to support 'clean technologies and non-fossil fuel energy solutions'. It's spending $100 million 'partnering with four world-class environmental charities to launch a ground-breaking five-year global programme to inspire action by individuals, businesses and governments worldwide'. The company's ranking on the Dow Jones Sustainability Index is trotted out as evidence of its place among the environmental vanguard of big business. Quotes from the CEO, going back nearly a decade, stress the importance of taking 'early action to reduce the impacts we are having on our fragile planet'.

Not everyone wants to tickle polar bears, so HSBC uses a variety of methods to reach you with its climate-friendly messages. In Hong Kong in 2008, it released a green credit card that 'complements the Bank's unwavering commitment to protect the environment'. The card featured a big G on the side, and for each transaction a small sum would be donated to environmental projects in the Hong Kong region. Celebrity environmentalist Leonardo DiCaprio flew over to launch the card. Huge billboards featured hedges and other greenery cut into the shape of 'g' for green. The clear message: if you sign up for a green card, you'll be helping Leo and HSBC to fight climate change.

HSBC's polished sustainability pitch makes it look as though a progressive big business is leading while government is procrastinating. The bank points to annual emissions of just 831,642 tonnes, all of them offset. Yet what many observers may not have considered is what the bank is doing beyond its in-house initiatives, sustainability report, slick websites and marketing. After all, the core activity of this $101 billion* company is investing in and lending billions of dollars to large corporations. So, the emissions associated with HSBC's *investments* are where the real carbon is to be found.

Take HSBC's stake in the mining giant Rio Tinto, one of the world's largest coal exporters. Rio Tinto's carbon footprint,

---

*   Unless otherwise stated, all references to money are in US dollars; and greenhouse gas figures are given in metric tonnes of carbon dioxide equivalent, where tonnes of different greenhouse gases are converted into the equivalent number of tonnes of carbon dioxide based on their global warming potential (GWP).

including what is generated when its coal is burnt, is nearly a billion tonnes of carbon dioxide annually. HSBC's 20 per cent stake in Rio Tinto Limited (the Australian-listed part of the dual-listed entity) does over fifty times more harm than HSBC's carbon-neutrality does good. HSBC isn't responsible for Rio Tinto's carbon footprint, of course, but its large stake in it could hardly be less consistent with the climate-friendly image the bank has spent so much effort crafting. Each year, with funds directed its way by HSBC, Rio Tinto is increasing its coal production, and the carbon footprint of that coal is growing by vastly more emissions than the bank is offsetting. In 2011, around the time when HSBC was hosting the 'Business Summit on Climate Leadership', Rio Tinto was using HSBC money to buy new coal projects in Mozambique. These additions *alone* will add another 67–80 million tonnes of carbon dioxide annually to global emissions. Rio Tinto is similarly expanding its number of coal mines in Australia, and it's searching for new coal opportunities from Mongolia to Namibia. Beyond Rio Tinto, HSBC owns large stakes in a host of big-emitting fossil fuel companies – 17 per cent of Woodside, 11.5 per cent of Caltex, 20 per cent of Oil Search.

As well as owning stakes in such companies, HSBC's global research team routinely spruiks coal and oil companies as good investments. Quite how this 'facilitates the transition towards a low-carbon economy via banking products and services' is a mystery. As is HSBC's heavy involvement in raising money for new projects. As a report co-published by Friends of the Earth (Scotland) found, HSBC provided over $10 billion between 2006 and 2008 to companies that are engaged in either the extraction or combustion of coal. This was around the same time as we were being asked to help protect the fun-loving polar bear's environment.

It's a similar story at other major banks, including the Bank of America (BOA), which not so long ago announced that it 'will phase out financing of companies whose predominant method of extracting coal is through mountain top removal' (MTR). The odium attached to MTR coal mining in Appalachia had increased to such an extent that the return on investment was apparently no longer worth the political flak. In the wake of BOA's announcement, the priceless kudos flooded in, with many environmentalists pointing to the decision as proof that big business was backing away from dirty energy.

To help green its brand, BOA also launched a green credit card of its own. The Brighter Planet™ credit card, emblazoned with green hues and a picture of planet Earth, was a 'practical and effective' way for its customers to combat climate change, and over 200,000 Brighter Planet™ cardholders have saved an estimated 105,000 tonnes of carbon dioxide equivalent. Meanwhile, around 4000 BOA staff bought hybrid cars, each receiving $3000 from their employer and saving a tonne of carbon dioxide equivalent annually. It's all part of 'the bank's 10 year, $20 billion environmental commitment', which BOA says saw the bank's total emissions cut by 7.5 per cent in 2010 alone. It sure sounds impressive.

But there's no way to know for sure how climate-friendly BOA is without factoring in the emissions being generated by the bank's investments. Notwithstanding its policy against MTR mining, BOA remains deeply enmeshed with fossil fuel production and use. The Rainforest Action Network estimates that BOA invested $4.3 billion in new coal projects in 2009–10. It's a major investor in the two largest US coal producers – Peabody Energy and Arch Coal – and through the latter, it has a stake in a proposal to export 72 million tonnes of coal to Asia

– equivalent to a 75 per cent increase in annual US coal exports. That coal alone will generate 100 times the emissions of BOA's worldwide operations, and all but negate the benefit of lower rates of coal use achieved within the United States in recent years. It's more than 2000 times the emissions saved by those 200,000 Brighter Planet cardholders, whose efforts at combating climate change suddenly look much less effective. It would wipe out the annual contribution of those 4000 hybrid-driving BOA staff in eleven minutes.

As well as funding new ports and mines for the rapid expansion of US coal exports, BOA is still keen to fund new coal-fired power. It is also among the largest lenders to tar sands projects – one of the most emissions-intensive forms of energy available – in company with other banks that announced plans to exit MTR coal mining, including Citibank, JPMorgan Chase, Wells Fargo, Credit Suisse and Morgan Stanley. Moreover, a few years after the much-promoted announcement, BOA is quietly continuing to finance MTR. Remember that qualifying phrase about the 'predominant method of extracting coal'? So long as companies pass that test, BOA's door is still wide open. Under the new policy the bank could not have funded Massey Energy – one of the world's largest MTR coal miners. However, when Massey was swallowed in 2011 by Alpha Natural Resources, a more broadly focused coal miner which BOA does fund, the bank was suddenly able to justify funding the United States' largest MTR operation. Indeed, it's estimated by the Rainforest Action Network that BOA still underwrites loans to companies responsible for 40 per cent of MTR coal mined in the United States in 2010. This mocks the company's Bank Better, Live Greener™ slogan and the CEO's claim that, 'At Bank of America, we are helping to create a more sustainable economy for future generations'.

In Australia, the major banks are guilty of the same hypocrisy, busily promoting their climate-friendly credentials while simultaneously funding a coal and gas rush that by 2020 could add more carbon dioxide than everything currently sold by BP, Chevron and ConocoPhillips put together. Toyota Priuses were branded with National Australia Bank (NAB) livery and the words 'Banking on a cleaner future'. The bank declared all its brands 'sustainable businesses' and announced that it would be carbon-neutral by 2010. NAB said it would cut the emissions associated with its operations to zero – by improving energy efficiency, buying up to 10 per cent green energy, buying hybrid vehicles and offsetting the rest. Even the credit cards that NAB issued would be made with carbon-neutral plastic. This sounds thorough but these assurances gloss over the reality that NAB's biggest impact on climate change by far does not come from the 790 branches and 158 business banking centres it had in Australia, its corporate headquarters or its offshore businesses, but from its investments.

In 2007, after NAB announced its intention to become carbon-neutral, it became a major shareholder in Centennial Coal, then owner of Anvil Hill coal mine. At the time, this was the largest new coal mine ever proposed in Australia. At full production, its coal will generate around 28 million tonnes of carbon dioxide annually – roughly 136 times as much as the bank is offsetting to justify its carbon-neutral tag. And that's just one project. The NAB has billions of dollars invested in coal mining in Australia and elsewhere, as well as in coal-fired power stations and other emissions-intensive enterprises. Even a cursory assessment shows that these NAB investments will do thousands of times as much harm as the bank's climate-friendly push does good. The claims that NAB is 'committed to supporting the transition to a low carbon economy' would be embarrassing but for the sad reality that the banking sector worldwide is engaged in the same charade.

Go to Barclays Bank's website, and you'll find a lament that 'Mt Kilimanjaro's ice fields may disappear by 2020'. There's lots of detail about how Barclays funds 'Solar Aid' in Kenya, works with the World Wildlife Fund and sponsored the first carbon-neutral professional basketball game. There's a carbon-neutral Breathe™ debit card. Once again there's the earnest claim, 'We not only take proactive steps to reduce the direct impact of our own operations on the environment, we also recognise that we have a greater impact through our lending and investment activities'. What you won't find anywhere, however, is Barclays disclosing its vast investments in fossil fuels. No mention that among the world's banks Barclays was the second-biggest financier of coal-fired power stations between 2005 and 2011. According to a study by BankTrack, Barclays poured over €11.5 billion in project finance and raised capital into coal-fired electricity and coal mining over that period. It's a spectacular double standard, carefully played down.

The same scene plays out with the Royal Bank of Canada (RBC). It sponsored a carbon-neutral 2010 Winter Olympics torch relay by buying 500 tonnes worth of carbon offsets. According to the bank, 'RBC's decision to make the longest Olympic Torch Relay in history carbon-neutral was an easy one'. Certainly, it would have been a much easier decision than, say, neutralising the emissions generated by the tar sands projects it finances. At the same time that RBC was basking in the carbon-neutral warmth of the Olympic torch flame, the bank was the largest underwriter of credit to tar sands companies. Presumably, RBC's decision to power 124 bank branches with certified green power was also an 'easy one' – much easier than not financing new coal-fired power stations and coal mines. The RBC's own emissions are a relative cinch compared with these projects. Coalspur's plans to build the largest thermal export coal mine in North America will result in a carbon footprint more than 100 times greater than that of RBC. Yet playing a lead role in raising capital for the mine and others like it seems to have been an 'easy one' too, for a bank that's looking anything but neutral on carbon.

Everywhere you look, bank windows are dressed the same way: lofty rhetoric from banking industry executives; in-house initiatives like green-powered branches, carbon offsets and glossy reports; conspicuous 'consumer-facing' products, including green credit cards, green mortgages and electronic bank statements; collaborations with business-friendly environmental groups like the World Wildlife Fund, the Nature Conservancy, Conservation International and the Climate Group; and enthusiastic participation in Earth Hour, Earth Day and World Environment Day. Some banks publish a long list of the clean energy projects they've financed (the sort of list they wouldn't dare release detailing their fossil fuel investments), but most keep it vague and perhaps mention that they are a signatory to the international 'Climate Principles' or the US 'Carbon Principles'.

Another obligatory feature is to rattle off accolades such as positive ratings on the Dow Jones Sustainability Index, the FTSE4Good Index or the Carbon Disclosure Project Leadership Index. But these types of indexes are also not always what they seem. Some are based on 'best in category' criteria, which in certain emissions-intensive industries means something like the 'best of a very bad lot'. Some don't examine whether environmental impacts are actually rising or falling, but simply whether companies tick procedural boxes associated with improvement: adopting climate change policies, publishing sustainability reports, submitting returns, etc. HSBC, BOA, RBC and NAB are all among the 'leaders' of the FTSE4Good and Dow Jones Sustainability indexes, and the Carbon Disclosure Project. These indexes have become another way for big brands to avert regulation by creating an illusion of transparency and improvement.

It's emblematic that the World Bank, whose investment principles spawned those now promoted by the banking industry, is greenwashing its own support for expanding fossil fuel use. For all its talk about 'contributing to a global solution' on climate change, the World Bank is investing in new coal-fired power stations from India to South Africa to Chile. Other publicly funded banks, such as the US Export-Import Bank and the European Bank for Reconstruction and Development, are doing much the same. This is also true of many sovereign wealth funds managed by publicly owned banks from Singapore to China to Saudi Arabia. Even the Norges Bank, which manages the sovereign wealth fund of Norway and is reputedly subject to impeccable ethical and environmental investment guidelines, deeply invests in fossil fuel companies like BP and Shell and coal-heavy fund managers like BlackRock (which, fittingly, recently bought a licence to promote the Dow Jones Sustainability Index).

The big banks would argue that they're cutting, and in some cases offsetting, their operational emissions, implementing many worthwhile projects and expressing the right sentiments. Of their large investments in emissions-intensive activity, they would probably say that they can't be blamed for servicing demand for capital and credit where the economic incentives drive it. But it's not clear that economic incentives *do* force banks to stay heavily invested in the big polluters. Their portfolios are sufficiently broad to prosper from a rapid transition to a clean energy economy. As RBC, for example, concedes, 'RBC has a diversified portfolio and the majority of our clients will not be impacted by future climate change regulations'. Indeed, RBC could offset all its operations for around $4 million – a mere 0.12 per cent of its first-half profit in 2011.

There are even a few banks demonstrating that you don't need to fund the fossil fuel business to be profitable. The Netherlands-based Triodos Bank has the obligatory eco visa card, but, unlike most banks, Triodos uses 100 per cent renewable electricity for its operations and offsets the remaining emissions. The biggest difference, though, is that 'Triodos Bank doesn't finance fossil fuel projects ... because of its negative impact on human health and the environment'. Friends of the Earth estimates that shifting a €10,000 deposit from ABN Amro (which has some of the most emissions-intensive investment portfolios) to Triodos saves as much carbon dioxide as not driving for six months. This is in such stark contrast to most of its competition in the banking sector that somehow it's easier to take this bank's eco credit card and 'Welcome to Sustainable Banking' branding seriously. You might even want to stroke a polar bear in a Triodos ad – except banks like Triodos don't seem to need such gimmicks.

beer

Let's imagine the scene. It's the marketing meeting at Tuborg in late 2009, and with the Copenhagen climate conference around the corner, everyone is going green. 'Ideas, people!' says the boss. 'Tuborg Green comes in a green bottle with a green name, but we need to look even greener. Who's got something?' A bright spark offers, 'How about we sponsor a carbon-neutral swimming pool at the Roskilde music festival? We can make people ride on a bike to generate energy before they're allowed in'. The idea was probably pitched as a swimming pool rather than a toilet, but let's face it, kids will be kids – especially kids with a belly full of Tuborg beer at a four-day rock festival. The carbon-neutral Tuborg Green Pool went ahead at Roskilde 2010, offering patrons some welcome 'relief'. Before entering the 512,000-litre pool, which was in the shape of Tuborg's logo, swimmers spent some time on the exercise bike, greenwashing a beer brand.

This is the common trick for marketing beer as climate-friendly: stick to gimmicks and awareness raising, and hope some green vibes rub off on the brand. Tuborg is an expert. In 2009, also at Roskilde, it sponsored a carbon-neutral Ferris wheel, and in 2011 it came up with an 'eco-friendly' aerial cable-way, partly powered by solar panels and rapeseed oil. The price

of admission to the cableway was a minimum of ten empty cans
for recycling. Let's set aside the self-serving nature of that price,
and the wisdom of encouraging young people to drink ten cans
before the ride (tragically, one woman fell to her death from the
cableway). From a marketing standpoint, it's hard not to marvel
at the way Tuborg has used Roskilde to appear green without
any reference to whether the carbon footprint of its products is
rising or falling.

Another way to achieve this result is to help consumers
make their own green statement, as Heineken did. In 2009, the
company started making eco-friendly canvas shopping bags by
recycling its old billboards in Puerto Rico. These bags, sporting
the slogan 'Green is the New Black' next to the company's logo,
were then sold on the Heineken website. The company wasn't
making any specific claim, but the clear implication was that
Heineken was going green. That implication was then spread far
and wide by shoppers – as the ad agency involved (JWT) says
proudly, 'Consumers become a walking billboard for Heineken'.
Yet when you delve into Heineken's sustainability and annual
reports, there's no indication that 'Green is the New Black'.
There's no 'green beer', no major switch to renewable energy, no
large purchases of carbon offsets. What's more, Heineken's operational emissions are increasing due to acquisitions and expanded
production, and that's without considering the carbon footprint
of the ingredients used to make its products. Of those ingredients,
the company says, 'We have no emissions data'. The 'Green is the
New Black' bag is a deft way of disguising this reality – it makes a
positive link between a green message and Heineken's brand
without making any specific claim about the beer.

Other beer brands with no green claim to make sometimes
go ahead and make one anyway. In 2007 Coopers, a brewer in

South Australia, started marketing its products with the slogan 'big beer – tiny footprint'. In ads placed in green lifestyle magazines, Coopers said it was making 'Australia's greenest beer' and that it was taking 'every step possible to ensure our beers have the least impact on the environment'. But when these claims were investigated by the Australian Competition and Consumer Commission, it emerged that there was nothing especially climate-friendly about Coopers' products, and some of its competitors were actually doing more to reduce their footprint, such as going carbon-neutral. Most surprising of all, Coopers hadn't even measured its carbon footprint before making the 'tiny footprint' claim. The ads were soon pulled.

A more common, and successful, approach is for a company with no intention of making its *whole* operation climate-friendly to green up just one of its many beers – or, for a multinational corporation, one of its microbrewery brands. Buying enough carbon offsets to market that particular beer or subsidiary as carbon-neutral is the easiest method. Cascade Pure (initially sold as Cascade Green) has been perhaps the most aggressively marketed 'green beer' in Australia. It featured a green logo, a 'Global Cooling' slogan and the words '100% Carbon Offset'. The beer got its own website as well, complete with forest noises to relax you as you read what the brewery was doing to reduce its carbon footprint. According to the company, all the emissions associated with the beer were offset, covering 'the full life cycle of the product – from harvesting the ingredients, to consumption and advertising'. The advertising even included billboard ads planted with living green shrubbery so that the wording on the sign was gradually reclaimed by nature.

The picture changed when you looked behind the greenery. Cascade Green is a tiny part of the Foster's beer, wine and spirits empire, yet Foster's eagerly used Cascade Green as evidence of the larger brand's climate friendliness. Cascade Green was one of the things the Foster's CEO mentioned in his letter introducing the 2009 Foster's sustainability report. The report cites the product as evidence of the company's efforts to 'promote a sustainable future', saying that through Cascade Green, Foster's is 'making it easier for beer drinkers to make a greener choice'. In its 2010 return to the Carbon Disclosure Project, the company said 'Foster's has explored climate-related products in the form of 100% offset beer – Cascade Green'. This is a classic example of a large corporation receiving a reflected green glow from one of its brands. Foster's makes over seventy beers (plus many other products), and the Cascade Green offsets accounted for less than 1 per cent of the emissions of these products. So while Cascade markets itself as 'the Brewery that gives back', very little is being given back in carbon terms by the company's owners.

Some brewing multinationals go well beyond 'one green beer', mixing a cocktail of spin, data and documentation that is all but indigestible to consumers. This dissuades people from digging too deeply, but leaves the impression that the company is on the right track. Whether it's SAB Miller (which now owns Foster's), Carlsberg (which owns Tuborg), Anheuser-Busch or Heineken, it's as if they're following the same template: glossy sustainability reports printed on carbon-neutral paper, breathless rhetoric about the importance of climate change, pledges to do the right thing, claims that emissions are falling, and limelight for the isolated instances of breweries powered in part by renewable energy. SAB Miller's response is fairly typical. The company says it's 'committed to sustainable development, from the grain that is a vital ingredient in our beers to the glass that holds the finished product for our consumers'. It cut its annual *operational* emissions by 450,000 tonnes between 2008 and 2011. Based on the figures that SAB Miller makes public, this looks like an unqualified success: a global company bucking the trend and cutting its carbon footprint by 16 per cent in three years.

But we're not being given the full picture by SAB Miller. Like the majority of multinationals in the consumer staples sector, most of the carbon footprint of SAB Miller's products is not generated by the brewing operations. It's tied up in the supply chain, the purchased goods and services – everything from cultivating hops, barley and various other ingredients in the beer to the raw materials used for packaging, and transporting these to, and ultimately from, the breweries. In spite of its 'grain to glass' commitment to sustainability, SAB Miller reports a tiny fraction of these emissions publicly. However, if we look at food and beverage companies that do report supply chain emissions, such as Kraft, we find that these emissions are over ten times greater than those generated by the company's operations. As production grows, so too do these emissions. Since 2004, SAB Miller's annual lager production volume has increased by roughly 60 per cent.

We catch just a glimpse of the consequences when SAB Miller admits that its transportation and distribution emissions rose by 19 per cent in 2011 in part due to 'production volume increase'. That increase alone almost wipes out the operational emissions saved by the company in 2011. But the supply chain emissions *not* made public are far more significant. If we conservatively assume that the carbon footprint of SAB Miller's supply chain is only over five times its operational emissions, it comes to around 12 million tonnes a year. If these emissions increase by 5 per cent annually – the rate of SAB Miller's recent production growth – then the supply chain is adding another 600,000 tonnes of greenhouse pollution annually that the company doesn't acknowledge. For roughly every tonne that the company saves in its own operations, perhaps four times that amount is added to the supply chain by the increased production. It's only by ignoring these emissions that SAB Miller can pretend that their carbon footprint is shrinking. If consumers were aware of the supply chain emissions, it's likely that SAB Miller would have a much tougher time getting away with vague statements such as: 'We're looking at using better measurement systems and investigating new technologies ... we're considering renewable technologies ... we will seek to switch to cleaner fossil fuels over time. We're monitoring developments in this area'. While they're busy looking, investigating, considering, seeking to switch over time and monitoring, some small-fry companies are 'doing'.

Eel River Brewing Company in California is the first certified organic brewery in the United States, and it gets all the power it needs to make its beer from a renewable source. The energy comes from waste timber from a miller nearby, and the brewery itself is housed in a closed-down old-growth timber mill. The timber waste is ultimately carbon-neutral because the trees absorb as much carbon when they grow as is emitted when the waste is burnt. Most of the ingredients also come from nearby, and much of the waste is used to feed cattle that produce the organic beef and cheese served in the company's restaurant, bar and beer garden complex on site. Like Cascade, Eel River has a 'green beer'. In 2011, it released a limited amount of 'Earth Thirst Double IPA', to help promote Earth Day. Part of the proceeds were donated to the California Certified Organic Farmers Association. The big difference here is that at Eel River all of the beer is made with 100 per cent renewable energy, a large step Cascade's owner shows no sign of taking. So, unlike SAB Miller, Eel River isn't using one green beer to prove its climate friendliness – it has no need.

Not far down the road from Eel River, in Boonville, California, is the Anderson Valley Brewing Company. It produces beer in similar quantities, selling 'Solar Powered Beer' – a reference to the solar panels installed in 2006 that provide 40 per cent of the brewery's energy needs. For a European example, there's Nørrebro Bryghus brewery in Copenhagen, which produced the first carbon-neutral Danish beer in 2009. To some, releasing Globe Ale in the lead-up to the Copenhagen climate conference may have seemed opportunistic, but the brewer has since made some impressive efforts to reduce the carbon footprint of its own operations and completely offset its entire beer range, the brewery restaurant and even its website. The company has also gone beyond the brewing operation and offset the supply chain and product use.

These small brewers aren't perfect. Eel River benefits from the fact that biomass power is on hand locally, powering the whole community; Anderson gets only 40 per cent of its energy from the panels, so the 'Solar Powered Beer' marketing may be a stretch. The Nørrebro Bryghus brewery doesn't have much publicly available information about its offsets. Even so, what these companies have demonstrated – and it's their lesson for the big multinationals – is that taking a few big steps goes a long way. Going 40 per cent solar, 100 per cent biomass or 100 per cent carbon-neutral (including all those supply chain emissions the big brewers ignore) proves that doing something meaningful to reduce the carbon footprint is a viable alternative to spending millions of dollars on gimmicks and spin.

big box grocery and retail

Put yourself in its shoes. You're Walmart, the world's biggest, boxiest retailing giant. Your 10,130 stores already cover 100 square kilometres and you're growing by over 10 per cent each year. In 2011 you added another 1160 stores, mostly outside the United States. About every eight hours, another store is added, and each one has a carbon footprint roughly equivalent to that of 165 homes. Your emissions are increasing as far as the eye can see. It's a no-brainer to make your response to climate change all about your suppliers and your customers. Get them to reduce *their* carbon footprint, and then claim the credit as if the cuts are your own.

In early 2005, Walmart president and CEO Lee Scott began to worry about the world his grand-daughter might inherit. Soon afterwards, he announced three *aspirational* goals for Walmart: to use 100 per cent renewable energy; to create zero waste; and to 'sell products that sustain our resources and environment'. Naturally, a new company logo followed – gone was the iconic star with 'Wal' on one side and 'Mart' on the other. What had once looked vaguely patriotic now looked decidedly environmental: an ambiguous yellow symbol, which could signify anything from a sunflower to the sun to a wind turbine. Then the marketing blitz began, with the help of a former Sierra Club president turned consultant, Adam Werbach.

Some Walmart TV commercials hint strongly that the company is well on its way to achieving that aspirational goal of 100 per cent renewable power. With the spin of a hand the Walmart logo becomes a collection of wind turbines, from which we go straight to a US map covered in spinning Walmart logos. The voiceover tells us, 'We're committed to one day powering every one of our stores in America with 100 per cent renewable energy'. It explains that the company is designing stores that are 20 per cent more energy-efficient. Another ad features a Walmart executive standing next to wind turbines in Texas explaining how using wind power helps him keep Walmart's prices lower. It concludes with the top of the company's windmill logo appearing above the executive's head like a golden halo.

Have a closer look at Walmart, however, and the halo quickly fades. Though the company says 'we've achieved a 12.74 per cent absolute reduction in greenhouse gas emissions', this excludes stores added since 2005. Count them and Walmart's annual operational emissions are up by 2.5 million tonnes since the company announced its aspirational goals. Buying 147,000 megawatt-hours of renewable electricity is significant, but it's only 1 per cent of the company's overall power consumption. The commitment to use 100 per cent renewable power was *aspirational*, after all, and that aspiration 'does not currently have a final target year'. Walmart can't even tell us how it's tracking, because it's still 'developing the detailed final metrics for progress toward this goal'. Some interviews given by the company suggest that renewables will need to 'match or beat grid parity' before it switches – Walmart, it seems, is committed to being

100 per cent renewable once renewables are as cheap as fossil fuels. The commitment to more energy-efficient stores is similarly vague. While the advertising says Walmart is 'designing' stores that are 20 per cent more energy-efficient, there's no word on how many of the new stores actually going in every eight hours are 20 per cent more energy-efficient – and no detail suggesting any significant impact on the company's total carbon footprint.

In other Walmart ads, the emphasis is on those customer and supplier emissions. One commercial asks how many tonnes of carbon dioxide could be saved if everyone in America washed their laundry in cold water. Another explains that Walmart is working with its suppliers to make DVDs less emissions-intensive. There are ads called 'The Secret Life of Sour Cream' and 'The Secret Life of Pizza', which show the steps being taken to reduce the carbon footprint of seemingly every product in the store. The company explains how it is working with its customers and suppliers to cut 20 million tonnes of carbon dioxide over the five years to 2015. Customers are told that by shopping at Walmart they are going to help the company reach that goal. Without a hint of self-awareness of the unnecessary consumption it feeds, the company even sells a DVD on the plan itself for the bargain price of $1. Walmart says that a saving of 20 million tonnes is equivalent to what 3.8 million cars produce in a year, and one and a half times the projected increase in the company's operational emissions over that five-year period.

What this statement glosses over is that those supply chain emissions will still be increasing very rapidly thanks to Walmart's continued expansion. The company wants it both ways: it doesn't want to count the growing supply chain emissions as its own, but it does want to claim 20 million tonnes of supply chain emission savings. A quick look at the numbers exposes the greenwash. Walmart claims around 21 million tonnes of greenhouse pollution per year, but if – as Walmart acknowledges – its supply chain forms 90 per cent of the overall carbon footprint associated with the brand, then the carbon footprint including the supply chain is about 210 million tonnes each year. When asked, Walmart confirmed that it did not expect supply chain emissions to contribute proportionally less of that carbon footprint anytime soon. It said it was fair to assume 'that Walmart and its supply chain make direct carbon footprint changes at an equal pace and the mix of the type of goods we sell remains fairly static'. With the company growing annually at 8–10 per cent, it's more than fair to assume that the supply chain emissions are growing by some 5 per cent annually. This means that by 2015, the *annual* emissions of Walmart's supply chain will have grown by 45–50 million tonnes.

It sounds bad enough that the growing Walmart supply chain might add twice the emissions that the company eliminates if it achieves its goal of saving 20 million tonnes. But it's worse than that, much worse. What's cleverly opaque in all the PR, and only clarified when you directly ask Walmart, is that the 20 million tonne saving being targeted is *cumulative* – spread over five years from 2010 to 2015. In fact, it's seven years if you factor in the 'deferred tons' the company has decided to count until the end of 2017 for projects with 'executive level buy-in' that promise 'transformational change' – what Walmart forgivingly calls 'game-changer' projects. Over that 2010–2015 period, the likely 5 per cent a year growth in Walmart's supply chain emissions would add over 145 million tonnes. So the 20 million tonne saving would be wiped out seven times over, which is not exactly the great turnaround that Ed Humes suggests in his recent book

Force of Nature: The unlikely story of Walmart's green revolution. It's not to say that Walmart's focus on supply chain emissions isn't a good thing – it's just a shame that this and so much other greenwash is being used to conceal the growing carbon footprint of what Walmart sells.

The UK supermarket Tesco is playing similar games. If you live in the United Kingdom, perhaps you've noticed biodiesel-powered trucks with 'Tesco – Less CO2' emblazoned on the side – you can even buy a toy version of one. The same slogan is painted on trains and barges. If you've shopped at Tesco, you've almost certainly bought one of the 525 products with labels that include a Carbon Trust–verified calculation of the product's carbon footprint. If you're a Tesco Card holder, maybe you've earned 'Green Points' for reusing bags, recycling mobile phones and printer cartridges, or for buying solar panels or home insulation. You may have surfed the 'Tesco Green Living' website with its list of green products, carbon calculator and tips on how customers can minimise their footprint. Perhaps you've sat enthralled by Tesco's plan to roll out 'zero carbon stores' across its vast global empire. Or, if you're in the United States, maybe you've noticed Tesco's subsidiary Fresh & Easy promoting itself as a 'lean, green savings machine'. Odds are, if you're in Tesco's orbit, its green messages have reached you.

As with Walmart, public statements by Tesco executives suggest the company understands the gravity of the threat posed by climate change. 'All the evidence is that climate change is a reality', said then CEO Terry Leahy in 2010, and 'Tesco has committed to fundamental change in how we do business'. The company's goals also suggest Tesco is serious: it wants to be a zero-carbon business by 2050 and reduce the emissions of its stores and distribution centres by 50 per cent by 2020. New 'carbon zero stores' have been implemented in the United Kingdom, the Czech Republic and Thailand. In Poland one store runs largely off wind and solar power. Tesco is trialling 'bio-methane' from landfill to power its grocery delivery vehicles. As with Walmart, though, the focus at Tesco is on enlisting others to make reductions – the potential cuts are vastly greater than what Tesco might achieve through addressing its operational emissions. However, whereas Walmart looks mainly to its suppliers, Tesco is looking primarily to customers. Tesco wants to cut its *customers'* emissions by 50 per cent by 2020 – and claim the credit. Leahy has stated that the 'energy and innovation of the market' could create a mass movement in green consumption, by encouraging consumers to 'go green' and choose products with low carbon footprints. Shoppers, not corporations, would save the planet.

The green marketing hides the fact that Tesco's own carbon footprint is rising. Between 2007 and 2011, Tesco's annual operational emissions rose by 1 million tonnes, to the carbon equivalent of putting another 220,000 cars on UK roads. That's perhaps not surprising given that the company has added over 2100 stores in the past four years (a new one every sixteen hours). The company points to an absolute reduction in emissions in the United Kingdom, but this deftly overlooks the fact that two-thirds of the company's store space is outside the United Kingdom, and these expanding markets account for more than two-thirds of Tesco's profit growth. As for halving the carbon footprint of stores and distribution centres, that's an emissions-per-square-foot measure which, at the rate Tesco is growing globally, doesn't amount to a cut in total emissions. And all this is before we even start on the supply chain emissions. Tesco makes no global estimate, but acknowledges that in the United Kingdom, 'supply chain emissions are at least ten times our direct footprint'. A fast-growing Tesco means fast-growing supply chain emissions too.

You might take Tesco's climate-friendly marketing seriously if its emissions were falling; or if its 'carbon zero stores' or bio-methane trucks were being rolled out across its vast and growing empire, rather than in a few well-promoted cases. And what are we to make of a company that spruiks its carbon footprint labelling as 'allowing customers to make a greener choice', only to dump the labelling less than a year later, reportedly because too few other companies adopted the idea? As with Walmart, Tesco is doing some good things, from labelling to shifting freight from road to rail and water. But so long as Tesco's own emissions continue to rise, its 'Shop the planet clean' vision of a customer-led green revolution will remain greenwash.

Whereas Walmart and Tesco want to make suppliers and customers responsible for reducing emissions, some more diversified companies use their more climate-friendly big box businesses to hide their less friendly investments. Wesfarmers in Australia is a good example. What started out as a conservative business squarely focused on agriculture is now chaotically diversified. Among much more, Wesfarmers owns the Australian operations of the big box retailers Kmart and Target; the largest Australian office supplies retailer, Officeworks; along with liquor stores, petrol stations and an insurance business. Wesfarmers owns Australia's largest home improvement chain in Bunnings, which gets 15 per cent of its energy from renewable sources and says it will go carbon-neutral by 2015. Wesfarmers also owns Australia's second-largest supermarket chain, Coles, which has a well-publicised 'green choice' range of products, a partnership with environmental organisation Clean Up Australia, and claims to have cut its greenhouse emissions by 40,000 tonnes in the past two years. While the larger Wesfarmers brand doesn't specifically market itself as climate-friendly, on the cover of its sustainability report you'll find smiley kids recycling plastic bags at Coles, along with Bunnings staff proudly clutching energy-efficient light bulbs.

These brands have enabled Wesfarmers to look greener by association, which is worrying given that the company's carbon footprint has more than doubled since 2007. Yet that fact only scratches the surface. Wesfarmers also owns a modest resources business, consisting mostly of coal mines. So while the supermarket business is going green and the hardware business is pledging carbon-neutrality, while the office supplies business is recycling printer cartridges and the company headquarters is mumbling about putting alternative fuels in its vehicle fleet, the coal side of the business is busy expanding production – and emissions – as if climate change isn't happening. You won't read this in the sustainability report, which gives the impression that it's the supermarket line pumping out nearly half of the company's emissions. The coal business's footprint looks positively non-existent, accounting for less than 10 per cent. What's missing is the carbon dioxide released once the 14 million tonnes of Wesfarmers coal sold annually is eventually burnt. Count it and Wesfarmers' carbon footprint is six times bigger than it says, and coal is around 80 per cent of it. This goes to show just how a few green apples can be used to hide an otherwise bad bunch.

Sometimes the green bunch hides one large bad apple. Whole Foods Market (WFM), which is consistently rated the greenest brand in America, began thirty years ago as a single store in Austin, Texas. Today it is nudging the top half of the Fortune 500 list of the biggest-earning US companies, with 300 stores – and 1000 in its sights. Along the way, it's arguably done more to raise environmental considerations when it comes to selling food than any other company. WFM sources relatively more organic and locally produced foods than its competitors, reducing the amount of transport and petroleum-based fertilisers used in its supply chain. It has solar panels at fifteen stores, and one-third of its distribution truck fleet now runs on biodiesel. Most significantly, WFM was the first Fortune 500 company to offset its entire electricity use with wind power credits. Last year it bought enough of them to cover 750,000 megawatt-hours of electricity, which is more than five times the amount of renewable energy Walmart says it buys in the United States – and WFM is less than a fifteenth of Walmart's size. So far, no other big box retailer has been willing to do anything like offsetting all their electricity use.

Even so, like most other big box retailers, WFM is struggling to reduce its greenhouse emissions while growing its business. WFM's exponential growth means its emissions (before offsets) are growing by 15 per cent *annually*. Perhaps not surprisingly, the company's plans to cut electricity use and greenhouse gas emissions by 25 per cent from 2008 levels by 2015 are expressed not in absolute terms, but per square foot of floor space. WFM says it hopes this might result in a 1 per cent absolute reduction in emissions by 2015, but that looks extremely unlikely. What keeps it ahead of the competition are the offsets: these erase nearly two-thirds of the company's carbon footprint. Aside from wind power credits, the most persuasive aspect of WFM is its lack of aggressive greenwashing. It's refreshingly open about its own inadequacies on these issues, and it spends relatively much less on marketing than its competition, relying instead on word of mouth.

So where's the bad apple in the bunch? Unfortunately, he's in charge. The founder and CEO of the greenest brand in

America is also a climate change sceptic. In 2010, in an interview for the *New Yorker*, John Mackey said that 'no scientific consensus exists' on the cause of climate change, and it would be a shame to allow 'hysteria about global warming' to cause us 'to raise taxes and increase regulation, and in turn lower our standard of living'. While his personal views may not reflect the views of his company as a whole, they taint its positive action and its Green Mission™.

So then, three things to keep an eye out for on your next big box shopping excursion: at Walmart, look out for a DVD called 'The Secret Life of Our Rising Carbon Footprint'; at Tesco, see if you can still find a product bearing the certified 'low carbon footprint' label – it's a collectors' item now; and at Whole Foods Market, look out for that climate sceptic CEO – and give him an earful.

cars

Let there be no doubt that Mother Nature truly exists because, according to Toyota's advertising, she drives a hybrid Prius. Maybe you've seen her loading groceries in the car park at the local supermarket, or dropping Baby Nature off to crèche; maybe Mother Nature has even cut you off on the highway. More likely, she wouldn't drive at all, let alone endorse Toyota. But Toyota assumes that we consumers will see its ad as just a bit of green-tinged fun.

Toyota is hardly alone among car makers in creating climate-friendly advertising so patently fanciful that it skates past any 'truth in advertising' laws, but still generates a green glow around the brand. There's a Honda commercial for the Hybrid Civic that shows a young couple clearly exhilarated by their purchase speeding through an idyllic rainforest, the car emitting nothing but nature: butterflies, seahorses, clownfish, chameleons, other pretty critters and leaves. And in a Ford commercial for the Mercury Mariner, a woman plants a Mercury badge into some decent soil, stands back and watches it grow, beanstalk-like, in a matter of seconds, into a glistening hybrid SUV. These ads are not meant to depict reality any more than is the Lexus commercial for its LS600h hybrid, which shows an invisible car leaving nothing but wind as it sweeps through a wheatfield. We know that Lexus isn't yet making invisible cars, just as Mercedes isn't yet selling the cars featured in their ads with water taps instead of tailpipes. Over-the-top fantasy in car advertising is not just entertaining for the viewer, it's a good way to avoid discussion about what might actually make a car company climate-friendly.

The most breathtaking example of the genre to date is Toyota's 'Harmony between Man, Nature and Machine' commercials. In one ad, a Prius speeds through a landscape in which everything is made of smiling people – the sun, the clouds, the grass, the trees, even a waterfall. This commercial is the car-advertising equivalent of the Opening Ceremony of the Olympic Games. It involved 200 extras in elaborate costumes, and it took advertising and production technicians from Japan, New Zealand and the United States months to put together. There is even a short film showing the making of the commercial, in which all involved pat themselves on the back about being involved in something so clearly good for the planet. The irony of a green ad being this resource-intensive seems lost on everyone involved.

Other car companies have found simpler ways to achieve the same goal. The quickest option, which again avoids advertising regulation by making no claims at all, is to toss a few green images into the mix. In a recent magazine ad for its turbo-charged G series Falcon sedan, Ford makes no mention of the car's (poor) emissions performance, but nine windmills on a grassy backdrop subtly reassure the consumer of the car's green credentials.

Another option is to tell only part of the story. Nissan's marketing of its electric LEAF is the best example of this. The convenient part of the story is that the 100 per cent electric LEAF has no tailpipe, so there are no tailpipe emissions. This is so spectacularly helpful in the fight against climate change that one

Nissan commercial shows a polar bear walking from the Arctic to North American suburbia to give a taken-aback LEAF owner an appreciative hug. It's what enables Lance Armstrong in another commercial to bemoan how 'in twenty years of cycling, even when I was ahead I was behind ... behind cars, behind trucks, behind those guys [motorcycles]. Tailpipe after tailpipe after tailpipe ... until now. The 100 per cent electric no tailpipe Nissan LEAF'. There's no false information in the ads, but what's not mentioned is that 'no tailpipe emissions' and '100 per cent electric' don't equal 'zero emissions'. Plenty of the electricity comes from power stations run on fossil fuels. So the LEAF *does* generate greenhouse pollution from fossil fuel, just not from a tailpipe. Nice for Lance perhaps, but not something polar bears would walk all that far to thank someone for.

Nissan sinks beneath half-truths when it drops the tailpipe talk altogether. One ad shows a LEAF with the words 'Zero Emission' on its side, a message that is also shown on the Sat Nav and number plate. The car drives by a grove of wind turbines, as if to suggest that the electricity powering it comes entirely from renewable sources. Maybe it does in this isolated instance. Either way, the electricity powering most LEAFs comes from non-renewable sources – mainly fossil fuels, so they're still generating carbon dioxide. This misleading 'Zero Emission' tag also appears in an infomercial about the making of the LEAF commercial featuring 'Aggie' the polar bear. Most LEAF ads end with Nissan's catchcry: 'Innovation for the planet, Innovation for all'. The truth is that the planet benefits less than is suggested and the company is doing anything but 'innovating for all' – the vast majority of its cars are conventionally powered, and the overall contribution to climate change from those cars is increasing. Still, Aggie's none the wiser, and neither are many of us.

Another common greenwashing technique is to advertise cars you are *not* selling. Ford promotes a hybrid F-550 that's not yet available, Ferrari flags a hybrid ... available in five years' time, Aston Martin is promising a hybrid Lagonda, but no time frame. In Australia, the website for Holden (owned by GM) has for years shown a Holden Volt, complete with the lion logo that Holden owners know, love and presumably have been very excited to see displayed on this cutting-edge electric car. Declaring it 'a new era in automotive transportation', the company explains that the Holden Volt will go 64 kilometres a day without any tailpipe emissions and comes with a 'range extender' combustion engine option: 'The Holden Volt is electric when you want it, petrol when you need it'. But not if you want it straightaway. As this goes to print, the Holden Volt is still not for sale, and when it does finally go on sale only about one in every five dealerships is expected to stock it.

In the United States, a GM Chevrolet website features a page that until recently showcased how its Equinox fuel cell–powered SUV emits nothing but water vapour, is blitzing the competition, winning green car awards and being lauded for running 'like a Rolex'. 'The best emissions strategy is a zero emissions strategy,' said Chevy. It's genuinely exciting until you read the fine print: 'Not available for sale'. Mercedes and BMW also promote hydrogen-powered vehicles that they won't sell to most of us. BMW has generated much publicity for its Hydrogen 7 by giving the 100 cars it has made to high-profile politicians and celebrities such as Jay Leno, Hilary Swank and Ed Norton. Mercedes has made fewer than 1000 F-Cells and commercial production is still years away. Almost all the major car makers have produced hydrogen-powered fuel-cell vehicles and/or plug-in electric vehicles, but it is invariably easier to use them for marketing purposes than to actually sell them.

Some auto companies decide to market cars that are not very green as eco-friendly. This technique is particularly popular in countries with serious addictions to SUVs and large sedans. In the United States, Ford ran ads in which Kermit the Frog sings 'It's Not Easy Being Green' only to conclude, to his surprise, that it can be if you drive the Hybrid Escape. It's not clear whether Kermit appreciated that this SUV has got efficiency slightly worse than the US average. Another 'big green car' is the Cadillac Escalade (owned by GM). Marketed grandly as 'the first luxury full-size hybrid SUV', it generates nearly 10 tonnes of carbon dioxide annually. That's twice what the average US car produces, but apparently it's climate-friendly enough for GM to declare, 'So much for the size theory. Apparently you can comfortably seat 8 and still be competitive on fuel-efficiency'.

In Australia, Holden aggressively markets 'Advanced Fuel Management' (AFM) with a suitably green logo. This is heralded as a breakthrough technology, which enables four of the cylinders in its V8 engines to switch off when not required and instantly start back up when acceleration is needed. According to the company, this can reduce fuel consumption by up to one litre per 100 kilometres, with commensurate reductions in greenhouse gas emissions. AFM is now an option available on all of Holden's V8 engines – and herein lies the problem. Not one of the top twenty greenest cars in Australia is a Holden. What the welcome improvement hides is that Holden wants to keep doing what it does best: making six-litre V8 engines that get woeful mileage even with one litre less per 100 kilometres. The AFM pitch just helps to keep the 'green police' at bay.

Which brings us to the 'green police' ad, which Audi (owned by Volkswagen) spent millions making and placing during the 2010 Super Bowl – the most prized position in the world of advertising because of its audience of over 100 million. Making fun of the upsurge in what is seen by many in America as environmental correctness, this ad spoofs an imaginary world in which 'green police' bust people for taking plastic bags at supermarkets, for throwing compostable waste in with the garbage and for using polystyrene cups. The ad culminates in a highway roadblock where, complete with 'sniffer anteaters', green police find a man in an Audi A3 TDI diesel wagon. As he's waved through while everyone else is stuck in the queue, the message is clear – drive a 'clean diesel' Audi and you're officially green. Audi's parent company, Volkswagen, runs another commercial in which a bikini-clad woman with a bodybuilder's physique and a weakling hippie man spot one another on a beach. It's love at first sight and, to Etta James singing 'At Last', they run towards each other in slow motion, finally embracing, with the woman swinging the man around in the air. 'Power and the Environment. Together at last', says the voiceover. 'The all new TDI clean diesel from Volkswagen – we've done the unthinkable.' The words 'ultra low emissions' flash across the screen.

These ads are like so much green car maker advertising – funny, creative and hard not to like. Yet, it's still greenwash because in reality, all commercials for a product also advertise the brand. While the focus might be on one particular car, the implicit message is that the brand is going green. What's 'unthinkable' is the deception: the operational emissions of Volkswagen (including Audi) are up 10 per cent in just two years – something which seems to have eluded the 'green police'. As for the emissions generated by Volkswagens and Audis once sold, when calculating this the company counts only new vehicles sold in the past year into the European Union, though these vehicles account for a small fraction of Audis and Volkswagens on the road. Overall, notwithstanding all the marketing of clean diesel as the solution, the number of cars sold annually by Volkswagen has risen by over 46 per cent in five years – much faster than efficiency improvements – which means the total emissions generated from new vehicles sold by Volkswagen (including Audi) are still increasing. So, power and the environment are not quite the happy couple that the TV commercial suggests.

The truth is that emissions generated by cars are increasing, not falling. Worldwide, there are now over 1 billion vehicles. Thirty-five million cars were added to the roads in 2011 alone. On average, each one produces around 4.5 tonnes of carbon dioxide annually, so even though cars are becoming more efficient, the overall carbon footprint of cars increases by over 150 million tonnes each year. The popular impression, reinforced by the advertising, is that things are moving in the right direction even if progress is slower than many would like. In fact, things are still moving in the wrong direction. Never before have more cars been added to the world's roads, and only a tiny fraction of those are hybrids or electric or hydrogen powered, let alone run on renewable sources of energy.

Toyota (including Lexus) makes much of the 4 million hybrids it's sold over the past fifteen years, but these figures need to be seen in context. Toyota hopes to sell 8.6 million vehicles in 2012 – that's nearly 3.5 million more vehicles than it was selling *annually* when the Prius was launched. More than 96 per cent of the more than 100 million vehicles that Toyota has sold over the same period have not been hybrids. Toyota sells nearly three gas-guzzling four-wheel drives, sports utility vehicles and utes for every hybrid. It's worse in the United States, where for all the marketing, hybrids account for one in a hundred cars sold by Ford. In 2011 half of them were Escape SUVs with their average mileage, and

Ford has now discontinued this model. It's even worse over at GM where 5000 hybrids and nearly 7700 Chevrolet Volts accounted for about 0.5 per cent of the company's sales. As for Nissan's LEAF, you find more 'leafs' on a single oak tree than in four years' worth of Nissan sales figures. By early 2012 about 27,000 in total had been sold globally. For every LEAF sold, meanwhile, Nissan is now also selling seven big Navara utes and twenty-seven SUV X-Trails and Dualises.

To appreciate just how dramatic a shift is needed for the auto industry to meet projected demand sustainably, consider this. The science suggests that an overall reduction of global emissions of 80 per cent or more is required by 2050. Right now, the average car ownership rate in Australia is around 550 per 1000 people; in China, it is 34 per 1000. If the number of cars in the world were to treble by 2050 – as is projected – emissions per vehicle would need to be cut by at least two-thirds just to keep things stable. That's almost impossible while most efficiency advances are being squandered to make larger and more power-ful cars. To make cuts of 80 per cent or more, car makers need to cut emissions by around 95 per cent across all their vehicles, not just the few that they use to showcase their green credentials. So far no car maker is taking that sort of leap. When these brands say, 'what drives us is not just to make the best cars in the world but to make cars that are the best for the world' (as Mercedes does), what they mean is that they are driven to make a very small number of cars that are a little better for the world.

Still, by all means buy a green car and enjoy the award-winning commercials. And if you do come across Mother Nature in her Prius, wish her luck – because she'll be needing plenty of it.

celebrities

When a star of stage or screen tells us to buy their latest release, or to buy the latest shampoo or car they're endorsing, everyone gets that this is driven mainly by their commercial self-interest. Yet, when a celebrity tells us to go green, it's different – this is supposedly something they believe in. What then are we to make of Jennifer Aniston flying in private jets while claiming that she saves the environment by installing solar panels and brushing her teeth in the shower; or talk show host Kelly Ripa selling green washing machines for Electrolux while she also flies in private jets? When it comes to eco-celebrity behaviour and the big brands they endorse, the procession of hypocrisy and double standards seems endless. Granted, many of the media reports turn out to be as baseless as most celebrity gossip. The worry, though, is just how many of the eco-celebrity faux pas are real. Some of the green celebrities are letting down the cause, and badly.

Oprah Winfrey is perhaps the best known face on television. Over twenty-five years, she has built an audience of over 50 million people across 145 countries, and in recent years she included climate change among the many causes about which she has been a strident advocate. She has given a convoy of

high-profile environmentalists one of the world's best media platforms to get the word out – scientists such as Michael
Oppenheimer, movie stars such as Leonardo DiCaprio, politicians such as Al Gore, and Hollywood fixtures such as Laurie
David and Mathew Modine. With DiCaprio explaining that
Americans are disproportionately responsible for climate
change, Oprah has urged US viewers to play their part. To help
them, she put together a Global Warming 101 page on her website. She shares ideas on how to reduce your carbon footprint:
drive a hybrid car, use energy-efficient appliances, install compact
fluorescent light bulbs. They're all sensible suggestions, which
presumably Oprah follows. What's not to be found on that list,
however, are some of the other choices Oprah makes. There's her
$46 million private jet, and her comments about it to an audience
of students: 'It's great to have a private jet. Anyone that tells you
that having your own private jet isn't great is lying to you'. There
are the new (non-hybrid) cars she gave to every member of one
audience; the hundreds of iPads she gave to another; and then,
most recently and spectacularly, the whole US audience she flew
to Australia for ten days, staying at luxury hotels, as part of a deal
with Qantas to promote long-haul travel Down Under.

How seriously can we take exhortations to change light
bulbs from someone who sets an example that is anything but
climate-friendly? How many efficient light bulbs and clean
appliances would it take to bring the carbon footprint of her
$50 million, 23,000-square-foot mansion in California, with its
fourteen bathrooms and ten fireplaces, back to anything remotely
normal? No-one begrudges Oprah promoting Australia as a tour-
ism destination, but was it really necessary to take 300 people
along for the ride? And to take her own private jet as well as the
two Qantas charter planes? Whether it's the product giveaways,

her own opulent lifestyle or commercials aired on her cable channel promoting emissions-intensive petrol made from Canadian tar sands, Oprah seems oblivious to the vast gulf between her rhetoric on the one hand and her actions and lifestyle on the other.

John Travolta was Oprah's celebrity companion on the recent mile-high pilgrimage from Chicago. It made great PR sense to involve him. The Hollywood star owns a retired Qantas 707 – it's one of various aircraft kept at his house in Florida, which features parking for five planes and a runway capable of taking 747s. Travolta has also been an 'Ambassador-at-Large' for Qantas for over a decade, presumably in a paid capacity (the Qantas media department was asked to confirm this but did not respond). He's featured in various promotions, and until recently even conducted the in-flight welcome and safety routine in Qantas pilot garb. Much of his marketing involvement is also hands-on, or more accurately, hands-on the throttle, racking up 35,000 miles in one year by flying 'goodwill' tours around the world. He's taken global flights with his family of five, plus a few staff, on the 707, a vintage plane with very poor mileage by today's standards.

Given Travolta's gargantuan carbon footprint, you'd expect him to say nothing on climate change. But there he is, not just acknowledging the problem (global warming 'is a very valid issue'), but telling the public *they* should reduce their carbon footprint ('Everyone can do their bit ... We have to think about alternative methods of fuel'). He both acknowledges and justifies his own emissions: 'I'm probably not the best candidate to ask about global warming because I fly jets ... I use them as a business tool, though'. Never mind that long-haul air travel is the world's fastest growing contributor to greenhouse emissions

– several private jets are apparently as essential to today's movie star as a spanner set to a mechanic.

More surprising than those celebrities you'd expect to keep a low profile on climate change are those who are mired in hypocrisy though they pride themselves on climate friendliness. Take Leonardo DiCaprio, one of the five biggest earning stars in Hollywood today by many reports. There isn't a more vocal advocate in show business of global action to reduce greenhouse emissions. He produced a hit documentary largely about climate change called *11th Hour* and established a foundation with his own money to advance climate protection around the world. He's taken every possible opportunity to publicise the cause – from announcing the greening of the Oscars with Al Gore to arriving at the ceremony in a hybrid rather than a stretch limo, to buying multiple hybrids of his own and trying 'as often as possible to fly commercially'. He's said, 'We don't want to be reliant on these ancient resources like coal and oil to power our civilization anymore. We want some drastic changes'. He bought a hybrid Prius for his girlfriend, who had been getting around in an SUV, and he bought himself a Fisker hybrid supercar. He's also worked with business to promote green products. There were TV commercials for the Prius in Japan, Bridgestone's Ecopia tyres and the HSBC green credit card in Hong Kong. Perhaps best known of all has been the new 'green' watch that DiCaprio supposedly co-designed with watchmakers Tag Heuer.

DiCaprio's contributions seem overwhelmingly positive, and there's no denying the amount of time and money he's given to the cause, considering environmental advocacy is not his day job. And yet the choices of even the greenest of celebrities are worrying. DiCaprio would no doubt argue that he is promoting a single product when he says, 'Bridgestone's Ecopia technology can help save the environment' or when he says, 'I own a Toyota Prius – it's a step in the right direction'; or when he says that the Tag Aquaracer 500M is built to minimise waste by lasting for generations. And yet he's not just endorsing the product, but the brand behind it. Why else would he say something like, 'Tag is a company that gets it', one that has 'a mission that is bigger than all of us – to protect our planet'. But the reality is that the carbon footprint of the products sold by all of these brands is still rising – at Toyota, at Bridgestone and at Louis Vuitton Moët Hennessy (LVMH), the multinational that owns Tag. At LVMH, between 2009 and 2011 there was a 28 per cent increase in operational emissions alone, with rising Tag watch sales a star contributor to the company's recent growth. And HSBC, the bank that DiCaprio praises for its green credit card, remains one of the largest investors in fossil fuel projects in the world. Associating with companies with increasing carbon footprints tarnishes the DiCaprio green brand, as do the lapses in the example being set by the Hollywood star, such as travelling to Johannesburg for the World Cup in a private jet, as he did with another top-notch celebrity climate change hypocrite – Paris Hilton.

It may come as a surprise to hear that Paris Hilton has thought deeply enough to form a view on the issue. It's not actually true that in 2009 she declared that food scarcity caused by global warming would have an upside – helping 'poor people look totally hot' – that was a satirical piece by a South African website. What is true, though, is that she made climate friendliness a central part of her candidacy for 'fake president' in 2008. This opportunistic pitch for publicity during the 2008 US presidential campaign was mostly light-hearted. There was a dance music video in which she featured in a skimpy swimsuit and high heels, saying, 'global warming is totally not hot', calling herself 'a proponent of clean energy' and pledging to 'ratify Kyoto today'. Perhaps pitching to undecideds, the would-be 'Commander-in-Bikini' added, 'You can ride in the motorcade in my hybrid pink Escalade'. There was a televised kitchen table chat with Martin Sheen (America's longest-serving fake president, as the star of *The West Wing*). And there was a fake presidential campaign commercial, in which – reclining by the pool in a swimsuit – she called for tax credits to encourage hybrid cars, along with off-shore oil drilling, to help America achieve energy independence. Hilton's 'energy policy' received widespread praise – with tongue in cheek, John McCain's campaign spokesman even praised it as superior to that of Barack Obama.

Along with the green pitch to fake voters, Hilton bought her own hybrid, leading to plenty of coverage – Paris caught texting as she drives her hybrid out of a multi-level car park; Paris running out of both electricity and gasoline in her hybrid, and having to be rescued by Charlie Sheen's then wife, Brooke Mueller, carrying a jerry can. While few people would be surprised by her misadventures, the fact that Hilton drives a hybrid and has a considered view on the economics and diplomacy of climate change does exceed expectations. Yet her lifestyle mocks this green image. Hilton doesn't just enjoy private jet travel on a regular basis, she flaunts it by posting pictures online. As for her green car, she didn't get a hybrid Hummer as was wrongly reported, but rather a huge GM Yukon which is more hybrid by name than by nature. The notion that she is going green is, well, clueless.

Another shining example is supermodel, self-styled Earth mother and UN Environmental Ambassador Gisele Bündchen, named 2011 celebrity environmentalist of the year by London's Natural History Museum. Through her green-coloured website, she implores the public to do the right thing by the planet. Bündchen promotes Earth Hour, posting videos of herself and her celebrity husband, the New England Patriots quarterback Tom Brady, enjoying the event by candlelight. 'Lights off, candles on', she instructs. The planet could hardly have more handsome advocates. Back in her home country of Brazil, she's funded the planting of 25,000 seedlings in the Amazon rainforest. She's putting together a kids' book to get the message out. This all sounds great, but of course it isn't her day job – when she's not busy greening her profile, she's working, and her work isn't so Earth-motherly.

Bündchen's career has been spent primarily encouraging people to buy more and more stuff. She's made millions promoting everything from Victoria's Secret lingerie to Volkswagens and Apple's electronic gadgetry to the luxury goods of Versace and Givenchy. Many of the companies concerned report dramatic increases in consumption as a direct consequence of her endorsements – and often these campaigns target people in developing countries, which means additional consumption and emissions, not just a shift in market share. Yet this huge and growing carbon footprint from the products she endorses is never mentioned in her green work. Not content with selling all this generic stuff for large corporations, Bündchen sometimes has her own line of products pitched as eco-friendly. Forbes recently reported that that 25 million pairs of 'eco-friendly PVC' sandals from the 'Gisele Bündchen Ipanema' range were sold in 2010. That's got to be just great for the environment.

Everyone has to make a living, and most of us are in the business of selling something. Perhaps we shouldn't be so hard on Bündchen. It's just that her lifestyle is utterly at odds with its eco-friendly façade: telling her fans to use less water and energy when she's flying on a private jet between Brazil and her residences in Boston, Costa Rica and a new 20,000-square-foot mansion in California, complete with its own elevator. It's great that she was able to get profits from flip flops sold under her name directed to fund the planting of 25,000 seedlings in the Amazon. But then for the $50 million pricetag of her Gulfstream 550 private jet, she could have afforded to plant at least 12 million trees or buy carbon credits equivalent to cutting 3.2 million tonnes of carbon dioxide. Instead, she bought one of the most emissions-intensive new vehicles available. Bündchen defends her lifestyle, telling CNN, 'I think in today's world it is more about finding ways to live in harmony with nature and to do steps, everyday steps, to make a difference'. She clearly wasn't thinking very hard the day she bought the Gulfstream jet.

Last, but not least, there are the green celebrity rock gods. Radiohead kicked this trend off in 2007 by having two North American tours carbon-audited. When it publicly released the results in a 36-page report, its transparency was punished, with critics suggesting the carbon footprint was outrageously high. However, the audit enabled the band to reduce its emissions on subsequent tours. Now the band tours less often and with less emissions, even adopting a 'no air freight' policy. In the United States, Pearl Jam is doing something similar: it's also cut back on tours, and it's offset its entire carbon footprint, releasing a 'carbon portfolio' with the details. The Dave Matthews Band has gone further still – and just as well, since it's played more than 550 shows to over 17 million people. But credit where it's due. In 2006, the band announced it would offset all emissions in its touring history, dating back to 1991.

However, despite the many feature stories like this on how musicians are going green – with a new hybrid or solar panels

– the more you dig, the more you find celebrity greenwash. Sir Paul McCartney is a typical example. A few years ago, the former Beatle started promoting hybrid cars for Lexus. Yet his own special-order $158,000 Lexus LS600h was flown over 11,000 kilometres from Japan, rather than being shipped like most imported vehicles. The carbon footprint from the flight was estimated to be 100 times higher than shipping would have been, cancelling out the emission savings McCartney might make over the car's lifetime. As a carbon credit company quipped at the time, 'It's like driving the car 300 times around the world'. The former Beatle was reportedly 'horrified after learning it was delivered by plane', but kept his close working relationship with Lexus. It was after all a longstanding collaboration, about much more, as it turns out, than endorsing green cars.

In 2005, the car company sponsored McCartney's entire US tour. There were no half measures: McCartney and his then wife were driven to the shows in black Lexus SUVs, and the Lexus logo was everywhere – on the concert posters, tickets and back-stage passes. A double CD of the tour, *Motor of Love*, was sold exclusively at Lexus dealerships, its cover featuring a Lexus car hood next to McCartney's signature. Magazine ads promoted a special edition Lexus hybrid SUV made in McCartney's honour, complete with a guitar painted on the side. Lexus's TV ads used McCartney's music, which was the first time the musician had agreed to such a deal. The climax of the tour was McCartney singing – you guessed it – 'Drive my Car' as part of the half-time show at the Super Bowl, the most watched event on American television.

At the time, McCartney was quoted as saying: 'It's good to be involved with a company that sees the value of an environ-mentally conscious product.' Here is a performer travelling to

America to put on dozens of concerts and teaming up with a car company for which the vast majority of sales are not hybrid vehicles. There's no indication that the concert tour's emissions were offset, and the total carbon footprint of Lexus vehicles rose in the wake of the McCartney tour, with Lexus sales rising to record highs in 2007 largely on the back of US sales. Sure, the hybrids were the focus, but the ubiquity of the Lexus logo meant that McCartney's relationship with the company amounted to an endorsement of the whole brand. As McCartney said himself, 'Lexus and I share the same philosophy and approach to creating the best work possible – me with my music and art and Lexus with the vehicles they create'. Strip the spin away, and it was just another celebrity greenwashing his brand and that of an emissions-intensive company.

So what's the answer for green-minded celebrities? Are their lifestyles so unalterably profligate as to be beyond redemption? Does their special brand of 'champagne environmentalism' help if it misleads millions of fans into thinking mansions, private jets and hybrid supercars can somehow be sustainable? For those determined to help, there are a couple of easy ground rules: don't tell people to change the little things in their life when you're not willing to change the big things, and don't take money to promote companies where the overall contribution that their products make to climate change is getting worse. Sure, it takes a little time and perhaps some advice to hack through the greenwash to work that out, but it will be cheap compared with private jets and hybrid supercars.

coffee

You wouldn't think we'd need reminding by Starbucks that we share this planet with them, and yet, since 2008, the ubiquitous Seattle-based coffee giant has run a Shared Planet campaign. 'Shared Planet' is trademarked, as if to remind us that they'll share Planet Earth so long as they retain all intellectual property rights. 'You and Starbucks – it's bigger than coffee', say the commercials, with the words 'Shared Planet' and a coffee bean logo appearing in green. The campaign has a sedative quality. One ad features footage of cloud forests, healthy macaws and toucans accompanied by a soothing voice explaining how Starbucks is working with its farmers to grow coffee sustainably and make 'more clean air for everyone'. Simply by buying Starbucks coffee, we're assured, we 'can easily help protect carbon-absorbing forests'. Another Shared Planet™ commercial starts by assuring us that Starbucks is a 'values company', and then, along with tranquil yoga music, we hear how exhilarated company executives are about making 'the whole company building plan green'. The pitch has three main elements: Starbucks is protecting forests by encouraging sustainable coffee farming, reducing its energy use by building green stores and buying a large share of its energy from renewable sources.

The forest protection claim is based on Starbucks' long-standing financial support for Conservation International's reforestation programs. Starbucks makes much of how this partnership has encouraged farmers to adopt 'shade-grown coffee' techniques to minimise forest losses and ultimately supplement their income by selling carbon offsets. Starbucks promotes pilot projects in Chiapas, Mexico, that it says have generated 21,189 tonnes in carbon offsets. The company says it has similar plans for programs in North Sumatra and Aceh, Indonesia. To aid (and promote) its collaboration with Conservation International, Starbucks introduced a Conservation International Starbucks Card. Bright green and made of 80 per cent recycled plastic, it triggered a five-cent donation to Conservation International every time the consumer made a purchase.

Energy efficiency is the second component of Starbucks' climate-friendly campaign. The two most prominent commitments are to 'reduce energy consumption by 25 per cent in our company-owned stores by 2015' and to build exclusively energy-efficient stores – as certified by the rating systems collectively known as Leadership in Energy and Environmental Design (LEED) – from early 2011. Starbucks' switch to renewable power is the final element. By 2011, the company pledged that it would 'purchase renewable energy equivalent to 50 per cent of the electricity used in our company-owned stores'. Having done so ahead of schedule, it has since revised that target upwards to 100 per cent by 2015.

Starbucks seems to be 'taking bold actions to reduce our environmental impact', and yet, when you look at the finer print, the sedative effect of the Shared Planet campaign wears off. The first alarm bell is the company's coyness about the size of its carbon footprint. Starbucks is coy with good reason. Buried deep in the company's 2011 return to the Carbon Disclosure Project, you discover the emissions from Starbucks' operations rose by over a million tonnes, or 11 per cent, between 2006 and 2010. Yet even in a little-read document like this, Starbucks can't bring itself to admit that its operational emissions are rising. Dancing uncomfortably around the issue, it says, 'Total energy use for the company could increase due to an increase in stores. It is therefore unclear whether there will be a decrease in absolute emissions'. They may say 'unclear' but they mean 'extremely unlikely'.

While Starbucks' Shared Planet ads claim credit for reducing emissions in the company's supply chain, with talk about how the company is working with farmers to protect carbon-absorbing forests, there's no interest in taking any responsibility for supply chain emissions. Never mind that these are by far the largest component of the carbon footprint of the coffee Starbucks sells. These emissions are left to the farmers, the coffee wholesalers, the freight companies and others, almost none of whom publish emissions data. Here's just some of what Starbucks doesn't count as its own: 'agricultural inputs such as coffee, cocoa, dairy'; 'packaging'; 'emissions from all modes of transport of inbound raw materials and goods, and outbound to stores'; 'waste to landfill'. It also disowns emissions from 'licensed stores' where Starbucks retains no financial interest in the store. So, while customers buying Starbucks coffee in Starbucks packaging from a Starbucks-branded store would naturally think, having seen the Shared Planet campaign, that Starbucks is dealing with the associated emissions, in the case of a licensed store the company is doing nothing of the sort. In reality, Starbucks only counts emissions from roasting, retail activity in company-owned stores and other corporate operations, while most of the carbon footprint of its products is excluded. It's impossible to take seriously a Starbucks CEO talking up 'our commitment to transparency' when the carbon footprint of his company's supply chain is totally concealed. Shared Planet does not mean shared information.

The Shared Planet commitments to energy efficiency and renewables involve the same tricks. The pledge for LEED-standard energy-efficient stores only applies to 'new company-owned stores' from 2011, not the 17,000 existing stores or the 47 per cent of Starbucks stores that are licensed. Similarly, the plan to buy renewable energy equivalent to 100 per cent of electricity use by 2015 also applies only to company-owned stores, as does the pledge to cut energy use by 25 per cent. Then you need to factor in Starbucks' viral expansion plans. The global recession torpedoed plans to expand from 17,000 to 40,000 stores, but rapid growth has now resumed, with another 800 stores planned for the 2012 fiscal year. With over two Starbucks stores being added every day, it's little wonder emissions are rising.

Starbucks is emblematic of coffee industry greenwash, though it's perhaps more visible because the brand is the same as the company. We think of brands with coffee, be it the name of the coffee house – Starbucks, Caffè Nero, Gloria Jeans – or the label on the jar – Maxwell House, Folgers, Nescafé. Yet in most cases, the brand we know belongs to a larger corporation. The four biggest coffee companies are Nestlé, Kraft, Cargill and Sara Lee. These companies may publish sustainability reports and have emissions targets, but the carbon footprint of their coffee operation is generally lost in the crowd of products. Behind them sit the companies that actually source the coffee – names completely unfamiliar to most coffee drinkers, such as Neumann Kaffee Gruppe, Volcafe and Esteve. The Indian conglomerate

Tata is well known for its cars and steel, but few people would realise it's also the largest coffee plantation company in the world.

About 25 million coffee farmers around the world produce the beans required to deliver nearly 600 billion cups of coffee a year. With each cup generating an estimated fifty-one grams of carbon dioxide, that's nearly 31 million tonnes annually, with rainforest destruction, agricultural production, freight and espresso machines all playing a part. But most of the carbon footprint is not claimed by the brands we know. In nearly every instance, the farm-based emissions – estimated by the industry itself to be around 40 per cent of coffee's total carbon footprint – and other supply chain emissions associated with coffee refining and distribution are not publicly disclosed. Coffee marketing gives us only a romantic glimpse at coffee's long supply chain. Mimicked over and over are the legendary TV commercials by Colombian Café featuring Juan Valdez, who's up at daybreak riding his trusty donkey to tend the coffee trees and smell the beans. It gives us the comforting sense that the brand takes responsibility for the whole production line. Yet while companies want us to think we're sharing the sunrise with farmers like Juan when we drink the coffee, they have no interest in sharing the emissions generated on these farms by clearing land, using fertilisers and burning petrol. There's no interest in sharing the emissions in the rest of the coffee production process either, except for the tail end: the roasting and retail.

It doesn't have to be this way, as some coffee companies are beginning to show. The founder of New England–based Dean's Beans, Dean Cycon, started out in Amherst, Massachusetts, in 1993 roasting beans in his barn and delivering them in his car. Now he roasts around 183,000 kilograms of coffee a year. His expansion is less impressive than Starbucks', and his marketing more homespun, yet his response to climate change is more credible. The main difference is transparency. Dean's Beans publishes a greenhouse emissions report that is relatively accessible and thorough for a company of this scale. Crucially, it covers many of the supply chain emissions that most of the coffee industry hides – from the freight emissions generated in bringing green coffee beans to the United States to the commute emissions of Dean's staff to UPS deliveries of his coffee to market. This is precisely the sort of information that seems beyond the capacity of a $41 billion company like Starbucks, and is also concealed by most other big players in the industry.

Like Starbucks and other coffee producers, Dean's talks up the money it spends on sustainable farming and forest protection in the countries where it sources coffee beans. The company says it has joined forces with Trees for the Future and the Pangoa Cooperative in Peru to plant 500 trees in Pangoa, which it expects to deliver 11.2 tonnes of carbon savings annually. The difference here, though, is that Dean's is more explicit in saying just what this will offset – in this case the entire life-cycle emissions only of a specific product called 'NoCO2 Coffee'. (Dean's encourages consumers to 'see if this hot coffee can help cool the planet'). The other big difference is that Dean's is refreshingly honest about the huge challenge posed by the growth of the business. Notwithstanding its best efforts – and the company boasts a creditable list of emissions-saving investments like a solar panel array that helped to cut electricity consumption at the roastery by 42 per cent – Dean's publicly acknowledges that the emissions generated by its operations are increasing as production rises. Having suppressed emissions in spite of growing sales for a few years, by 2011 the company's emissions were above its 2005 levels and rising fast.

Another company showing up Starbucks and in an important respect going further than Dean's Beans is Green Mountain Coffee Roasters (GMCR). With a green logo and the slogan 'brewing a better world', the company lists plenty of impressive initiatives involving renewable energy, and for many years GMCR has been a coffee industry darling for green consumers. What was once a small coffee shop on Waitsfield village green in Vermont has become a $10 billion business, selling 135 types of coffee through nearly twenty brands. The emissions being generated by GMCR doubled between 2007 and 2009, in line with the doubling of its coffee purchases. Since then, the company's sales have doubled again. Ironically, the growth has been driven in part by the company's good environmental reputation.

Like Dean's Beans, GMCR publicly details at least some of the emissions tied up with its supply chain. Even more creditably, and uniquely, it's offsetting all of *these* emissions as well as operational emissions, and with credits generated from renewable energy rather than distant forest protection. At over 40,000 tonnes worth of carbon offsets in 2009, this investment is on a vastly greater scale than that of Dean's Beans – not in Starbucks' league, but an indication of what's possible for a listed public company. Even so, GMCR's expansion has brought new challenges. In 2006 the company expanded into the business of coffee-brewing machines and single-serve coffee 'pods'. As well as encouraging the use of yet more energy-intensive appliances in the home, GMCR is now selling roughly 2.9 billion disposable portion packs for these machines, and says, 'we want to sell more of them'. For some observers the company's green halo is starting to fade, and certainly GMCR's heavy reliance on carbon offsets looks to be a short- to medium-term solution at best. In the meantime, GMCR's transparency and willingness to offset all of its carbon footprint, including the supply chain, is a rare good news story.

Unfortunately, there aren't many good news stories, given the ease with which the coffee brands can disown most of their emissions. Keep in mind that the companies discussed here are the ones bothering to market themselves as green. Dozens of familiar coffee companies, such as Caffè Nero in the United Kingdom, are making no effort at all. In short, when it comes to climate change and coffee, we shouldn't let the cloud forest imagery lull our senses. After all, coffee's there to help us stay awake.

earth hour

Imagine if every year on the same day around the world, 1.3 billion people chose not to light ... their cigarette for one hour. As 'Quit Hour' started in each new time zone, there'd be suitably exhilarating warm-up acts involving celebrity smokers, such as Robbie Williams, Bono and Pink. Between sets, inspiring video montages would show former nicotine addicts telling of their struggle. Then famous smokers from the worlds of politics, sports and entertainment would link arms and chant a count-down – perhaps Barack Obama and Raul Castro sharing a cigar in DC, maybe David Beckham and Kate Middleton in London, Nicole Kidman and Shane Warne in Australia. At the end of the countdown in each location, the VIPs and the huge assembled crowds would extinguish their cigarettes as one.

As happens when large groups of people are plunged into darkness momentarily at major events, the crowd would inhale simultaneously before erupting in the usual whooping fashion, with a brief lapse to tread their cigarette butts into the ground. Fists with stained fingers would punch the air, accompanied by slightly husky screams. As the large thick grey plume drifted slowly away in the breeze, leaving this mass of humanity enjoy-ing the novelty of clean air, those present would realise that this day, much like the tar in their lungs, would last forever in their memories. Once Quit Hour passed locally, attention would turn to the next time zone, the satellite feed and the big screen ... and, with Quit Hour done, attention would also turn to that gnawing craving to light up. A new grey plume would form.

Cynics would probably say the event had had little impact: if every smoker in the world went without two cigarettes during Quit Hour, that'd just leave 5.97 trillion cigarettes that would still be smoked this year, and an even greater number next year. The tobacco industry's expansion into the developing world would continue. A few right-wing columnists would seize on such statistics to label Quit Hour a 'futile gesture' and 'yet another cause célèbre for socialists looking to encroach further upon our personal freedom'. Some think tanks still denying the link between smoking and cancer would remind us that tobacco is a naturally occurring product that has been smoked for centuries without all this 'political correctness gone mad'. Quit Hour organisers would retort that the event wasn't about the number of cigarettes not smoked on the night, but about raising awareness and encouraging people to 'go beyond' Quit Hour and make smoke-free changes in their daily lives. Between the sheer goodness of that sentiment and the persuasive skills of the event's promoters, Quit Hour would emerge with its own near-sacrosanct brand.

Would we care if the world's best known tobacco companies were among Quit Hour's strongest supporters? If the most tobacco-friendly politicians in the land were appointed as official Quit Hour ambassadors? If the advertising agency that dreamt up Quit Hour made much more money helping to sell cigarettes? If the organisation responsible for Quit Hour had been funded by Big Tobacco for years?

The real-world precedent of Earth Hour suggests not. The number of smokers worldwide is around 1.3 billion, the same number of people that reportedly participate in Earth Hour. Just as the number of smokers globally is predicted to increase to 1.7 billion people in spite of a decline in the west, greenhouse gas emission increases in developing countries are erasing many times over the modest savings being made in a few developed nations. Many of the industry-funded think tanks and front groups that denied the science and fought tobacco regulation every step of the way do the same on climate change. And the parallels run much deeper. The emissions cut by Earth Hour really are minuscule, the event has taken on a sacrosanct aura, some of the biggest-polluting corporations are among Earth Hour's greatest supporters, the advertising gurus behind Earth Hour make serious money working for the carbon lobby, the official ambassadors do include some of the world's most fossil fuel–friendly politicians and the organisation behind the event is funded by companies with rising carbon footprints.

Let's begin with the emissions. When the World Wildlife Fund (WWF) launched Earth Hour in 2007, it talked up the savings generated by everyone turning off the lights for an hour. In Sydney's CBD, 'an impressive 10.2 per cent drop in energy usage' was 'double the anticipated energy saving' and 'the equivalent of taking 48,613 cars off the road for an hour'. WWF-Australia's national communications manager, Andy Ridley (now the global boss of Earth Hour), said, 'We are thrilled with the participation and energy reduction results on the night which have been [sic] greatly exceeded our original expectations'. The organisers had aimed for a 5 per cent energy reduction. Back then, the emissions impact clearly mattered.

That tune quickly changed as people worked out just how small the impact was – by some estimates, the event may even involve a small increase in emissions, thanks to everything from people travelling to attend the event to fossil fuel–based candles and firing up power stations when the lights come back on. Setting this aside, the benefits are still tiny. Those 1.3 billion people only switched off their lights, not their fridges, air conditioners, heaters or big screen televisions, which were left on to watch the live coverage of Earth Hour. Worldwide, lighting generates around 1.9 billion tonnes of carbon dioxide each year – about three times as much as commercial aviation. If 1.3 billion people, or nearly 20 per cent of the world's population, switch all their lights off for an hour, this amounts to roughly 38,000 tonnes of carbon dioxide saved. If participating businesses save a similar amount, the combined total of less than 80,000 tonnes of carbon dioxide saved is like pausing global coal use for about two minutes, or Australian coal exports for fifty-five minutes. The event's organisers, realising that it's harder to critique what isn't measured, now say: 'Earth Hour does not purport to be an energy/carbon reduction exercise. Therefore, we do not engage in the measurement of energy/carbon reduction levels'.

Instead, the promoters have emphasised other goals. Earth Hour could encourage business to lead in addressing global warming. It overwhelmingly hasn't. It could lead to political action in Copenhagen. It didn't. All this left was the awareness-raising value of going lights-free for 1/8760th of the year. So, in 2011, there were new slogans: 'change the way you live' and 'commit to actions that last all year long'. The logo was tweaked from a big '60' to '60+' to signify the new emphasis on doing something beyond sixty minutes. Had over a billion people taken that message to heart, we'd see proof that 'together our actions add up' in falling emissions statistics. Instead, after five years, emissions are still rising almost everywhere that Earth Hour is celebrated. In 2012, the concept was made more amorphous still – what had really been all about global warming was now a movement to protect the planet, with climate change relegated to fine print at the very bottom of the Earth Hour website front page, and disappearing from TV commercials altogether. But what's the problem, you may ask, if 1.3 billion people are helping to raise awareness about climate change? The chief problem is that beyond the grand futile gesture, Earth Hour and its 1.3 billion participants are unwittingly helping to greenwash a great deal.

Let's start with the companies. If you run through the 20,000 businesses that signed up to support Earth Hour in 2010, in Australia you find companies whose contribution to climate change is getting worse – from Coca-Cola to IBM to McDonald's to Starbucks to Toyota and many more of the greenwashers featured in this book. You find banks such as ANZ, the largest financier of new coal projects in Australia, and investment funds such as BlackRock – the most ubiquitous buyer of coal stocks worldwide. You find lots of fossil fuel companies too: from Rio Tinto to BHP Billiton, Vale, Woodside Petroleum and Origin Energy. As they increase their fossil fuel production, the carbon footprint of what each of these companies sells is also increasing. The supporters list also includes the world's largest coal-mining contractor, Leighton, which is busy expanding the frontiers of global coal production in Indonesia, Mongolia and Mozambique; steel companies, such as Bluescope Steel, which have strongly fought carbon pricing; and emissions-intensive electricity generators that overwhelmingly rely on coal, such as Country Energy and Stanwell Corporation.

Similarly, in the United States, event organisers don't bat an eyelid at Southern Company 'going dark' for Earth Hour, even though it is the fourth-largest emitting power company in the world and one of the most coal-dependent, and it has also funded climate sceptics. None of these things is an obstacle to participating, so for sixty minutes, the lights at Southern went dark while some of America's oldest and dirtiest coal-fired power stations churned on. It's the same story in South Africa, where Eskom, the second-largest carbon-emitting power company in the world, enthusiastically backs Earth Hour. Its press statement spoke about the importance of individual consumers reducing *their* carbon footprint, but Eskom has no such plans itself – it has 9000 megawatts of coal-fired power stations on the way, and is reportedly on track to increase its emissions by 50 per cent to nearly 300 million tonnes of carbon dioxide annually, with almost no renewable capacity. In India, Tata Power was an equally enthusiastic, if confused, participant. It didn't know – or seem to care about – the difference between Earth Hour and Earth Day (which is held in a different month and doesn't involve switching off lights). Tata's website declared: 'On this Earth Day, Earth Hour ... commit to a clean and bright future ... This Earth Day, let's pledge to switch off the lights for 1 hour on the 27th of March from 8.30 to 9.30pm'. 'Earth Day, Earth Hour, whatever!' seems to be the attitude – an apt display of eco ignorance from a company busily building 7030 megawatts of coal-fired electricity at three new power stations.

These reprehensible credentials seem not to concern the Earth Hour recruiters. So long as you're willing to kill the lights for an hour in your corporate office on a Saturday night, you're in: coal miners, coal-fired power generators, car companies, steel makers, banks financing new fossil fuel developments, celebrities with private jets. The companies and celebrities are included on the official Earth Hour supporters lists published in newspapers and online, they can publicise their participation far and wide, and everyone can pretend they're part of the fight against climate change. Come one, come all, to the greenwashing free-for-all.

The extent to which political 'brands' are greenwashed by Earth Hour is similarly absurd. Almost everywhere that you find political leadership backing expanded fossil fuel production – especially coal – you also find politicians cleansing themselves at Earth Hour with WWF's backing: in Mozambique, Mongolia, Indonesia, Russia ... the list goes on. In Australia, WWF even made Anna Bligh, then premier of Queensland, an official Earth Hour Ambassador. When Bligh was not dimming the lights for Earth Hour, she ran the most coal-friendly jurisdiction on Earth, and boasted about how she was helping to 'supersize' the coal industry. If Queensland's coal production increases as projected, it will treble Australia's exports within a decade, creating a carbon dioxide exporter twice as significant as Saudi Arabia is today. It's as if Earth Hour has a 'don't ask don't tell' recruitment policy.

In Pakistan both the president and prime minister have been involved in turning off the lights and lighting candles. In Karachi, the regional government declared Sindh an 'Earth Hour province' and worked with WWF to raise billboards. Yet the 'Earth Hour Province' is home to some of the world's largest coal reserves, which the provincial and Pakistani governments both want to develop as fast as possible, pushing the idea of using over half a billion tonnes of coal annually for thirty years to run some 100,000 megawatts of new power. This is equivalent to increasing the number of cars used globally by about 25 per cent. In March 2010, then Pakistani prime minister, Syed Yusuf Raza Gilani, launched Earth Hour by calling it an 'opportunity for us to demonstrate that it is within our means to make a difference'. Later that same year, he hosted Chinese premier Wen Jiabao and among other things put the wheels in motion for greater Chinese involvement in mining much more coal in Earth Hour Province. Not a candle in sight.

Just as galling is the way the advertising agencies responsible for Earth Hour drape themselves and their brands in it. When the Leo Burnett agency first came up with the campaign, it didn't just leave the interviews to its client. The company's chairman in Sydney, Nigel Marsh, spoke on Sky News as if it was Leo Burnett's event and cause, not WWF's: 'We've got 2000 companies which have signed up which is fantastic, 60,000 people have signed up and I reckon there's a chance to show the world what Australia can do, like with the Olympics, and a chance to actually draw a line in the sand and say, "Let's take some action"'. When Leo Burnett won a 'Titanium Lion' for the Earth Hour campaign at the advertising industry's annual awards in Cannes, the agency spruiked its efforts in a video, saying: 'Leo Burnett Sydney created a symbolic event that could become a movement'. It highlighted media quotes such as 'the night an ad agency turned the lights out on Sydney' and 'Leo Burnett is setting an example other agencies and their clients should be following'. This supposedly in-house video is now posted on the internet for all to see, further reinforcing the agency's brand with Earth Hour. The two admen who came up with the concept go by the curiously concomitant title of 'Earth Hour co-creators'.

Both 'co-creators' are relatively well known already – Nigel Marsh through his books such as *Fat, Forty and Fired*, and Todd Sampson through his starring role in *The Gruen Transfer*, a popular Australian TV show about advertising. Their careers need no boosting. Even so, the pro bono association with Earth Hour has clearly been a great opportunity for both to green their personal brands. Both Marsh and Sampson have given their association with Earth Hour prominent treatment in a host of media interviews, and in their personal profiles with speakers agencies. Sampson's profile until recently featured him wearing a green shirt with 'Turn off the lights' on the front. Marsh told the *Sydney Morning Herald*, 'The climate change issue fundamentally changes everything. There are a few things in life than can make you change your world view ... The green issue, once you get it, is one of those things. Once you understand the extent to which the human race is in peril, it makes you ask different questions ... The world cannot live like it's been living'.

At times, Marsh's and Sampson's apparent need to talk up their association with Earth Hour is as palpable as their lack of perspective. Sampson's official profile says that Earth Hour has been 'recognised as one of the best ideas in the world' – presumably right up there with the smallpox and polio vaccines, and perhaps even all that electric light, which is briefly being extinguished. In another interview, detailing his lifelong passion for the environment, he says his agency had, 'in a short space of time, created the world's greatest environment movement'. He discusses his eco-friendly lifestyle, the greener office that Leo Burnett has moved into, and how people 'switch the lights off when they leave the building'. An airline magazine feature on Leo Burnett explains how 'the bright sparks at Leo Burnett' won an 'Effie' award for persuading hundreds of millions of people to turn off the lights. Again wearing the 'Turn off the lights' shirt, Sampson is pictured next to Earth Hour billboards with co-workers nursing little inflatable planet Earths. The impression is that these admen are themselves environmental champions working for a climate-friendly ad agency – the Earth Hour brand, the Leo Burnett brand and the personal brand of the event's co-creators are all wrapped up in the pitch.

But just how green is Leo Burnett? This is a company that brought us the Marlboro Man and advised tobacco company Philip Morris on how to combat the perception that passive smoking is dangerous. It works for Shell (one of the most prolific greenwashers) and the Emirates National Oil Company. It markets big screen televisions and many other products for Samsung; it sells energy-hungry gadgetry and games for Nintendo. It does ads for McDonald's, which doesn't even mention climate change in its own Sustainability Scorecard, let alone disclose its carbon footprint anywhere. It sells cars for GM, Buick, Suburu and Alfa Romeo, including gas-guzzling four-wheel-drives such as the GMC Sierra pick-up – one of the least efficient cars on the road. Marsh says he doesn't see it as his role to tell clients what to advertise; Sampson says he isn't telling people how to live or not to drive Hummers. And well he might say that – at the same time as Leo Burnett was promoting Earth Hour, it was advertising Hummers, from Russia to the United Arab Emirates.

Leo Burnett is not the only ad agency greenwashing itself in Earth Hour. Another keen supporter is Ogilvy, which creates lots of WWF advertising, but has no problem with helping the Australian Coal Association to market 'clean coal'. The company that WWF used in India was Burson-Marsteller – the same PR company that Exxon used to defend itself in the wake of the Exxon Valdez oil spill, the same company hired to manage the PR fallout after the radiation leak at Three Mile Island. During the 1990s Burson-Marsteller ran successful campaigns against a carbon tax in the United States, and it still works for oil companies such as BP and Chevron, car makers such as Ford and GM, and General Electric, one of the world's biggest suppliers of coal-fired power station turbines and jet engines. This is the same PR company that Union Carbide used to navigate the media storm that followed the chemical disaster at Bhopal that killed 15,000 and injured over half a million Indian citizens. Then it popped up in 2009, cloaking its brand in green by running award-winning Earth Hour campaigns, using Facebook to count itself among the event's proud supporters and encourage people to participate, and using Flickr to post pictures linking itself with Earth Hour.

This isn't to suggest that ad agencies and PR companies must choose between large companies with big carbon footprints and environmental groups. But they can't expect double standards not to be noticed, just as they would be if agencies simultaneously worked for tobacco companies while running Quit Smoking campaigns. Companies draping their brands with the green cause need to be less cavalier about their double standards. If there's a cavalier comment that sums up the marketing people behind Earth Hour, perhaps it's this one from Sampson: 'I actually think greenwash is a good thing. Some action has to be better than no action, even if it is a largely symbolic action, an awareness-growing thing'. So greenwashing the world's biggest polluting companies, the politicians that cosset them and the PR firms that defend them, is just fine, so long as there's some real action, albeit tiny.

What then should we make of WWF, itself a large multinational organisation that spends millions each year promoting its own brand globally, with much of the focus on Earth Hour? There's no doubt that WWF is an organisation that does good work across a range of environmental issues, whose concern about climate change is real, and whose desire to raise awareness and build momentum is genuine. Underpinning its Earth Hour brainchild, however, is deep faith in the idea that big business is driving a green revolution, and that many of the companies with which WWF has built close collaborations are leading the charge. The more sober reality is that Earth Hour is being used to greenwash many of the worst polluting big brands. Worse, still, WWF accepts tens of millions of dollars annually in undisclosed donations, some of it from emissions-intensive companies whose contribution to climate change is worsening. In embracing and promoting their collaborations with WWF, these companies are being encouraged to greenwash their brands with the WWF logo. At the very least, it raises questions about the efficacy of WWF's climate change campaigns and whether its determination to generate the appearance of a green revolution has undermined its campaigns.

The genius of Earth Hour is that it allows anyone to look climate-friendly – politicians, corporate polluters, ad agencies, celebrities, citizens and, of course, WWF. Until Quit Hour really does come along, Earth Hour remains unparalleled as a marketing campaign that attracts corporate and government support and gives the most culpable an opportunity to absolve themselves. This is not the greatest social movement of all time, but it may well be the biggest greenwashing campaign of all time.

electricity

By the time electricity reaches your wall sockets, it's been greenwashed more thoroughly than just about anything else you can buy – especially if coal has been burnt to produce it. The company that owns the coal mine, the contractor that digs up the coal, the companies that handle freight and electricity generation, the company retailing the electricity, and their various lobby groups and industry associations – all are busy selling the industry that contributes the most to climate change as clean and green. Let's look at the most absurd selling points made by the least climate-friendly industry.

Since sex sells, and coal is as dirty as it gets – perhaps it was inevitable that a marketing genius would put the two together. In 2006, GE, presumably with its ecomagination™ running wild, ran now infamous TV ads depicting coal as sexy. To the dulcet tones of Tennessee Ernie Ford's 1950s hit single 'Sixteen Tons', we enter a mine full of sweaty male models gripping big tools, while pouting girls in sooty sports bras confidently ride jackhammers in slow motion. Against this soft-porn backdrop, coal is 'looking more beautiful every day', thanks to GE's 'emissions reducing technology'. Coal was becoming as clean as these models were sexy, which seemingly meant one thing: carbon capture and storage. But back then, as now, there were no commercial-scale power stations fired by this 'clean coal' technology. Then, as now, GE was one of the biggest suppliers of turbines and other equipment essential to running conventional coal-fired power stations. And although the equipment is undoubtedly becoming more efficient, total emissions from power stations using GE's technology are going up. That's mainly thanks to rapid increases in dirty coal use in countries such as China and India (where GE is also busy running ads that promote coal as clean). Not that you'll hear GE acknowledge this – the company says it would be too burdensome to gather data on the emissions from the equipment they manufacture. Too hard, and maybe not so sexy.

If clean coal can be sold as sexy, though, then why not also sell it as 'cool'? Peabody Energy, the world's largest privately owned coal company, did just that with ads showing a chunk of coal wearing sunglasses. To further emphasise coal's cool credentials, Peabody ran another ad reminding the youth of today that coal is 'The rock behind today's rock music'. A teen, wearing a green shirt, listens to music on his laptop, while sitting on, of all things, a great big block of coal. 'Play a tune. Flip a switch. Send an e-mail', the ad beckons. 'The technologies that surround your life are fuelled by clean coal.' A group called Americans for Balanced Energy Choices pushed a similar line in its 'Coal is Cool' TV commercials, the familiar shades-wearing block of cool coal belying the impression that this Peabody-funded group is independent or 'balanced'.

Another approach is to portray fossil fuel as green. Some coal union bosses even artfully describe coal as organic thanks to its origin in fossilised plants. But the green claims mostly relate to burning coal more efficiently than fifty years ago and the mirage-like prospect of zero-emissions coal. Peabody routinely refers to 'green coal' – it funded a website called 'Coal Can Do That', which won energy-industry marketing awards for ads claiming that 'green coal is the solution'. One ad says: 'At Peabody it's not just about being the world's largest coal company. Our aim is to become a leading worldwide producer of sustainable energy solutions'. The company's actions suggest otherwise. Peabody has no renewable energy investments of any scale, its spending on carbon capture and storage is minuscule, and it expects to account for a sizable part of the more than 50 per cent increase in global coal use expected by 2030. When the company's vice-president says that 'using more coal to generate electricity is good for our health and good for our wealth', he's really speaking of Peabody's health and wealth.

It's a struggle to see coal as sexy, cool or green, which is why the industry wants stubborn free-thinkers to know that it too is switching to renewable energy. Tokenism is the consistent theme here. An ad by Leighton Holdings features nothing but solar panels and the sun setting behind a hill, with the line: 'More than today's power ... we're about tomorrow's ... As the world hungers for more reliable and sustainable power sources, we never stop generating innovation.' Yet, Leighton's involvement in solar power is infinitesimal by comparison to its involvement in fossil fuel extraction. Leighton was part of a consortium looking for government funds to build a solar power station a few years ago, but it is yet to build a single solar power station of any scale. Meanwhile it digs up hundreds of millions of tonnes of coal annually, and the list of new mines keeps growing.

Australian companies are showcasing other ways to dress up fossil fuel–based electricity as green, such as buying a few hybrid or electric vehicles. In New South Wales, Country Energy (now called Essential Energy) had a fleet of bright green

Toyota Priuses with its name and 'plug-in hybrid electric vehicle' emblazoned on the side. Further north, in Queensland, Ergon Energy has half a dozen Mitsubishi i-MiEV electric cars running around sporting the company's name and logo, and lots of green paint. The core business of both companies is selling coal-fired power, but these cars are moving billboards that hint strongly otherwise. Ergon even has billboards featuring the green i-MiEVs prominently displayed at airports with the words: 'You're driving Queensland's future'. Another technique is to plant a few trees, like the electricity utility now called Endeavour Energy. Though they're also mainly in the business of selling coal-fired power, they saw fit to run a full-page magazine ad with 'Plant Power' as the headline. Given the smiling man planting seedlings and the words 'sowing the seeds for tomorrow', you'd think the electricity flowing along power lines in the ad's background must somehow be generated from plants, but of course it isn't. Endeavour is merely spending a tiny fraction of what it makes from selling coal-fired power to sponsor a revegetation project in western Sydney that it grandiosely calls a 'greenhouse forest'. On the company's own figures, the project absorbs 'around 50 tonnes of greenhouse gases each year' – equivalent to the emissions of just four or five houses. Meanwhile, the electricity sold annually by the company generates around 11 million tonnes of greenhouse pollution – about 230,000 times as much as the revegetation project's saving. No mention of that in the ad, though – the company instead claims boldly to be 'offsetting carbon emissions and helping to ensure a brighter future for generations to come'.

Around the same time as the Plant Power ad, Endeavour cottoned on to another neat greenwashing trick for a coal-fired power company: pledge to go carbon-neutral by 2020, but don't count the emissions produced to generate your electricity in the equation. It's the electricity equivalent of a cigarette company vowing to operate a completely smoke-free office by 2020, while disavowing the lung cancer caused by its product because it didn't grow the actual tobacco. Yet whether it's Ergon, Essential, Endeavour or quite a few others, the reality being hidden is the same – over 90 per cent of what's being sold is electricity from fossil fuels – and mainly coal.

An even more brazen alternative to dressing coal up as climate-friendly is to ignore climate change entirely while still claiming to be 'green', 'eco-friendly' or 'sustainable'. It's similar to the way Reynolds American tobacco company markets Natural American Spirit 'organic' cigarettes without any mention of the lung cancer risk. So long as the Indonesian coal-mining company Adaro ignores the 143 million tonnes of greenhouse gas emitted annually from the coal it sells, its ads can feature a hand cupping a tree above a 'Caring for the Environment' banner, talk about mine rehabilitation being a 'prime focus', and claim to sell 'the world's most environmentally friendly solid fuel' – on the grounds that its coal is 'ultra low' sulfur, ash, dust and Nitrogen oxides.

Anglo American is on to the same trick. As Anglo is one of the world's largest multinational coal exporters, by far its biggest environmental impact is the nearly 275 million tonnes of greenhouse gas generated annually by its coal. Yet there's no inkling of this in the marketing. Instead, Anglo runs heartwarming ads about planting trees and saving fish. One full-page newspaper ad declares that 'good mining is good fishing'. The fine print next to a close-up of an earnest-looking coal miner reveals that Anglo is planting thousands of endangered redgum trees along the river near one of its mines, 'and even building wooden fish hotels'. The ad claims, 'Environmental considerations are at the heart of all our mining operations' – so long as you're happy to ignore climate change.

Still not buying coal as sexy, cool or green? How about the idea that coal-fired electricity just makes common sense? So much so that energy companies are trademarking common sense itself. Coal-fired Southern Company has actually trademarked the slogan 'Powered by Common Sense'. In a move reminiscent of Chevron's fanciful assertion that it is powered by 'human energy', the world's fourth-largest polluting power company now seems to be claiming a monopoly of sorts on common sense. Southern's marketing has included full-page ads in which the company argues, 'Common sense says don't eliminate what you can make cleaner ... common sense says, if you're looking for the best energy solution, start with what's under your feet.' The ads explain that Southern is 'working towards' building the first zero-emissions coal-fired power station and spending just over a billion dollars a year cleaning up coal use. They don't mention that much of that money is spent on making more efficient use of coal rather than zero-emissions coal, or that Southern gets a mere 2 per cent of its electricity generation from renewable sources, or that its overall emissions are still increasing. Common Sense™ says play that down.

For those who remain unpersuaded by the power of Common Sense™, the coal-fired industry has a few final entice-ments, such as nationalistic fervour and faith. Leading up to the 2008 US presidential election, the American Coalition for Clean Coal Electricity ran TV ads urging Americans to 'believe' in clean coal technology. In the space of sixty seconds, actors said 'I believe' an impressive seventeen times. 'We can' or 'We will' were thrown in fourteen times to bolster the case that 'believing' could foster national energy independence, environmental protection, limited greenhouse gases, affordable energy costs and the use of 'cheap and clean' coal. This faith-based case for clean coal was interspersed with an emotional appeal to patriotic pride – 'I believe we can use American energy resources'; 'I believe in energy independence'; 'I believe in technology'; 'I believe in American ingenuity'. The ads stop short of asking Americans to close their eyes, click their heels and chant 'there's no place like clean coal'. Perhaps that is still to come. Yet no matter how faithful or nationalistic we might be, there is no clean coal utopia. Four years on from those ads, there's no commercial-scale clean coal power stations in sight and scientists warn that if we continue to burn the world's remaining coal at current rates, global temperature increases of four degrees, or worse, look very likely.

In fairness, not all electricity being delivered is heavily greenwashed – there are a few companies that mostly use renewable energy sources. There are some that can say their business is genuinely helping to reduce emissions and combat climate change. But most electricity companies selling themselves as green and, for that matter, the companies selling most available green power, are still overwhelmingly reliant on fossil fuels. So while it makes lots of Common Sense™ as individuals to buy green power where we can, it makes as much sense to be wary of the greenwash that usually comes with it.

fashion

'Look hot while discussing global warming', says the Levi's poster. If there's going to be a debate about climate change, then apparently the crucial thing is not what you say or do, but that you look the part in a pair of Levi's Eco Jeans. Featuring 100 per cent organic cotton, recycled buttons and zippers, and a green tab instead of the usual red, is there an item of clothing other than Levi's Eco Jeans that could possibly exude more green cachet? Well, Italian fashion label Diesel certainly thinks so. Back in 2007 it ran an advertising campaign called Global Warming Ready, which depicted the usual pouting models in a series of casual poses, surrounded by visual evidence of catastrophic climate change but still enjoying the high life – sunbathing on the rooftop of a Manhattan skyscraper that has been partly submerged under 500 feet of water; swimming with penguins in a snow-free Antarctic; lazing on a palm-fringed beach next to the flooded Mt Rushmore; feeding South American macaws in St Mark's Square in Venice; picnicking in tropical forests under the Eiffel Tower; and driving a speedboat straight into the open seas from central London. Rising sea levels and encroaching deserts are nothing to worry about, the ads seemed to say, and here are the fun things we'll be able to do in a warmer world – while wearing fashionable gear. Did their colleagues scoff? Not on your life. The advertising industry awarded the campaign a Silver Lion at its annual Effie Awards in Cannes.

When Diesel was widely criticised by others for making light of climate change, it pleaded innocent, saying the campaign was 'consistent with Diesel's tradition of generating attention and provoking discussion of serious societal issues with a tongue-in-cheek ironic voice'. Diesel became a partner of the advocacy group 'stopglobalwarming.org' and it urged its customers to get active: 'there is still time to turn the tide. Maybe. Get informed, get in touch and get involved. This is the cause of our lifetime and the fight of our generation. It's not just trendy. Green is the new black. Join the virtual march'. The company posted a list of things its customers could do: 'having sex (quietly) to cut down on heating; walking to the shops; turning off lights; insulating homes with recycled denim; never taking a shower; unplugging electric guitars at the wall; giving fashion magazines to grannies, friends or anyone; hanging up towels; planting trees; and eating steak in a restaurant (to make it possible to get rid of the fridge at home)'. Presumably much of this advice was tongue-in-cheek. But since Diesel claims to be serious about climate change, surely it would publicly advocate deep cuts in emissions world-wide and lead by example by reducing its own carbon footprint? Well, no. Diesel seems not to have mentioned the issue since that ad campaign, and it doesn't publish any information about its own carbon footprint. That's presumably tongue-in-cheek irony too, or perhaps just tight-lipped opportunism.

It's not quite this bad over at Levi's, where at least it wants to discuss global warming ... while looking hot. The company's sustainability report highlights how it has reduced the amount of water used in manufacturing – not so long ago softening a pair of

Levi's jeans was akin to running the tap for over an hour and a half. Levi's has joined coalitions pushing for energy independence in the United States, backed emissions trading legislation and lots more. It also claims a relatively tiny carbon footprint of around 80,406 tonnes, which it says it's cut by nearly 6 per cent in just one year, mainly through big renewable energy purchases in Europe. Sounds like a good news story, until you dig a bit deeper and discover how much more there is to the carbon footprint of Levi's products. The cultivation of the raw materials used, assembly and garment finishing, and transport and distribution generate around 4 million tonnes, and then there's another 3.3 million tonnes generated annually to clean and iron the end product. In all, the company is claiming as its own just over 1 per cent. And with Levi's doing its best to encourage people in developing countries to dress like westerners, it's hardly surprising that the company can't – or won't – say whether those indirect emissions are rising or falling, any more than it's saying how many of those Eco Jeans it's selling.

What about some of the well-known eco-clothing labels, such as Patagonia? For many, the outdoor clothing company based in Ventura, California, is an exemplar of green corporate behaviour. Visit its website, and you may well conclude that this is an environmental activism outfit rather than a commercial enterprise. The site is dominated by its environmental philanthropy and projects, recounting the millions of dollars being contributed annually to hundreds of worthy green causes, such as blocking large-scale hydro power schemes in vulnerable parts of the Patagonian wilderness from which the brand takes its name. The company's interest goes beyond writing cheques, though – it also publishes lengthy, almost scholarly, essays on environmental issues and philosophy.

It is therefore no surprise to read that the company has switched to renewable energy and offset the remaining emissions at its distribution plant in Renoor, and that it has installed solar panels at its head office, which also double as car park shading. Patagonia also launched a Footprint Chronicles™ initiative allowing customers to view every conceivable aspect of the environmental impact of individual products it sells, including the greenhouse emissions. It even allowed the public to follow the impacts right through the supply chain: from farm to factory to shop across continents. The Footprint Chronicles couldn't tell you how much methane you'd emit from a pair of organic jeans or shorts over its lifetime, but the Chronicles could tell you to within a few grams how much greenhouse gas was emitted before you put them on. It also features a global map detailing all of the company's suppliers.

Whereas most companies go to great lengths to demonstrate the sustainability of their enterprise and painstakingly avoid words like 'pollution', Patagonia openly acknowledges that virtually everything it does causes pollution, even doubting whether a company can become truly sustainable. In admitting that its growing business is struggling to be sustainable, it is much more honest than most, which makes it easier to take seriously the positive steps it's taking.

The implication of the Footprint Chronicles, the solar panels, the carbon offsets and the essays is that Patagonia is reducing its carbon footprint in an effort to be a beacon of environmental leadership for the business community. Yet what's missing among the mountain of material is any mention of Patagonia's carbon footprint – total emissions, whether they're rising or falling, and what the company's plans and timetable are for reducing its contribution to climate change. The

Footprint Chronicles might tell you about the carbon footprint of a pair of pants, but not how many pairs the company sells. Because Patagonia is a privately held company, there are no publicly accessible annual reports. It's as if Patagonia's total carbon footprint is the only one it won't chronicle. Write to Patagonia asking for this information, and you are referred back to the Footprint Chronicles website. Point out that you're looking for the carbon footprint of the company itself, and ask whom to speak to for more information, and the media department suddenly stops answering. You can enquire to your heart's content, but the media department doesn't want to know. In spite of a prolific record on a range of environmental fronts, on the biggest issue of all – its own carbon footprint – the greenest-looking fashion brand may also be one of the shrewdest greenwashers.

Timberland is another fashion company that markets itself as climate-friendly. It ran an advertising campaign dubbed Earthkeepers™, which featured light-hearted TV commercials in the United States with the heroes that 'nature needs'. One depicts a man seeing a stray water bottle blowing past in the wind, then chasing it down, James Bond–like, riding the top of a train, scaling waterfalls, etc. before catching the bottle and disposing of it in a recycle bin. Right when he thinks the chase is over, another piece of litter blows past, and presumably he's off again. Other ads by the company tell us that each pair of Earthkeepers boots contains as much recycled PET as one and a half typical water bottles – so in effect, buying some new shoes helps to reduce litter. When the boots aren't reducing litter they're planting forests, with another ad pledging that Timberland will plant a tree for every new pair of Timberland footwear purchased. 'Plant one on us' goes the slogan. But just how does Timberland's climate friendliness stack up? What targets has it set itself and what progress is it making?

In 2005, Timberland announced it would become carbon-neutral by 2010, zeroing out the emissions for which it is directly responsible by cutting energy use and buying renewable energy and carbon offsets. But there's wiggle room in the previous sentence, as the carbon-neutral pledge and the very ambitious emission reduction targets that go with it apply only to facilities that Timberland *owns and operates*. Happily, Timberland admits that this covers a mere 4 per cent of the carbon footprint of its products: not the factories run by others that produce its boots and clothes, not the transport involved in moving all that clobber around the world, etc. So, when Timberland says it is carbon-neutral, it means that 4 per cent of the carbon footprint of its products has been neutralised. Meanwhile, Timberland still gets a decidedly unheroic 87 per cent of its electricity from non-renewable sources. With the company targeting increased volumes over the next decade, those supply chain emissions it disowns are going to keep rising, as the company itself acknowledges, saying, 'As we open new stores and expand our international presence, we expect our emissions will grow' ... with 4 per cent of it carbon-neutral. Nature needs heroes alright – Timberland could use a few more too.

The more fashion brands you look at, the more a worrying picture starts to emerge: in almost every case, the brand we see relies on other contractors, mostly based in developing countries depending on relatively more emissions-intensive energy sources. This enables the big brands to escape any responsibility for the vast majority of emissions generated in the manufacturing process. It allows them to report a small carbon footprint and focus on promoting green initiatives, most of which are concentrated in the developed country markets where public interest and scrutiny is greatest. In many cases, though, the situation is far murkier because the brands we know don't even report a carbon footprint. They're owned by larger companies, of which most of us have never heard, and whose businesses are so broad that any overall reporting is meaningless.

Take the world's largest fashion group, Spanish company Inditex – which owns brands such as Zara, Pull & Bear and Bershka. It has more than 4600 retail stores in seventy-seven countries. In 2011 it opened another 436 stores. But if you try to follow the carbon footprint of the Zara brand, there is hardly even a trail to go cold. Zara itself provides no information and a visit to the Inditex site results in a massage of greenwash. The company relaxes you with assurances that 'reducing greenhouse gas emissions' is one of its main goals, then prods you gently with comforting initiatives – from greener vehicle fleets to solar panels on its sprawling logistical centres. You hear soothing words about a new tree planting project in the Sierra Gorda Biosphere Reserve, in Mexico. Then comes the news to unwind any remaining tension: the company does release an annual disclosure of its carbon footprint. You leave feeling great about Inditex, unless you've twigged that the company takes responsibility only for the emissions from transporting products to their shops and selling them to you, not the much greater emissions tied up in *making* what it sells.

PPR is another relatively unknown fashion giant whose brands are household names: Gucci, Yves Saint Laurent, Puma. PPR releases data on the size of its carbon footprint and even claims that its emissions are falling thanks to its emissions-reduction activities. However, the emissions reported are mainly tied up with its stores, offices and warehouses in developed countries – it excludes the emissions generated in making what it sells. In 2011, however, PPR allowed Puma to lift the veil somewhat, with what the company called its 'environmental profit and loss statement'. Like various large companies, Puma had analysed the greenhouse gas emissions generated not just by its own operations, but by all of its supply chain. The analysis found that Puma's operations accounted for just 15 per cent of the carbon footprint of its products. With the help of PricewaterhouseCoopers, the company then applied an estimate of €66 per tonne to come up with what it considered to be the ecological cost of the greenhouse emissions tied up with its products. A similar analysis is being done of other environmental and societal negatives as well as economic and social positives associated with the business. Along the way there is to be lots of stakeholder engagement and one suspects the result will be a rigorous conclusion that Puma is a wonderfully sustainable outfit.

What's missing in all this so far, however, is any evidence as to whether the carbon footprint of the products sold by Puma (and PPR) is decreasing. This seems pretty unlikely at the rate Puma is increasing its sales of footwear, apparel, golf clubs and much more. So there's good reason to look behind the environmental profit and loss statement to investigate the emissions trail back to the factories and raw material suppliers. Try doing so, and you run into trouble. Puma cooperated with one recent study, but refused to disclose the location of a factory in southern China. (Other companies, including Nike, Asics, Saucony and Brooks, refused to participate at all.) When you do manage to trace the factories, what you find is many well-known brands buying clothing made by the same companies, of which few of us have ever heard – and which are even less inclined to disclose their carbon footprints.

Esquel, one of the world's largest manufacturers of cotton shirts, is one example. Based in Hong Kong, it produces well over 100 million garments a year. The company runs some fifteen factories in six countries from China to Mauritius, and also owns its entire supply chain, right down to the cotton farms. The company's revenues roughly doubled between 2004 and 2010, mainly by servicing well-known western fashion labels. Esquel paints itself as a leader in sustainable corporate behaviour. Esquel's CEO is a former director of Conservation International, and the company runs a robust campaign to promote its green credentials. Rattling off a long list of initiatives, Esquel says its customers 'can sleep at night' knowing that their brands are going green. More likely, customers are sleeping well at night for a different reason: among all the green PR by Esquel, you will not find any information about the size of its carbon footprint, or any target or timetable to reduce it. The company says it's saved 164,000 tonnes of greenhouse gas by using over 20 per cent less energy to make each shirt – but as all the figures are 'per piece' and the number of pieces being made by Esquel is spiralling, it doesn't tell us much about the total carbon footprint of the enterprise. Esquel is the emissions equivalent of a Swiss bank account or offshore tax haven. And who are the brands sleeping soundly under roofs like Esquel's? Whose emissions vanish every year into this carbon dioxide Bermuda Triangle? Well, let's see: there's Patagonia, Levi's, Nike, Gap, Zara, Yves Saint Laurent, plus big box retailers such as Walmart, Tesco and Marks & Spencer. Many other household-name clothing brands shelter here too, including Abercrombie & Fitch, Esprit, Gant, Nautica, Hugo Boss, Brooks Brothers, Nordstrom, Banana Republic, Ralph Lauren and Tommy Hilfiger.

When you buy clothes at a well-known department store, at a shopping mall or on the local high street, the brand may well be telling you a green story, but it is almost certainly hiding most of the carbon involved somewhere in China or some other developing country, with companies totally unknown to you. And we've focused here only on the companies with greener reputations. You can guess what's going on elsewhere. When it comes to the fashion industry and climate change, it *is* mostly about *looking* hot.

fast food

'What if making the world a better place was as easy as eating a sandwich', says a Subway commercial. A bright green backdrop and whimsical piano music help you ponder the question. It goes on, 'What if helping the environment was as easy as giving up a hamburger'. We'll return to the hamburgers, but let's stick with the sandwich for now. 'What if making the world a better place by helping the environment was as easy as going to your local Subway'. In case the lack of question marks didn't tip you off, you're being told, not asked. Subway is so certain on these points that the ad concludes with a new logo: one that adds 'Live Green' to the existing 'Subway – Eat Fresh' slogan. But what evidence is there to support the idea that eating a Subway sandwich is good for the environment?

First up, let's look at the environmental impact. People are already so enthusiastic about saving the planet by eating a Subway sandwich, a new store is opening about every 3.5 hours. Worldwide, the brand (owned by Doctor's Associates Inc.) has over 36,000 locations in ninety-eight countries. It is the second-largest fast food company in the world behind Yum! Brands, which owns KFC, Pizza Hut and Taco Bell. Its signature dish is a foot-long sandwich, and that's something unlikely to change any time soon – which can't be said of Subway's rapidly growing carbon footprint. The exact scale of Subway's total greenhouse emissions is unknown, as the company doesn't make this information public. However, one safe assumption with this many restaurants, and over 2000 new stores opening annually, is that it's a large and growing number.

To show you the leap of faith involved in believing that Subway's sandwiches make the world a better place, consider this: of the 22,000 stores that make Subway the largest takeaway chain in the United States, the company deems a mere fourteen to be worthy of being called 'Eco-Stores'. The Eco-Stores sound great – lots of energy-efficient innovations, water-efficient technologies and recycled materials – but for each one, Subway has 1500 or so non-Eco-Stores. On its corporate website, Subway mentions a few other green initiatives, including changing to energy-efficient light bulbs, switching its cups from polystyrene to polypropylene and using 100 per cent recycled napkins. The company says, 'In 2010 alone, our initiatives in North America cut carbon emissions by 104,586 metric tons'. What's not provided to customers, however, is context. If we conservatively assume that a Subway store uses just half the electricity of a KFC restaurant, this would roughly equate to 184 tonnes of emissions annually per store. On that basis it would take only 568 new stores to erase Subway's 2010 carbon savings in North America. With the company adding over 2000 new stores annually, Subway is adding perhaps three times as much greenhouse pollution as it saves. That's before we even think about the supply chain emissions tied up in producing the sandwich ingredients used by Subway.

The paucity of detail to support Subway's 'Live Green – Buy Subway' pitch is staggering. As well as concealing the size of its carbon footprint, and having announced no plan for reducing it, Subway says nothing about when, if ever, it plans to start using renewable energy on any meaningful scale to power its stores. The lack of attention to these issues could hardly be in starker contrast to Subway's steely determination to grow as fast as possible. The company aggressively markets franchising opportunities around the world, spoon-feeding would-be franchisees with free seminars, cost breakdowns, contacts with lenders and lots of 'Why Subway?' marketing. There is even a University of Subway available 24/7 to train and assist would-be franchisees. The expansion is so great that the store growth achieved by Subway's founders in their first ten years is now matched every three days.

Fittingly, for a company this oblivious to its carbon footprint, Subway boasts, 'You can enjoy a foot-long turkey breast sub with your choice of a variety of vegetables and condiments served on bread baked right in the restaurant in Jamaica, then travel to New Zealand and get the same foot-long turkey breast sub'. I'm sure the company isn't seriously suggesting lunch in the Caribbean and dinner in New Zealand, but it certainly makes you wonder whether two Subway sandwiches would still be 'helping the environment' if they require a flight halfway round the world. Which brings us to the hamburgers Subway wants us to avoid. Just how bad are they?

Let's start with McDonald's, which decided to paint its golden arches bright green in 2009 'out of respect for the environment'. If this marketing decision wasn't reflected at your local Macca's, that's because McDonald's did it only in Europe. In the lead-up to the 2009 Copenhagen conference, the clear message was that McDonald's was going green. This was out of the ordinary for McDonald's, whose previous use of the word 'green' generally related to new menu items with a counter-intuitively high salad quotient. The company has had many environmental headaches over the years, from the polystyrene clamshells in which it once packaged its burgers to the Amazon forests destroyed to feed the cattle and chickens providing the meat. McDonald's dealt with these challenges as they arose, but never seemed to aspire to green leadership. Once the company painted its arches green, its claim to consumers was clearly that McDonald's was now on the planet's side.

McDonald's serves over 64 million customers every day in over 33,500 restaurants in more than 119 countries. From 2005 to 2010, and in spite of the global financial crisis, it managed to add more than a new restaurant every single day. In 2011 it increased that pace to over two new restaurants a day. Growing that fast, and with every cheeseburger generating around three kilograms of carbon dioxide, the company obviously needs much more than green arches to reduce its carbon footprint. Perhaps aware of this, it now publishes a thick compendium of in-house initiatives, called 'The Best of Green'. Along with spruiking its LEED-certified restaurants (a grand total of four by 2012, though the company says it plans to add twenty-five by 2015), and details of its alliance with Greenpeace to save Amazonian forests, the pages are brimming with heartwarming examples of McDonald's franchisees and staff saving the planet.

As a corporate scrapbook of greenwash, this document is almost without peer. What makes it so effective is the way the local focus obscures the bigger picture. We learn all about how organic waste from McDonald's restaurants in Switzerland is turned into biogas to run environmentally-friendly trucks, and how enough energy is being produced from the landfill waste of eleven restaurants in Sheffield, UK, to heat 130 homes. What's studiously neglected, however, is the cumulative impact of these actions for the brand worldwide. Nowhere does the company say how large is its total carbon footprint. It lodges a return with the Carbon Disclosure Project at the request of institutional investors, but it will not make the data or the accompanying detail public. McDonald's says it has had 'a global commitment to the environment since 1990', but apparently its commitment to the environment does not extend to telling us what contribution its activities make to climate change.

But don't for one minute think you're going to save the environment by taking your business across the road to KFC, which these days is owned by Yum! Brands rather than Colonel Sanders. With over 38,000 restaurants in more than 117 countries and territories, Yum! Brands is a juggernaut of even greater size than McDonald's. Most of KFC's green claims relate to the packaging it uses – the green-coloured wrapping around its Chicken Fillet Burger has a picture of a tree and the words 'great taste, less waste'. 'Renew, Re-use, Rejoice' has been added to its logo, with a small green-coloured leaf. As part of efforts to promote its 'award-winning' reusable salad containers, KFC put up posters in stores declaring, 'We're going green'. KFC cites 'smart energy use' as one of the various ways the company is going green. Yum! Brands, meanwhile, is emphatic on its website and in posters displayed in stores that 'Reducing Carbon Footprint' is one of its four main sustainability objectives.

Try clicking on the 'Reducing Carbon Footprint' icon on Yum!'s website, however, and the problems begin – there is no link from it to more information on how the company is reducing its carbon footprint. Another page features the 'Reducing Carbon Footprint' icon with a little detail, but the font is so small as to be almost completely unreadable. Search further and you notice the company's pledge to 'reduce global energy consumption by 10 per cent by 2015'. Then you ask yourself: how can Yum! possibly cut its total energy use worldwide when it adds a new store about every six hours? That commitment, it turns out, is not at all what it seems. It sure sounds like a 10 per cent cut in the total amount of energy used in Yum! Brands stores. Yet, as Yum!'s Public Affairs department confirmed when asked, it actually means a 10 per cent reduction in the energy use of *company-owned stores* relative to 2005. This still sounds impressive, until you discover that the number of company-owned stores is less than it was in 2005. During the same period the number of *non–company owned stores* not subject to the energy target has increased by over 470 per year! Between 2009 and 2011 the pace nearly doubled: the company added over 1700 new stores while also reducing the number of company-owned stores by 3 per cent. So, reducing the number of company-owned stores, for reasons that have nothing to do with the environment, helps Yum! to meet its narrowly defined energy target. By 2015, if Yum! succeeds in cutting energy use in company-owned restaurants by 10 per cent, that will be akin to 760 less restaurants compared with 2005. Yet, at the current rate, Yum would have added a whopping 6200 restaurants – almost all non-company owned. Given the magnitude of expansion, it's hard not to conclude that the overall energy consumption and carbon footprint of Yum!'s brands is increasing rapidly. It's greenwash of a spectacular order.

What makes it doubly remarkable is Yum!'s firm view that its global expansion is an environmental positive: 'a great opportunity to make a meaningful impact towards environmental sustainability'. Like Subway and McDonald's, it points to one or two green stores to showcase the company's leadership, including a joint KFC–Taco Bell site in Northampton, Massachusetts, which has been 'LEED Gold Certified', using LED lights, solar hot water, increased insulation and an unstated number of carbon offsets. The site even features a 'solar wall', which is designed to absorb more heat than normal walls so it can reduce the building's energy requirements. According to the company, this store 'demonstrates the Company's commitment to increasing awareness of renewable energy, as well as Yum! Brands' emphasis on corporate responsibility and environmental stewardship'. That's some commitment too – one green store out of 38,000!

Note that the emphasis is on Yum! Brands' commitment to 'increasing awareness' of renewable energy, not necessarily using much of it. After all, why switch to renewable energy en masse when doing so on a well-promoted, isolated scale can earn disroportionate green kudos? The solar wall initiative in Northampton will save just 245 tonnes of carbon dioxide (less than one carriage full of coal). But it was enough to prompt the company that built the solar wall to gush, 'In an era where a lot of companies are talking green, Yum! Brands is walking green'. Even the head of the US Green Building Council was sufficiently impressed with one building to declare, 'KFC–Taco Bell's LEED certification demonstrates tremendous green building leadership'. Beyond the sole green store, Yum! points to the energy-efficient interior lighting installed at company-owned KFC restaurants, saying it equates to taking 763 cars off the road for a year. Efficient air conditioners with thermostats save as much carbon dioxide as 532 American homes produce in a year.

To get an idea of just how insubstantial these green initiatives are, let's again consider Yum!'s projected growth. The company brags that it introduced franchising to China, and it has some

3400 restaurants there now, with another 20,000 planned in the long term. The other international expansion is just as daunting – in 2010, for the tenth year running, the company opened more than 700 new restaurants outside the United States and China. The average KFC restaurant uses 350,000 kilowatt-hours of electricity per year, some forty times that of the average home, involving 367 tonnes of carbon dioxide emissions (assuming renewable energy is not used). So adding 1000 new restaurants is the same as adding over 80,000 cars to the road. Even with the benefit of the energy target applying to company-owned stores, the carbon footprint of Yum! Brands restaurants is on track to increase in the next decade by around 20 per cent. Yum! is not kidding when it refers to its business as a giant cash machine – but it's also a giant carbon machine.

Perhaps not surprisingly, making the world a better place is not as easy as eating a Subway sandwich or Big Mac, let alone KFC's 'Double Down' burger – which involves two chicken fillets with bacon and melted cheese in the middle. Fast food companies trying to persuade us otherwise are doing their reputation for selling junk no favours.

flights

Not so long ago Air India announced that within a year it would become that country's first green airline. Announcing the plan, the company made clear it was absolutely committed to cutting greenhouse pollution. There were none of the usual greenwashing stunts – no trademarked green logo or slogan, no painting the tail and wingtips green. Air India was serious: it would introduce an e-filing system to reduce the company's paper use. Cue the canned laughter. Yes, the airline would go paperless, except where it was legally required to do otherwise. True, major airlines are more renowned in environmental circles for the emissions coming from their planes than their paper use, but presumably this is one of those single steps with which every large journey is supposed to begin. Even so, it's hard to think Air India's journey will be a climate-friendly one, with another thirty new planes on order.

Commercial aviation is good at not seeing the forest for the trees. At Singapore's Changi airport you'll see advertising on recycling bins claiming that the airport has saved lots of trees through its recycling initiatives. It's wonderful that the airport is encouraging patrons to recycle their newspapers, but some perspective wouldn't go astray. As of late 2010, the tally of trees saved stood at 1832. This saves perhaps 500 tonnes of carbon dioxide once the trees are fully grown, which is about the emissions generated on a one-way Singapore to London flight, of which there are more than 2500 every year.

The industry takes breathtaking mental leaps to create the impression that aviation is already green. Easyjet argues that flying on one of its jets is more climate-friendly than driving a Toyota Prius. The rationale is that when the number of kilometres flown is divided among passengers, flying an Easyjet airliner produces less carbon dioxide. Clearly, people should all replace their hybrid cars with 737s.

Over at Boeing, where they're making the 737s among much else, the green talk is similarly upbeat. Ads show a pair of eyes staring into a crystal ball – the Earth is etched into the ball which is held in cupped hands. It explains that Boeing is 'committed to finding those great ideas to enhance ... the life of the planet' and to becoming 'better stewards of the environment', as if it's already a good steward. The company's annual report suggests its carbon footprint is shrinking. A graph called 'Environmental Footprint Reduction' shows emissions declining for nearly a decade. On the same page, the company claims to have cut them by 31 per cent and to be 'on track to achieve aggressive five-year targets for 25-percent improvements in greenhouse-gas emissions intensity'. Boeing says it's working towards carbon-neutral growth, and it wants new generations of its planes to be 15 per cent more carbon efficient than the last. Arguing that biofuels should be set aside for aviation, rather than other transport modes, it says, 'Airlines are ready to use biofuels now'.

Yet a closer look at the numbers suggests that the industry is not going nearly as green as it suggests, and that carbon-neutral growth is extremely unlikely. At Boeing, the impression given that emissions associated with its business are falling is nothing but smoke and mirrors. The 31 per cent improvement claimed is 'on a revenue-adjusted basis', so, metric tonnes of carbon dioxide equivalent per unit revenue – not a concept most people even understand. The same is true of the 25 per cent emissions reduction target. It doesn't necessarily mean less emissions overall, especially if the company is making lots more planes.

More importantly though, the much-promoted performance and ambitious-sounding targets apply to Boeing's operational emissions, not the more significant emissions emanating from the planes it sells. About every eighteen hours a new Boeing jet is being added to the skies, and Boeing is delivering nearly two-thirds more commercial planes a year now than in 2005. The total number of commercial aircraft out there is on course to nearly double by 2030, while the total number of kilometres flown collectively by all paying passengers (passenger kilometres performed) is likely to treble. So while Boeing and other plane manufacturers are building much more efficient aircraft, and while they may be on track to reach their targets, that track doesn't lead anywhere near carbon-neutral growth. Instead, the overall carbon footprint of the aircraft they've produced is increasing.

GE is on the same track, with perhaps even more confidence in its climate-friendliness, marketing jet engines as 'Eco-magination – imagination at work™'. A TV commercial for the company's NX aircraft engine shows cranes (of the feathered variety) receiving permission from an airport control tower, then taking off after a long run-up to the sound of jet engines at full tilt. As one the birds banks gracefully over a pristine tropical archipelago at sunset, the ad asks us to imagine a way of flying 'that not only helps save millions of gallons of fuel but actually *reduces emissions'*. The ad doesn't claim that GE jets emit as little carbon as the birds, but it certainly gives the impression they're well en route to mimicking nature. In reality, though, the GE NX engine can't 'reduce emissions'. To do that, it would need to inhale greenhouse gases and exhale something more benign. But, of course, had you watched the ad in slow motion you would have taken in the 'compared to the engines it replaces' qualification that flashed up in fine print for a second.

Another piece of vivid 'imagination at work™' is the GE magazine ad in which a jet engine turbine is made to look like a sunflower, surrounded by golden petals and complete with buzzing bumblebee. This time, there's no claim that the engine will 'reduce emissions', and we are given time to absorb the fact that the NX engine is '15 per cent more efficient than the one it replaces'. What's glossed is that by 2015 GE is expecting to have 62 per cent more of its jet engines flying. So, while the new engine may be more efficient than the one it replaces, the number of jet engines being added is vastly greater than the number being replaced. Elsewhere GE boasts proudly on billboards that 'Today, GE and its partners will transport 3.5 million people with our jet engines'. It's left to us to 'ecomagine' the emissions consequences.

For many airlines green paint is the preferred greenwashing technique. An Air New Zealand jet does a biofuels test flight, and green paint appears on its tail; Air Canada launches a carbon offset program to enable passengers to buy a certified emissions saving to neutralise their own flight – on goes the paint. It's not clear why ANA painted one of its tailfins green – perhaps it simply wanted to emulate the rival Japan Airlines (JAL), which had painted the tailfin of one of its Boeing 777s bright green and dubbed it the Eco-Jet. JAL promoted it heavily and got lots of great media coverage, and die-cast toy Eco-Jets went on sale too. And yet, while the 777 is slightly more efficient than its predecessors, there is nothing particularly 'Eco' about this one. JAL's main reason for painting the tailfin green was reportedly to 'raise people's awareness of the importance of the Earth's environment'. Beyond that, it runs a voluntary emissions offset scheme and is gradually replacing older aircraft with more efficient models, but this is nothing special. Nor is there anything terribly impressive about its emissions performance. But JAL has retained the Eco-Jet livery all the same.

Meanwhile, dozens of airline companies around the world are promoting offset programs as evidence that they are doing something about climate change. Perhaps the most absurd case is that of Qatar Airways, the national carrier for a country whose economy could hardly be more dependent on fossil fuels. It runs ads declaring that its antelope mascot, the oryx, 'flies green – Qatar Airways' commitment to a sustainable future'. That Qatar Airways' green commitment seems to start and end with an offset program makes it hard enough to take seriously. That the company is growing at 30 per cent a year and planning to expand its 100-strong fleet with 250 new planes makes it impossible. Green tailfins are probably not far off, but the way things are headed, antelopes will fly before the oryx flies green. Offsets have become the airline greenwash tool of choice because they put the onus on the customer to cut emissions, and the airlines don't have to make public any information on the quantity of emissions offset. Most airlines supress this information, and you can see why. British Airways revealed that in 2008 passengers offset 55,000 tonnes of emissions from their flights, but this was reportedly less than 0.5 per cent of the airline's total emissions in that year. On average, it's estimated that less than one in fifteen passengers chooses to offset their flights – a 3 to 4 per cent take-up rate is considered good. So, perhaps not surprisingly, most airlines' carbon footprints are growing.

One notable exception is a small airline in Costa Rica. Nature Air bills itself as the world's first carbon-neutral airline on the basis that it offsets 100 per cent of its emissions, no matter how many passengers fly. It's not clear that its offsets from forest protection deals are all that reliable, but they're probably no more dubious than those used by other airlines. What's different in this case is that the airline is taking rather than off-loading the responsibility.

If United Continental did that, it might be justified in painting its wingtips green and running its 'Eco-Skies' marketing. This was a Continental campaign, before it merged with United, and one infomercial posted on YouTube kicks off with: 'Some think green, others talk about going green – at Continental Airlines, we are green'. Snapshots of Continental aircraft are shown with the words 'powered by sustainable bio-fuel' and assurances that the company 'is committed to reducing our carbon footprint'. Bright green recycle symbols flash across the screen, as the company explains how it became the greenest airline in America by investing $13 billion in more than 300 fuel-efficient aircraft. Much is made of the switch from fossil fuels to electric energy in the ground support equipment. Then, with footage of bright green Eco-Skies rubbish bins, the focus shifts to waste management, and how recycling more in-flight and food service–related aluminium saved 8500 tonnes of carbon dioxide in 2009 – equivalent to 100,000 trees or enough aluminium to build thirteen Boeing 777s. Continental jets sported a new Eco-Skies logo – a leaf with the words 'Commitment to the Environment', all in bright green.

A volunteer offset program was, of course, in full swing, this time offered to freight customers as well as passengers.

There's plenty of talk about how the Continental fleet is 38 per cent more efficient for every passenger mile travelled compared with 1997. Yet a quick look at the annual reports suggests that the number of passenger miles flown increased by 73 per cent between 1997 and 2008, so the overall amount of fuel burnt and carbon footprint generated across those eco-skies were still getting bigger. At no point did the airline reveal how many tonnes of carbon have been offset by its customers. Amid all the hype about the airline's green leadership, just one Continental flight in total was 'powered with sustainable bio-fuel'. The emissions savings from the switch to electric ground equipment and from recycling were at no point put into context for the public – the recycling savings made over a full year across the Continental fleet were about the same as what that fleet emitted every six hours.

Before the merger, United also touted its own environmental credentials. It trademarked a 'Make a difference – every action counts' slogan and set up an offset program, with the help of environmental group Conservation International. Though it was passengers rather than United paying for the offsets, United nonetheless claimed that the program was part of its effort to 'reduce our impact on the environment'. At no point does the company appear to have disclosed how many tonnes of greenhouse pollution were offset under the program. The merger provided United Continental with a temporary get-out-of-jail-free card, by generating a one-off set of efficiency improvements that enabled the company to claim that its emissions fell slightly in 2011. What this ignores, though, is the company's growth. The merged entity now flies over 1200 planes on 5605 flights a day to 375 airports on six continents, and the plan is to add another 125 new aircraft before 2020. So, it seems likely that the company will be making more carbon footprints across the 'Eco-Skies', not less.

Then again, why fly on airlines such as United Continental when well-heeled tree huggers have the option of flying 'environmentally sound' private jets? Or so says American company Avantair, which bases its boast on having the 'industry's lowest carbon emissions'. The truthful part is that its planes – the Italian Piaggio Avanti – are much less emissions-intensive than most private jets. The jets favoured by eco celebrities such as Gisele Bündchen, Oprah Winfrey and the late Steve Jobs emit as much as four tonnes of carbon dioxide per hour they fly – four times as much carbon as Avantair's plane. Avantair also buys carbon offsets for all of its new customers (though the proportion of the airline's total carbon footprint being offset is not specified). To help more Americans enjoy that green private jet experience, it has come up with the idea of 'fractional ownership', similar to timeshare arrangements for beachside apartments. Rather than buying a plane, you can buy a slice of flying time. And therein lies the greenwash. Avantair wants more Americans to fly on private planes. The relative efficiency of its planes is ultimately a side issue – the net effect is to exacerbate the problem for an industry whose emissions are already growing by 3.5 per cent annually.

If you thought greenwashing private jets would be as bad as it gets, think again, and think Richard Branson, and the way he has carefully cultivated the impression that his Virgin Group enterprises are going green. In Branson's 2011 book, *Screw Business as Usual,* he discusses Virgin's 'journey to transform itself into a force for good for people and for the planet', and calls for a green revolution, saying, 'My message is a simple one: business as usual isn't working. In fact, it's "business as usual" that's wrecking our planet ... We have to fix it and fast'. Back in 2006, Branson announced with great fanfare that he was devoting the profits from his aviation and locomotive businesses to clean energy investments. Over ten years, $3 billion would be devoted mainly to the development of renewable fuels, if need be drawing on the profits of Virgin's mobile phone and other businesses. While cynics would have noticed that robbing Branson to pay Branson to build a biofuels business was hardly altruistic, it sure looked green, especially amid other charitable pledges such as the Virgin Earth Challenge, through which Branson offered $25 million to support technologies that might remove emissions from the atmosphere.

Branson's announcement of a Virgin Atlantic 300-kilometre test flight between London and Amsterdam on biofuels was great television. Soon after, he released a blueprint for changing the way aircraft operate, which he said could reduce emissions by around one-quarter if implemented industry-wide. It looked as if Virgin Atlantic was leading a global crusade. It's what the PR hides that is a worry: the biofuels flight was a one-off – covering less than 2 per cent of the distance of one Virgin flight from London to Sydney, a route it flies five days a week. Put another way, the flight was 0.0002 per cent of the 145 million kilometres the airline flew in 2011. The company claims that its emissions are falling, but perhaps that's because the airline is flying hundreds of thousands less passengers annually than it used to – we'd expect fewer aircraft hours and seat kilometres to mean less emissions. More significantly, Virgin Atlantic is just one of many airlines in which Branson has a stake – his Virgin Group is the largest shareholder in Virgin Australia, and it has a

25 per cent stake in Virgin America and 10 per cent in Air Asia X. Factor in the growth in these businesses, and the overall carbon footprint of Branson's aviation business is almost certainly increasing. Most spectacularly, Branson plans 'very environmentally friendly' joy-rides to space through his Virgin Galactic venture. Even on the company's numbers, which are hotly disputed and largely unsupported, this is a practice that would generate more than six times as much carbon dioxide each hour per passenger as does a typical London to New York return flight today. No doubt, however, it will bear a green tailfin, a voluntary offset program and its ads will claim that Virgin Galactic is more climate-friendly than driving a hybrid car ... into space.

The real shame about commercial aviation's insatiable appetite for greenwash is that it goes against the industry's own interests. The industry is growing at an astonishing speed, and finding sustainable aviation alternatives to fossil fuels is a particularly complex challenge. Renewable electricity for commercial aviation is a long way off, and many of the biofuel alternatives being touted face problems – from destroying forests to establish palm oil plantations, to encouraging greater coal use to produce waste carbon dioxide that helps grow algae from which jet fuel can be made. If the aviation industry expects governments around the world to take the challenge facing it seriously and invest in solutions urgently, it needs to be upfront about the task. Feeding political complacency with green tailfins, wingtips, offsets, paperless filing systems and other disingenuous greenwash isn't helping.

A grateful polar bear gives a Nissan LEAF owner a hug for buying a 'zero tailpipe emissions' car. For every LEAF sold, Nissan sells 27 X-Trail and Dualis SUVs, and 7 Navara utes among many other carbon-intensive vehicles.

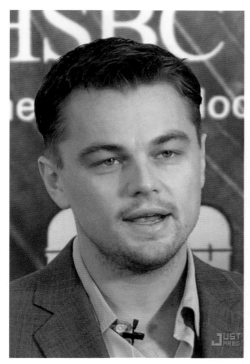

Eco-celeb Leonardo DiCaprio launches a green credit card for HSBC and co-designs greener watches for Tag Heuer.

Diesel's Global Warming Ready campaign highlighted some upsides of catastrophic climate change – in this case, lots more sun in Manhattan. The company says it was tongue in cheek, and that it's all for stopping global warming. But it won't say what's happening with its own carbon footprint.

Climate-friendly marketing helps ad agencies green their brands. Here, Leo Burnett staff pose with globes and Earth Hour banners. Earth Hour co-creator Todd Sampson wears a green shirt with the words 'Turn Off the Lights'.

A well-promoted tree-planting collaboration with an environmental group in a distant land creates the impression that a big brand is offsetting much of its carbon footprint.

'This billboard absorbs air pollutants', says the sixty-feet-square billboard in Manila featuring 3600 fukien tea plants potted in recycled PET bottles. To offset its growing carbon footprint Coke would need a sign as long as Manhattan and over eight times higher than the Empire State Building.

Many car makers promote hydrogen-fuelled cars, but they're not selling them to the public. The BMW Hydrogen 7 is given away to celebrities like Hilary Swank; others like the Chevrolet Equinox Fuel Cell are marketed with 'Not Available for Sale' in the fine print.

AFL stars Nick Reiwoldt and Luke Hodge decked out in 'Green for Footy' gear. Collaborating with Origin Energy helped the league go carbon-neutral and recruited thousands of new Green Power customers. However, the benefits are set to be erased many times over by Origin's expansion into coal seam gas.

Barges, trains and a few electric trucks involve less carbon dioxide than alternative transport modes, but that doesn't mean Tesco's carbon footprint is shrinking.

The impression is that eBay's offerings are mostly green – that it's 'the biggest engine for re-use on Earth'. Having the public write eco-statements and pose in front of eBay Green Team signs enhances this illusion for a company with a fast-growing carbon footprint, and a business now dominated by selling new products.

IT'S TIME
OIL COMPANIES
GET BEHIND
THE DEVELOPMENT OF
RENEWABLE
ENERGY.
WE AGREE.

Thomas Gideon
Executive Vice President, Timberlands
Weyerhaeuser Company

Desmond King
President, Chevron Technology Ventures
Chevron

Chevron
Human Energy™

Something's got to be done.
So we're doing it.
We produce more renewable geothermal
energy than anybody in the world.
Our venture capital arm is investing
millions in alternative energy start-ups.
And we're partnering with Weyerhaeuser
to commercialize cellulosic biofuels.
We're not just behind renewables.
We're tackling the challenge of making them
affordable and reliable on a large scale.
Learn more at chevron.com/weagree

Chevron Solar logos feature in the company's TV commercials, website videos feature Chevron staff next to huge solar power arrays, and newspaper ads suggest the company is all for oil companies investing in renewable energy. But you almost certainly won't find Chevron solar happening in your neighbourhood.

ecomagination

GE dresses up its latest jet engines as sunflowers – convincing enough to confuse a bumblebee. The new engines are more efficient, but GE hopes to have 62 per cent more of its jet engines flying by 2015.

"I guess it is easy being green."

Kermit the Frog explains that it is easy being green, so long as you drive a Ford Hybrid Escape. Or was until Ford stopped making them in 2012. Around one in a hundred Fords sold in the United States is a hybrid, and this one gets slightly worse mileage than the average US passenger car. In 2011, the company sold sixty gas-guzzling F-Series trucks for every Hybrid Escape.

Typical Comparison

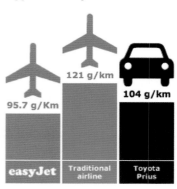

121 g/km

104 g/km

95.7 g/Km

| easyJet | Traditional airline | Toyota Prius |

= Data based on 1 person

A 'typical comparison' if you usually drive from London to the Canary Islands. In the world of greenwash, comparisons are often anything but real-world. Here, the carbon footprint of an EasyJet flight compares well with a Toyota Prius on a per kilometres basis. Richard Branson uses similar arguments to portray Virgin Galactic jaunts to space as 'very environmentally friendly'.

(Above) Smokestacks emitting flowers. Shell greenwash at its very best. (Below) A giant Shell billboard outside RFK Football Stadium in Washington DC suggests that carbon capture and storage is going to be as easy as swinging a butterfly net. Yet widespread deployment of the technology to clean up fossil fuel use is looking anything but probable.

freight

Imagine the year is 1780. You're standing at the docks in Jamestown, Virginia, as the slave traders' ships arrive. You're pondering what horrors the occupants have endured on their trip from Africa to help keep cotton production cheap. Many have not made it, having died of the diseases that come with being crammed below deck for months. Suddenly, you notice some bold lettering on the ships: 'We are an equal opportunity employer and we have an aspirational goal of freedom for all men'. OK, so it's unlikely that such signs were on slave ships. What we know for sure is that the environmental equivalent is precisely what's being pulled today by railway companies whose core business is hauling coal.

Take QR National, an Australian railway company that proudly carries the most coal in the country. When the former government-owned corporation was partially floated in 2010, it ran with the slogan 'Something Big' against backdrops of coal trains, boasting that it carries around 200 million tonnes of coal a year. A coal-laden train leaves a station somewhere in eastern Australia every nineteen minutes, each one carrying around 25,000 tonnes of carbon dioxide closer to its pyre. QR National already has a hand in more than one of every sixty tonnes of

carbon dioxide emitted *globally* each year. What's more, it plans
to build new railways to reach a clutch of mega coal mines proposed for the Galilee Basin in central Queensland. If the mines
and railways proceed, QR National could be hauling twice as
much coal – and nearly a billion tonnes of soon to be released
carbon dioxide – annually. It's hard to think of a company that
has so deliberately bound its future to the expansion of emissions-
intensive fossil fuel use.

Yet even with this much coal dust on its hands, QR
National enthusiastically maintains that it is an environmentally friendly business. It says that transporting coal by rail and
ship generates fewer emissions than using other transport
modes. Technically, trains probably do generate less emissions
than the alternatives – but then how plausible are the alternatives for the purpose of a real world comparison? Just imagine
200 million tonnes of coal being moved by truck along a few
major roads, or perhaps being carried by jet with FedEx or UPS.
In any case, this still avoids the reality that coal gets burnt no
matter how it travels, and getting burnt is what causes coal's
biggest environmental impact.

Like a slave trader talking up an aspirational goal of freedom
for all, QR National even has an 'aspirational goal of ZERO
Harm to the natural environment'. The emissions generated by
coal burning are not part of that calculation, of course – that's
assumed to be someone else's 'harm to the natural environment'.
QR National even runs carriages with 'EcoFab' emblazoned on
the side – these particular carriages are designed to suppress
dust from the ore being carried through suburban neighbour-
hoods from BHP Billiton's silver, lead and zinc mines. Given the
rising concern about coal dust in many communities, it wouldn't
be surprising at all to soon see QR National introducing EcoFab

coal carriages. It would fit right in with the rest of their claim to environmental friendliness.

In the United States, a similar hypocrisy is playing out with Burlington North Santa Fe, better known as BNSF, and even better known since the world's third-richest man, Warren Buffett, made it the largest purchase of his career, his company Berkshire Hathaway spending $26 billion to acquire it. BNSF's commercials talk about the environmental friendliness of rail, with the company boasting that it can move a ton of cargo 495 miles on one gallon of diesel. Against a backdrop of carriages carrying wind turbines, the ads claim that 'BNSF is moving a new generation of clean energy safely across the United States'. Some ads finish with BNSF's new green slogan: 'The Cleaner Road Ahead'. The clear impression created is that Buffett's company is at the forefront of a clean energy revolution – buffalo roaming on prairies full of windmills brought there by BNSF.

What the commercials don't say is that BNSF is spending much more of its time moving a new generation of dirty energy across the United States. In 2010, BNSF transported 300 million tonnes of coal – more than Australia exports to the world – and all the carbon dioxide in that coal is headed for the atmosphere. BNSF's advertising doesn't mention that revenues from coal haulage are the fastest growing area of its business. Nor will you find BNSF bragging that it is central to the plans of companies such as Peabody and Ambre to turbo-charge coal exports to Asia out of America's north-west. The ads don't broadcast Warren Buffett's opposition to carbon regulation in the United States in recent years, either. What you will find, however, if you hunt down the fine print of the company's annual reports is an acknowledgement that carbon regulation is one of the biggest threats to BNSF's future prospects. Perhaps

EcoFab carriages will rumble through America's north-west soon too.

Shipping lines are also taking up the challenge to present their business as climate-friendly. Nippon Yusen runs one of the world's largest such businesses, with NYK cargo ships a familiar sight the world over. The 'NYK Cool Earth Project' features a polar bear in its logo and seems to have two main features: to launch the NYK Super Eco-Ship, with 70 per cent fewer emissions per container, by 2030; and to become a zero emissions company by 2050. Though the Eco-Ship is still a long way off, it's being marketed as if it exists already. As one corporate video says: 'She is a shining example of NYK Line's commitment for achieving a cleaner and better future for all'. The company also recently launched a 'solar power assisted' ship with great fanfare.

Yet in its 'Cool Earth' promotional material, NYK doesn't talk about how it's positioned to cash in on expanded fossil fuel production. The 7 million tonnes of coal that NYK already ships annually generates nearly 20 million tonnes of carbon dioxide. While NYK talks up Eco-Ships, it's also tripling the size of its 'capesize' fleet (ships which carry over 150,000 tonnes), citing rising Indian demand for coal imports. The company has also recently dived into the deepwater oil transport business, with a plan to increase its number of VLCCs (very large crude oil carriers) by about 20 per cent. Soon after the BP oil spill in late 2010, NYK bought the world's second-largest operator of tankers serving deep sea drilling operations.

Meanwhile, NYK's excited PR about renewable energy is similarly selective but seems wholly unjustified by the scale of the projects involved. So, for example, there's great enthusiasm about solar panels at NYK's Tokyo terminal, even though these will generate only 1 per cent of the terminal's power. There's much fanfare about NYK's 'solar power assisted' car carrier, though the panels provide just 1 per cent of the ship's electricity needs and 0.05 per cent of the ship's propulsion power, saving a mere 36.3 tonnes of carbon dioxide per year – roughly the equivalent of what seventeen Japanese households would emit in that period. This, meanwhile, is a ship carrying up to 6200 cars at a time, which once delivered will generate some 25,000 tonnes of carbon dioxide annually. The irony of a few solar panels on a ship carrying thousands of new cars run on fossil fuel doesn't come through in the PR. And this is one of the few vessels even getting 'solar assistance' among the hundreds in the NYK fleet.

Under the circumstances, the prospect of an unspecified number of Eco-Ships in 2030 seems about as convincing as NYK's declared aim of 'rapid but clean transport services'. For now, NYK's emissions seem relatively stable – falling through the global financial crisis before increasing by nearly 4 per cent between 2010 and 2011, because of 'an increase in handling volumes' and 'additions to the fleet'. As the fleet size and volumes expand further, emissions seem likely to rise, and that's without considering NYK's role in facilitating other emission increases through the cargo it carries – more oil, coal and cars.

Of course, most of us don't deal directly with railway companies and shipping lines. The brands we know are those whose vans bring goods to our door. These companies have also been eager to jump on board the climate-friendly bandwagon. The tactics of three of the best known couriers – UPS, DHL and FedEx – are pretty similar. First, there's the rhetoric. UPS is adamant that 'addressing climate change is important' and 'being green isn't just good for the planet, it's good for business'. Against a backdrop of melting glaciers, polar bears, windmills, rainforests, waterfalls and rousing words from Al Gore, DHL says it feels 'a particular obligation to accept ecological responsibility'. The company pledges to 'deliver value to the environment' (a wonderfully unquantifiable Key Performance Indicator, the creator of which has no doubt been promoted). A green slogan is a must: FedEx has a green-lettered EarthSmart logo, which appears on the side of its new 100 per cent electric delivery vehicles.

There are ambitious emission targets: DHL aims to improve its 'carbon efficiency' by 10 per cent by 2012 and 30 per cent by 2020, compared with 2007. Next up are the voluntary carbon offset programs, such as DHL's GoGreen. Customers who choose to offset their item's carbon footprint have GoGreen stickers placed on their package and receive a GoGreen certificate. Over at UPS, carbon-neutral shipments are available in thirty-five countries – rather than stickers, the package features an eruption of green leaves – and the company even matches the carbon offsets purchased by customers. There are countless other initiatives. In FedEx's glossy Global Citizenship Report, for example, you can read about the company's new green data centre in Colorado and its installation of one of the largest arrays of solar panels in the United States at company headquarters. None of this is surprising in the clamour of green marketing by freight companies.

What is surprising, however, are the carbon footprint figures, none of which are rising rapidly. Both FedEx and DHL have recorded falls in their operational emissions in recent years, and the increases at UPS are relatively small. DHL, to its credit, acknowledges that a significant part of its improvement was the result of 'declining airfreight shipment volumes', with the global financial crisis and a reduction in its fleet size both playing a role. And UPS details the extensive range of *non-operational* emissions tied up in its business, acknowledging that once these are factored in and given projected business growth, there's no prospect of a reduction in the total carbon footprint of the brand in the near term.

Renewables, meanwhile, remain a relative sideshow for these companies. DHL talks up its renewable electricity use, but factor in all that transport fuel it uses and renewables account for less than 10 per cent of total energy use. UPS has 2600 vehicles in its 'green fleet' running mainly on gas, yet the company has 92,000 other vehicles running on regular petroleum. The solar power plant at UPS's facility in California cuts the firm's reported 22 million tonne footprint by 500 tonnes. FedEx offsets just 1.8 per cent of its electricity use with renewable energy certficates, and while it talks about four solar power installations, telling us that this cuts the company's carbon footprint by 4000 tonnes a year, it's peanuts against the company's annual footprint of 14 million tonnes. As of mid-2011, FedEx had just forty-three all-electric delivery trucks out of a fleet of 70,000. There's no knowing what proportion of these companies' emissions are being neutralised by their voluntary offset programs – presumably not much or else the figures would be promoted publicly rather than concealed. Of course, these offsets are being paid for mainly by customers – the company contribution to offsets is minuscule – in UPS's case, it capped its annual contribution to carbon offsets at $1 million.

Under the circumstances, it's hard not to wonder whether these companies can maintain relatively positive emissions results in the longer term. Clearly there's potential to switch to less emissions-intensive delivery trucks and vans, to improve logistics, and to use more renewables at distribution facilities.

But most of these companies' carbon footprints come from the planes, and although these planes are becoming more efficient, they're also becoming more numerous and they all run on fossil fuel. Round-the-clock worldwide delivery remains one of the most emissions-intensive business ideas ever conceived. Every day, UPS delivers 15 million packages across 220 countries, which takes 200 planes and some 750 flights to over 370 international airports. FedEx and DHL run similar operations, and in all cases, the plan is to expand. UPS has even acknowledged that without major breakthroughs in technology, it can't reduce emissions in absolute terms without turning business away. As heavily reliant as these businesses are on fossil fuel–powered aviation and road transport, and given their enthusiastic plans for expansion, it's difficult to see how they can be characterised as climate-friendly.

After all, how would we characterise a slave-trading company boasting that it had cut the number of slaves it carried per ship by 5 per cent over two years and planned to cut the number by another 10 per cent in the next decade? We'd see that as a modest (and extremely inadequate) change – especially if the number of ships in its fleet was growing faster than the slave per ship reduction. It's not something we'd expect the company to advertise as SlaveSmart™ or GoingFree™. Given the dire consequences of climate change, today's freight industry should not get away with similar tricks.

home appliances and entertainment

In the time it takes you to read this chapter, some 7000 people will have ducked out to buy a new television. Tens of thousands more will have acquired an air conditioner, fridge, washing machine, dishwasher, stereo or game console. Surprisingly large amounts of energy and materials have gone into making each one and getting it to its new owner. They will all be plugged into the wall and start sucking down electricity. Depending on the electricity source, buying a large new appliance is akin to signing a contract to emit a significant amount of carbon dioxide. A reverse-cycle air conditioner in Australia might produce seventeen tonnes over its lifetime. The average Australian household produces close to ten tonnes of greenhouse emissions every year, and around half of that comes from whitegoods, home entertainment and other appliances.

These appliances are getting more efficient, but this benefit is being eroded by the rapid rise in numbers being sold. Across the developing world, people are enjoying many modern conveniences for the first time as part of an unprecedented increase in affluence. The carbon footprint of appliances in these countries is relatively small today, but the projected growth is ominous. Currently, household emissions in Chinese cities are around one-fifth of the western average, but over a few decades the world's urban population is expected to nearly double as a billion people trade rural village life with minimal electricity for apartment city-living with the usual accoutrements. In China, 150 million large household appliances are being added each year, a figure that has been growing by around 25 per cent annually. But even though the Chinese are buying close to 100,000 flat screen televisions every day, TV ownership levels would need to double to match those in many western countries.

And it's not even as simple as matching western standards, because western affluence itself is increasing. We're not content with basic modern conveniences – as well as upsizing those, we're buying a seemingly boundless constellation of gadgets, from home theatres to temperature-controlled wine cabinets, icemakers, rice cookers, bread makers, café presses, coffee grinders, juicers, electric blankets, towel warmers, humidifiers, air purifiers, electric toothbrushes, nose-hair trimmers and foot massagers. There has been a near ten-fold increase in the number of espresso coffee machines sold in Australia annually over the past decade, while 18 million of them are sold in Europe every year. Over the next five years 221 million game consoles are expected to sell. Not so long ago a barbeque involved a few bricks, a hot plate, some firewood and matches. Now it is often a second kitchen, replete with stainless steel, the centrepiece of which is an automated 6–8 burner monster run on gas, as is the outdoor heater nearby. Appliance companies call the process by which they continually redefine the 'normal' roster of appliances as 'extending' or 'going beyond' their 'core business'. Whatever you want to call it, it's happy days for the industry, but not for the climate.

It's especially bad news given that the emissions intensity of electricity supply in China and India is roughly twice that of Europe, the United States and Japan. So for every new appliance purchased in these countries, the carbon footprint is potentially twice the size. And with more manufacturing also shifting to these countries, a similar problem applies to the making of the product. Under the circumstances, you might expect the appliance industry to keep a low profile when it comes to green marketing, yet it features some of the largest players in the greenwash game. Appliance companies have some of the most ambitious-sounding targets and claim to be making great progress. Some claim not only to be slashing their emissions, but also those from the use of their products. If it all sounds too good to be true, that's probably because it is.

Let's begin with Panasonic, whose solemn-looking president stood in front of a forty-foot-wide picture of Planet Earth in 2010. On each side of the planet was a bright green leaf logo featuring the trademarked term Eco Ideas. The same green Eco Ideas™ logo now features on almost all of the company's marketing – even on the front cover of its annual report. Billboards subsequently declared Panasonic to be 'connecting with the earth' and, among much more, A$780,000 went to establishing the Panasonic Chair in Environmental Sustainability at Macquarie University in Sydney, a post currently held by scientist and author Tim Flannery. But in the very year that Panasonic announced its green plan and the Eco Ideas marketing hotted up, the company also sold 123 per cent more flat screen televisions than in the previous year – over 200 million in all. Still, if Chevron can be powered by Human Energy™ (not oil and gas) and Southern Company by Common Sense™ (not coal) there's no reason to let people suffer under the misguided impression that Panasonic is in the business of selling millions of energy-hungry appliances and gadgets to plug into walls. Much better to sell Eco Ideas™.

One of the company's big claims is that it 'will endeavour to ensure that [carbon dioxide] emissions from its entire business operations – not only from its own production activities but also from the use of its products by customers – peak out by 2018', its hundredth anniversary. As part of this plan, the company says that *product use* emissions from its annual sales in 2013 will be cut by 50 million tonnes compared with 2006, mostly through more energy-efficient products. So far, says Panasonic, the annual reduction in product use emissions is 38 million tonnes, 5 million ahead of schedule. So it's surprising to learn that the carbon footprint of Panasonic's products is still growing – and will continue to grow after 2018 even if Panasonic hits all its targets. That reality is hidden behind mathematics and semantics: which emissions Panasonic counts and which it ignores; and which words it carefully chooses.

When the company says that it will cut annual product use emissions by 50 million tonnes compared with 2006, it doesn't mean that these will be 50 million tonnes fewer than in 2006. It means that, had Panasonic not lifted a climate-friendly finger since 2006, by 2013 product use emissions would have been 50 million tonnes higher than will be the case thanks to the company's green efforts. By 2018 the aim is to have the combined total of production and product use emissions back to 2006 (and current) levels, which is roughly 90 million tonnes. There's no denying that if Panasonic hits this target it is an impressive achievement relative to most large manufacturing companies.

However, though it may sound as if the total carbon footprint of what Panasonic produces will stop rising from 2018, that's actually not what it means. That's because a lot of emissions are deftly shunted out of the 'peaking out' equation.

For one thing, the *product use* calculations are a bit misleading. They're not an estimate of the emissions actually generated annually by all the Panasonic products out there, but an estimate of the lifetime emissions generated from the energy use of products sold in the most recent year. So in 2018, along with the Panasonic products sold that year, there will still be lots of less efficient Panasonic products out there also generating emissions. Then there are the emissions associated with producing the materials used in Panasonic products – from the steel, aluminium, copper and rare earths to the oil extracted to produce the plastics, to the glass. Panasonic does not yet make any estimate of these and other supply chain emissions, which it confirmed in writing are also not subject to the peaking out target. The reason this matters is that the volume of products being sold by Panasonic is spiralling upwards – sales increased by 17 per cent in 2011 alone. Lots more products means lots more materials which means lots more emissions to produce and transport the materials. As people throw their old appliances away, it also means lots more emissions from product disposal – once again not counted in the numbers or subject to the targets. It's by owning up to only production and product energy-use emissions that Panasonic greenwashes this larger reality. In the longer term, Panasonic seems to pin its hopes on energy-smart ideas, such as PanaHomes™, 'zero carbon' houses sporting solar panels, sophisticated batteries and much more energy-efficient appliances. As sustainable concepts go it's impressive, but it's similar to the company's plans for electric-vehicle charging stands: they're nice concepts that lie somewhere between R&D and niche commercialisation, which are unlikely to form the company's core business any time soon.

What *is* the company's core business, meanwhile, is selling hundreds of millions of appliances into developing countries as quickly as possible. Of India, Panasonic says 'we have begun earnest efforts to fully develop this huge market', and it hopes to double sales in India in a mere twelve months. The company is pushing for 20 per cent annual growth in China and 40 per cent growth per year in Brazil. The investor presentations focus less on Eco Ideas when discussing these markets and much more on building factories to produce air conditioners, washing machines and refrigerators. Panasonic may well reach its stated targets in time for its centenary, but even if it does, the carbon footprint of its products is likely to increase for many years. As Eco Ideas go, that's not as impressive as it initially sounds.

Panasonic's main competitor Sony has been equally keen to build a climate-friendly reputation. In an infomercial posted by the company on YouTube, the company's chairman, Howard Stringer, says, 'Sony is united in its efforts to achieve a zero environmental footprint while continuing to enrich our customers' lives and protect the planet we all share'. One senior executive adds, 'Although eco-friendliness has not always been communicated as our main goal, the path we've taken in development has inevitably been easier on the environment. This is somehow instinctual at Sony'. It's a sort of environmental sixth sense.

Sony's words are backed up with impressive environmental marketing, which only looks dubious initially because of its vague and distant aim of having 'zero environmental impact' by 2050. Legendary Japanese longevity notwithstanding, it's hard to believe this is an environmental target for which any current senior personnel will be held accountable. But let's not be distracted from the detail of the commitment. Sony plans to reduce its emissions and those generated using its products to zero, and to use 100 per cent recycled materials. Its Road to Zero™ campaign features YouTube videos with phrases such as 'curbing climate change' shown next to wind turbines. Sony is 'minimizing emissions at factories and offices, and in product life cycles [by] utilizing renewable energy'. In Europe, most of Sony's sites are reportedly powered by electricity from 100 per cent renewable sources, and the company saves 100,000 tonnes of carbon dioxide annually, partly by spending a billion yen on renewable energy certificates. It's developing dye-sensitised solar cells, sugar-based bio-batteries, and lithium batteries and 'storage servers' to give people more scope to store intermittent renewable energy for later use. And, of course, Sony's appliances are becoming more efficient all the time. The company claims it is intent on introducing 'a more sustainable lifestyle to consumers'.

If only. Sony generates around 1.4 million tonnes of carbon dioxide equivalent annually and says it has reduced its own emissions by nearly 600,000 tonnes – or close to 30 per cent – since 2000. But that's only a tiny part of the story. Sony doesn't estimate the emissions tied up in its supply chain or the 1.3 million tonnes of material that go into its products each year. Getting the products to customers produces another half a million tonnes of greenhouse gases. Like Panasonic, Sony provides a product-life carbon footprint estimate for the new products sold each year rather than an estimate of the footprint of the much larger number of Sony products out there. Even so, we get a sense of the scale of the emissions problem – energy use by the products sold by Sony this year will generate emissions around fifteen times that of the company's annual operations. That product use emissions estimate is 10 per cent higher than last year, with Sony's explanation being: 'Although each unit is more energy-efficient than the previous year, the number of LCD TV units have dramatically increased, contributing to the increase of total product-usage related [carbon dioxide] emissions'. In other words, the amount of stuff being sold is outstripping efficiency gains, and the company's expansion into developing country markets leaves little doubt that maximising stuff sold is the main priority. Citing 40 per cent per year sales growth in the BRIC (Brazil, Russia, India and China) economies, Chairman Stringer says, 'Sony views the emerging markets as vital to our growth strategy'. When he visited Mumbai in 2011, Stringer said he was 'particularly pleased to see bold "Sony BRAVIA" bill-boards along roads abuzz with speeding cars and auto rickshaws'. He wasn't specific about which roads those particular billboards are on, but they were certainly not the Road to Zero.

The saddest thing about appliance industry greenwash is that the greenest names in the sector are actually performing better than those in many other industries. Sony and Panasonic are a chance to stabilise their operational emissions this decade, and that's not something many companies can say. What this chapter highlights, though, is the relative insignificance of these emissions compared with those created by supply chains and consumer use. Neither company yet estimates or reports the emissions tied up in their respective supply chains, though Panasonic confirms it has plans to do so. Moreover, it's hard to see how the positive energy-efficiency gains being made can catch up with an expanding range of upsized appliances being sold in rapidly growing volumes. While consumers collectively downsizing their overall demand for appliances is nice in theory, that's not the world in which we live. Nor is it one in which

PanaHomes will be snapped up by the masses in any hurry. The only conceivable way to reduce the emissions of appliances rapidly worldwide is to support energy-efficiency gains with a dramatic increase in renewable electricity as a proportion of the power used to run appliances. That won't happen without government policies that force a rapid shift away from fossil fuels. The best Eco Idea for this industry, then, is to stop pretending it's on a Road to Zero and start communicating this reality to governments around the world.

hotels

So, you want to help fight climate change? Why not jump on a plane to Stockholm and enjoy an acoustic concert at the Hilton – unplugged out of respect for the environment? If that doesn't grab you, what about flying halfway around the globe for one of the Hilton Hawaiian Village's climate-friendly candlelit dinners? Whether you come to the Hilton London Kensington or the Hilton Cartagena, you'll find 'special drinks and menus with a "green" theme' and 'only cold menu items'. It's all to celebrate Earth Hour and it's 'another step in Hilton Worldwide's commitment to sustainability'. Believing that hotels that depend on attracting long-haul travel are fighting climate change by engaging in such token activities for one hour annually is quite a leap of faith. But perhaps tokenism is a good fit for the Hilton, which as hotels chains go, is not a zealous green marketer. However, what it lacks in volume it makes up for in speciousness.

The first indication to hotel guests that Hilton has an interest in the environment is its 'We Care' ads, featuring a bright green leaf with a delicate drop of water hanging from it. This logo was added to polite suggestions that guests use a towel more than once before having it washed. More recently, the company received good publicity when it claimed that it had already cut per guest carbon emissions by 7.8 per cent in just two years, and that it aimed to reduce them by 20 per cent by 2015, mainly through its Lightstay™ initiative. Lightstay is an in-house management system that measures the environmental impacts of hotels. Hilton said in early 2010 that it was driving dramatic improvements around the world, and by the end of 2011 it had been deployed at 3600 hotels worldwide.

In a typical example of the scant details provided, the Adelaide Hilton said it had been 'carbon measured' by Carbon Planet, yet neither the results of the audit nor the trends in the hotels' emissions seem to have been made public. Across the chain, Hilton assures us that its Lightstay system has been independently audited by a quality assurance outfit called KEMA, which declared the Lightstay system 'rigorous and user-friendly'. The impression given is that Hilton is reducing emissions through an independently verified system.

How misleading impressions can be. It's what the Hilton doesn't say that is crucial. Hilton does not publicly disclose its carbon footprint, release a sustainability report, or participate in the Carbon Disclosure Project. It does not say what a 7.8 per cent reduction in carbon output actually applies to: total emissions, emissions relative to those without Lightstay, or emissions per guest, per metre squared or per available room. Without saying what the 7.8 per cent applies to or what the savings are relative to the company's overall footprint, it is completely impossible to assess the claim. The same goes for its target to cut emissions by 20 per cent. It's hard to reconcile this with the company's rapid growth. Even if it cut its total emissions by 7.8 per cent over two years, that's about half the rate at which Hilton's portfolio has been expanding, so the emissions savings are unlikely to keep up. It's extremely hard to see how Hilton can meet its 20 per cent reduction goal unless that target (and the cuts it claims) relate to something other than the company's total emissions.

You might expect the quickest way to cut through the ambiguity would be to contact Hilton. After all, Hilton's website says, 'Get in touch with us – we'd love to hear from you'. Yet when you email the vice-president of Corporate Responsibility seeking to clarify what targets the company has, there's no response – and none from the quality-assuring KEMA, either. It becomes clear on studying the 'third party audit' of Lightstay that it was the management system being certified, not the 7.8 per cent reduction. It's a user-friendly system, alright – the main users being the spin doctors working in Hilton's PR office. But although it might satisfy them, it shouldn't satisfy anyone else that the carbon footprint of Hilton Hotels is shrinking, or that it will in the near future.

Another hotel chain that prides itself on climate friendliness is Carlson, whose best known brands are Radisson Blu and Park Inn. The company first attracted attention as a likely greenwasher when 100 of its properties took part in Earth Hour in 2010. It wasn't that it took part in the event so much as the way that its Earth Hour activities were then promoted as evidence of the company's commitment to the environment. These activities included 'blind' champagne tastings (in the dark) and even a 'gastronomic master class' on preparing meals without electricity. Here was another company asking for closer scrutiny.

Back in 2001, Carlson launched its Responsible Business campaign – catch-all marketing to portray itself as ethical in everything from combating climate change to preventing child prostitution. 'Reducing our negative impact on the environment' was listed prominently among the priorities. The company counts among its achievements releasing its first environment policy in 1989; pioneering carbon offsetting by hotel guests in 2007 (in 2008 alone, Carlson offset 10,000 room nights); and planting 1000 trees in support of the billion-tree-planting campaign by the United Nations Development Program. In 2008, the CEO and president of Carlson were among 100 business leaders who jointly called for a 'rapid and fundamental strategy by governments across the globe to bring about a low-carbon world economy', with Carlson president Hubert Joly saying: 'Our group of 100 CEOs is committed to seeking ways to diminish *our* carbon footprint while serving the demands of a dynamic, global economy'. Five years on, Carlson shows no sign of a 'diminished' carbon footprint.

Carlson does not publicly release data on its carbon footprint. The closest we can get is the responsibility report of Rezidor, of which Carlson owns 50.1 per cent, and which includes the Radisson Blu and Park Inn chains. The report makes worrying reading. The company says that 22 per cent of its hotels use renewable energy, but gives no figures on *how much* renewable energy these hotels are using – it could be 0.1 per cent. Energy use per square metre is worse than in 2008, which the company blames on 'increased occupancy', ironically citing the Copenhagen climate conference for a spike in its Nordic region. The responsibility report concedes bluntly: 'Our carbon footprint has thus increased in absolute terms which is to be expected with the large number of hotels opened last year'. By 'large', what it means is that Rezidor is the world's third-fastest-growing hotel company – growing from 59,000 rooms in 2007 to 88,000 rooms in 2010. According to its majority owner, Carlson, most of that growth is occurring in developing countries such as India – places where electricity is more likely derived from coal and other fossil fuels. The likelihood of a diminished carbon footprint while adding 10,000 hotel rooms a year: probably very low.

Next we come to Wyndham. With over 7200 properties, it is probably the largest hotel chain in the world, its Ramada brand being one of the best known. Climate change was not on Wyndham's radar for many years, but once the alert was sounded the company pulled out all stops. It's as if they were offered the full menu of corporate green initiatives and, like greedy Mr Creosote in Monty Python's *Meaning of Life*, said, 'I'll 'ave the lot'.

First up, the company launched its Wyndham Green campaign. No, it wasn't a new line of eco-hotels – the ambitious suggestion was that the entire chain had gone green. There is a Green Kids program with curriculum suggestions for teachers, parents and kids; a Champions of Green panel of environmental over-achievers; green teams in the company; and a blog to post green comments, with space for the public to discuss their own green ideas with Wyndham. There's lots of information on why environmental issues matter, and even an encyclopedia of green terms. The message seems to be: no need to lecture us about the environment – we're experts.

Then there's the more substantial stuff, such as the hefty Wyndham Green *Global Best Practices* report and a similarly voluminous 2011 return to the Carbon Disclosure Project – the first one that the company has made publicly available. These documents contain much more on the company's seemingly endless list of green initiatives – from staff uniforms each made of twenty-five recycled plastic bottles to a Ramada Hotel in New Jersey drawing 80 per cent of its electricity from a solar farm. There's some data on the size of the company's carbon footprint: Wyndham says it generates around 400,000 tonnes of greenhouse gas across its operations globally, though the numbers would be a bit more elucidating if they included the over 7000 franchised hotels bearing Wyndham's brands. The numbers would also be more useful if for all the green marketing, the company could tell us whether its emissions are rising or falling. That Wyndham is devoting significant resources to environmental initiatives, has started measuring its carbon footprint and made the details public is laudable. However, while the awareness-raising and proliferation of individual programs deserve praise, they're ancillary to what should be the overriding priority: reducing Wyndham's carbon footprint specifically, and its environmental impact more generally. For now activity and promotions seem to be trumping tangible results.

So, could Marriott be showing Wyndham the way? First impressions aren't great – lots of the usual greenwash boxes are ticked. For many years Marriott has crafted a green image in which climate friendliness features prominently. Like others mentioned here, the company has a green slogan – in this case Spirit to Preserve™. Guests at Marriott hotels will see a picture of two supple hands cupping Planet Earth next to a list of the company's green credentials. Marriott also encourages 'green meetings' for guests keen on 'A deeper shade of green'. There's all the usual stuff: ambiguous-looking claims, such as a commitment to install solar power at forty of its hotels by 2017 that doesn't say *how much* solar power will be generated, and a partnership with Conservation International involving among much else a $2 million donation from the company to help protect rainforest in the Amazon. And, as with other hotel chains, there's the same sort of staggering growth. Marriott has over 3500 properties in more than seventy countries. In 2010, Marriott added 29,000 new rooms and units – and it has 700 hotels and 105,000 new rooms in the 'development pipeline'.

It all seems tailor-made greenwash, but for the pretty clear impression that Marriott is reducing its total emissions. In spite of its rapid growth the company says it has managed to achieve a 20 per cent reduction in energy use per available room, resulting in an 11 per cent reduction in its absolute emissions. The company appears to be walking the walk better than most and certainly it's been busy: retrofitting the hot water, heating, ventilation and air-conditioning systems at some of its largest properties, achieving energy savings of between 5 and 25 per cent. The emissions-intensity improvements (19 per cent since 2007) seem to be happening fast enough to result in significant overall emission reductions. This makes the forest protection and other activity look more creditable than usual.

Until, that is, you stop and look at the fine print and realise that Marriott's claim of a falling carbon footprint relates to its 'managed estate'. This excludes the 53 per cent of rooms in properties bearing its brands that are franchised. With the number of franchised rooms growing four times as fast as managed rooms, Marriott is effectively off-loading its fastest-growing source of emissions. So, while it's impressive that the company was able to reduce the emissions of its managed properties (while adding some 10 per cent more of them) the broader Marriott brand is still being greenwashed. The inexorable pace at which this industry is expanding, and the importance of long-haul travel to the business model, makes imagining a climate-friendly hotels industry very hard. Then again, it makes those once-a-year candlelit dinners and acoustic concerts much easier to understand.

luxe punting

OK, so combining luxury cruises with gambling holidays was never going to be the easiest chapter to name – but each involves 'punting' on a very grand and carbon-intensive scale.

First, let's set sail with the cruise ship industry. With the world's chances of avoiding dangerous climate change rapidly going the way of the *Titanic*, it seems unfair not to take a closer look. Royal Caribbean Cruises Limited (RCL) fancies itself as a climate-friendly company – its emissions reduction efforts are all part of a trademarked Save the Waves environmental campaign that dates back to 1992. If you go to the company's website, you'll see ships with solar panels and green roofs, and a corporate video in which a ship's captain reassures us that, 'At a time of great global climate concern, I'm very proud to know that environmental issues are at the forefront of our work at Royal Caribbean'. The company's stewardship report leads with a letter from the vice-president of Environmental Stewardship, declaring, 'Global climate change is perhaps the defining environmental issue of our time, and as a result, we recognise that we need to be part of the solution'. In an interview, he tells how friends warned him about working for the 'dark side' after years in the environmental movement with Conservation International. Having seen the company's environmental commitment at close quarters, however, he clearly feels vindicated – saying he is 'extremely proud' and 'impressed on a daily basis' and wants us to join RCL 'as we cruise toward a sustainable future'.

Before we look more closely at RCL's efforts, let's first absorb the scale of its operation, which accounts for over a quarter of a global market that has boomed – cruising, to quote the company, has moved from being 'a sexy glamorous industry' to a 'mainstream choice vacation'. Each year, RCL's forty-two cruise ships carry more than 4 million guests to over 400 destinations. At any one time it can cater to around 92,000 people. The vast majority of the company's carbon footprint is tied up in running those ships – and there's a great deal more to run than just the engines when you're taking the scenic route in luxury. Imagine cross-breeding a floating hotel with a power station and you get a cruise ship: it has the largest, most rapacious appetite of any ocean beast. Weighing in some cases over 100,000 tonnes, carrying over 6000 people in its belly, and standing twenty storeys high, it devours electricity, which, like the engines, relies almost exclusively on fossil fuels. As these cruise kraken have grown larger and more numerous, shipping has become the fastest-growing source of greenhouse emissions behind commercial aviation.

So, it was certainly eye-catching when RCL decided to install solar panels on one of its largest ships – the gargantuan *Oasis of the Seas*, which features everything but the date palms you might expect. The ship's solar panels were promoted far and wide, receiving plenty of positive press coverage. The company that installed the panels, quoted at length in RCL's stewardship report, went so far as to say, 'This demonstrates Royal Caribbean International's commitment to environmental protection and the company's forward thinking approach to reducing their consumption of fossil fuels'. This commitment to solar sounded serious – apparently the solar panels would power 7000 LED light bulbs and generate enough power to meet the needs of the 'Royal Promenade and Central Park Areas', which sure sound big. When you investigate further, reality sets in. The solar panels generate a mere 1 per cent of the energy used by the *Oasis of the Seas*. So what wasn't going to be run by the solar panels? Well now, not the shopping malls, the casino or the simulated surfing, to name a few of the onboard services. Not the beauty salons, the exercise and spa facilities, ice-skating rinks, lounges, bars, Las Vegas–style entertainment or cinemas, either. Nor would the ship's engines run on the sun, let alone the rest of the RCL fleet.

For the switch to solar power to be this pathetic and the ex-greenie vice-president of Environmental Stewardship to be feeling so good about his new job, presumably there had to be more to RCL's climate-friendly pitch. And there was: another RCL ship called *Celebrity Solstice* featuring a 'green roof' was apparently the first cruise ship equipped with solar panels, and it also had a dedicated environmental education venue on board – the 'Team Earth Lounge', created in partnership with Conservation International. In 2008, the company also appointed an environmental officer to each ship. Nice, albeit fluffy stuff. Still, RCL also points to more tangible progress: the *Allure of the Seas* emits 30 per cent less carbon dioxide per person per day than ships built a dozen years ago. Such improvements underpin claims like 'As an environmentally conscientious company, we are setting rigorous emissions targets for ourselves', with RCL's rigorous target being to 'reduce its overall emissions by one third' by 2015 relative to 2005 levels. Reading the company's PR, you are assured that the company is making good progress.

Yet, look closely and you notice that RCL's plan to cut emissions is per Available Passenger Cruise Day (APCD), meaning 'the number of lower berths on a ship times the number of days that those berths are available to passengers per year'. Since 2001, RCL has more than doubled APCDs to over 33 million, growing by 7.5 per cent between 2010 and 2011. At that rate, even if RCL cuts emissions per APCD by a third by 2015, its total carbon footprint will still be much higher than in 2005. The company's emissions are actually *increasing* by more than 6 per cent a year. RCL puts this down to more ships – in 2010 it added four. Yes, these ships are much more efficient, but because they're not replacing four older ships, the fleet and emissions are growing. RCL does come clean: 'As we build new ships and expand our fleet, we design our ships to be as energy efficient as feasible. This is demonstrated in that from 2005 to 2015 our fleet capacity is expected to grow by 57 per cent yet *our emissions are projected to increase only 25 per cent*'. That's right, if it hits that rigorous target its overall emissions will go up only by 25 per cent. However, this estimate excludes emissions generated to manufacture new ships. By some estimates, a vessel the size of *Oasis of the Seas* might add another half a million tonnes of carbon dioxide. RCL's numbers also exclude purchased goods and services from its 'quite expansive' supply chain network, the emissions from which the company admits could add another 5 to 10 per cent.

As for 'reducing their consumption of fossil fuels', as RCL's excitable solar panel installer was led to believe, the opposite is happening. Most of the climate change section of the company's stewardship report is spent explaining why there's no real alternative to diesel. It's a 'damned if we do, damned if we don't' explanation as to why the company has all but given up on biofuels. RCL calls it a 'paradox of biofuels', as if to say, 'It might help cut emissions but the environmentalists don't want their rainforests destroyed to grow the stuff'. Alternatives are dismissed in turn leaving a between-the-lines message amounting to, 'We'd really love to save the planet but all these people will want to take a cruise, so what choice do we have?'. The annual report makes for very different reading – in ninety-two pages, there's none of this hand-wringing. There's one passing mention of climate change and greenhouse emissions, in a paragraph warning bluntly that bad PR from environmentalists about climate change might lead to more government regulation, which could increase the cost of doing business. It's a world away from the captain in the corporate video and his pride in 'environmental issues being at the forefront of our work'. Just how the vice-president of Environmental Stewardship feels so vindicated as this band plays on is a beguiling mystery.

For a very different type of 'luxe punt', how about a Vegas holiday? Ever seen a commercial for a solar-powered slot machine? Didn't think so. You'd think at least one of those behemoths in Las Vegas would be en route to becoming a Solar Casino. With so many bright lights to power, why not put all that sun in the Nevada desert to work? For that matter, with so many people sitting in front of the slots for hours on end, why not put *them* to work? You could plant an exercise bike in front of each machine and use pedal power to run them – people might leave with lighter wallets, but toned thighs. It would save the gaming companies millions. OK, perhaps a mandatory workout would dampen the gambling urge, but surely someone, somewhere, is putting some form of renewable energy to work in the gaming industry? Gambling may not immediately seem a likely greenwashing candidate, but it has its reasons. There are currently around 7.2 million slot machines operating worldwide, about one for every 1000 people. Largely thanks to LED light bulbs, the energy efficiency of the machines is improving: the average slot machine uses 250 watts of power compared with 400 watts a decade ago. Even with the improvements, the global fleet of slot machines uses roughly the same amount of electricity as a city of over 3 million people, such as Madrid.

One of the companies buying the slot machines is Caesars Entertainment, which is by far the greenest marketer in the gambling industry. Caesars is the world's largest 'gaming entertainment company', best known for Caesars Palace, Harrah's, Bally's and the World Series of Poker. It has fifty-two casinos, including fourteen casino brands in the United States alone. Across five continents it runs 40,000 hotel rooms, 1.5 million square feet of conference and meeting space, celebrity chef restaurants, retail shopping complexes and slot machines. Every year it rakes in $10 billion in revenue, and its rewards scheme has 40 million members. Twenty years ago, says Caesars, it was 'the first casino company to address problem gambling', and on the issue of climate change it is 'striving for the same kind of industry leadership'. Ominous as that parallel may sound, the company maintains that it has 'incorporated environmental sustainability programs into all of its properties and activities'. This is all aggregated under Caesars' internal brand CodeGreen™, with the slogan, 'driven by earth urgency'. Caesars says that CodeGreen is 'designed to embed a sustainability ethos into every corporate function', and CodeGreen teams have been set up at all of the company's casinos.

The company says that it's 'driving down' greenhouse gas emissions. In the past seven years, it's shaved its annual emissions by 106,000 tonnes to around 1.1 million tonnes per year. It's also reduced the electricity consumption of its operations by an estimated 163 million kilowatt-hours per year. Caesars says this is 'the equivalent of 122,000 roundtrip flights from Los Angeles to New York not taken'. This has been win-win, says the company, saving Caesars $10 million a year too. Along the way, Caesars offset the carbon footprint of the World Series of Poker, and guests at fifty properties worldwide have the option of carbon-neutralising their stay. When the company switches off external and decorative lighting for Earth Hour, it calls this 'a manifestation of our long-standing and steadfast commitment to environmental sustainability'. For good measure, Caesars collaborates with WWF, Conservation International and Clinton Global Initiative, and the Natural Resources Defense Council (NRDC).

But there are just enough signs that this CodeGreen is too good to be true. First, there are the little things: why would a company that is so serious about climate change offset only the *final* of the fifty-eight events held in the World Series of Poker? And how many tonnes of carbon have been offset by the company and its guests? Caesars isn't saying. The fine print of the emissions figures disclosed by Caesars also reveals that the 1.1 million tonne carbon footprint claimed covers only US operations, and for an international company this is usually a good hint that closer scrutiny is worthwhile.

Upon closer analysis, Caesars' claim that it's 'driving down' emissions looks very dubious. The company boasts that it has made, 'An EPA-approved commitment to achieve a 10 per cent absolute reduction in greenhouse gas emissions for our US properties by 2013'. But then, just because the EPA approves of the commitment doesn't mean it will be achieved. More importantly, there is so much not even covered by the target Caesars has set. Put yourself in the shoes of the person taking a Vegas holiday – the flight there, a stretch limo perhaps, all the ingredients in those grand buffets, all those celebrities and entourages being flown in to entertain them, stocking all those shops in the malls, everything from the cards to chips to flower arrangements essential to keeping casinos ticking over. None of the carbon footprint of these things is counted in Caesars' carbon footprint or its targets. All that's counted are on-site emissions and energy use. So, the emissions generated by Caesars' products are vastly more than its stated carbon footprint suggests. At the moment Caesars hosts over 100 million guests a year, and as it encourages more and more people to travel from around the world to blow their money amid the dazzling glare of its casinos, that number is growing fast. As a result, the emissions equivalent of new trips being created is much greater than the 122,000 that the Code-Green activity claims to save.

Caesars' exclusive focus on US emissions also glosses over the fact that overseas development is the most rapidly growing part of the business. In early 2011, the company set up Caesars Global Life: 'a non-gaming division created to develop and manage branded luxury hotels, resorts, residences, villas, retail and entertainment destinations around the world'. Its aim is to increase the company's presence in Asia – particularly India and China – and Latin America. In late 2011, Caesars announced, 'The company's goal is to develop 25 hotels and resorts in China over the next five years'. The 106,000 tonnes of carbon dioxide the company saved in the United States through CodeGreen will be wiped out quickly by offshore growth on this scale. What we're left with is a company pretending that its improved energy efficiency in the United States amounts to a reduction in its overall carbon footprint.

It's then perhaps no surprise to learn that Caesars' owners are deeply invested in industries exacerbating climate change.

In 2008 the company was bought by Hamlet Holdings, a joint investment vehicle of two private equity takeover artists, Apollo Management and Texas Pacific Group (or TPG). These companies also own power utilities that are heavily dependent on coal, not to mention cruise lines, hotels, travel companies, airlines and many more emissions-intensive businesses. Here was Caesars telling us how serious it was about saving the planet, and its co-owner TPG was, through its Asian partner Northstar Pacific, trying to take a 35 per cent stake in Bumi, Indonesia's largest coal-mining group, and the world's largest exporter of thermal coal. The emissions from Bumi's coal production wipe out the emissions saved in the United States by Caesars many, many times over. So, while Caesars is celebrating how it's cut emissions by 106,000 tonnes, its co-owner backs a company whose plan to double coal production will add an extra 46 *million* tonnes or so of carbon dioxide annually. It's 'CodeBlack' trumping 'CodeGreen'.

The greenwash is best explained by Caesars itself: 'climate change presents the company with an opportunity to strengthen its reputation and brand ... We anticipate that over time this will lead to increased market share and revenues'. In the end, it's about looking green to increase profits, just as it is for Royal Caribbean. Super-sized gondolas and gaming don't have a whole lot in common at first glance, but as very different types of luxe 'punt', cruise lines and casino companies are surprisingly similar when it comes to their growing carbon footprints.

media

You'd think media companies would find it relatively easy to go green compared to, say, oil companies, airlines, cruise lines and car makers. Sure, newspapers, TV stations and movie studios rack up emissions – there are reporters to be deployed to all points of the globe, celebrity tours, petrol for car chases and explosive stunts, and a plethora of electronic equipment to run. But compared with most, media companies are well placed to lead by example in reducing their carbon footprints. They can also use their disproportionate reach to give scientists, economists and others a platform to explain the problem; reinforce the need for governments to act; and inspire audiences to do their bit. Making sure the business itself doesn't undermine the climate-friendly future being advocated would also seem relatively straightforward. It must be harder than it looks.

In 2006, after years of scepticism that human activity was driving global warming, News Corporation's Rupert Murdoch came around. The patriarch of the world's second-largest media conglomerate said that while he wasn't 100 per cent convinced, 'the planet deserves the benefit of the doubt'. His son James, who at the time was well on the way to making BSkyB carbon-neutral in the United Kingdom, had seemingly persuaded him that there was enough evidence to justify an urgent response.

Murdoch used his first worldwide webcast to staff in 2007 to launch the News Corporation Global Energy Initiative, one of the most conspicuous publicity drives any company has taken to prove its climate friendliness. The company's 'long term vision', said Murdoch, is to 'grow our business without growing our carbon footprint' and to 'power our operations with clean electricity'. Its logos have since been reworked: News Limited had one done up in green paint telling the public to 'Get the news on being green'; Fox went with 'Fox, Green It, Mean It'. The Emmy Awards went carbon-neutral, climate change documentaries abounded on the News Corp–owned National Geographic channel, and seemingly every News Corp business went green. Fox Studios bought hybrid trucks and solar golf carts, while News International bought 70 per cent of its electricity from hydro energy in Scotland, and staff were offered financial incentives to buy their own hybrids.

In December 2010, News Corp announced it had achieved carbon neutrality worldwide, by cutting annual emissions from 700,000 to about 640,000 and offsetting these completely with carbon credits ticked off by the likes of WWF. Murdoch then wanted to go further, saying he appreciated that the company's own emissions were relatively small. The carbon footprint that the company really wanted to 'conquer' was that of its audience, which News Corp estimated to be 7 billion tonnes annually. The extent of the company's ambition was encapsulated in the 1 Degree campaign run in Australia by News Limited. Intended or not, the 1 Degree campaign implied company support for containing global temperature increases to less than 1 degree above pre-industrial levels. It's an ambitious position since we are already over 0.8 degrees above those levels – and the science suggests 1 degree is probably unattainable even if we stabilise emissions almost immediately. Full-page ads appeared in the *Australian* depicting a grinning young executive riding a bicycle (briefcase in hand, popping a wheelie), and asked: 'How do you take the equivalent of 7086 cars off the road? Start with one'. The ad explained that News Limited had taken many small steps over three years to cut emissions by 27,100 tonnes, and through offsets, 'for every bit we still put into the air, we now take a bit out'.

Now it was the public's turn. Having got their own 'house in order', said Murdoch, 'We can then do what we do best: educate and engage our millions of readers, viewers and web users around the world'. This has taken various forms, from News Corp triathlon and tree-planting teams decked out in '1 Degree' uniforms to Green Awards featuring celebrities, to handy tips on the News Corp website to help people manage their own carbon footprint.

In spite of it all, there's a big problem with News Corp's stated ambition to 'no longer be a company that contributes to global warming': its businesses play a central role in undermining a climate-friendly future. Perhaps a few members of the public have been inspired by News Corp's Global Energy Initiative, but it's reasonable to assume that the company's audience is more influenced by what News Corp actually publishes and broadcasts about climate change. And both before the Murdoch conversion and since, News Corp media outlets have fostered climate change denial and delay. Flagship brands like Fox News, the *Australian*, and the *New York Post* have consistently lent credibility to a tiny minority of climate sceptic scientists and non-scientists.

At Fox News, talk show hosts such as Sean Hannity and Glenn Beck have argued that anthropogenic climate change is among other things 'the greatest hoax in human history'. Upon hearing that Murdoch had offset News Corp's emissions, Hannity ridiculed the idea: 'You go cheat on your wife and then say, "Honey, don't worry, I bought an offset." Good luck'. In the lead-up to the Copenhagen climate conference, just as News Corp was becoming carbon-neutral, Fox News' Washington bureau chief issued these written instructions to reporters: 'We should refrain from asserting that the planet has warmed (or cooled) in any given period without IMMEDIATELY pointing out that such theories are based upon data that critics have called into question ... It is not our place as journalists to assert such notions as facts, especially as this debate intensifies'.

News Corp's newspapers are at it too. The *New York Post* ran an editorial in August 2011 called 'The (Polar) Bear Facts', arguing that 'the catastrophic scenarios pushed by warming alarmists are way off'. It also ran Op Ed pieces with headlines such as, 'Warming Not! Climate change theory faces sudden collapse'. While the News Corp websites refer people to Al Gore's film *An Inconvenient Truth*, *Post* columnists referred to it as a 'scare-umentary'. Over at Murdoch's *Wall Street Journal* in 2010, columnist Bret Stephens declared 'global warming is dead', dismissing it as an 'apocalyptic scare'. While News Corp was going carbon-neutral, its main communication channels – in a country responsible for nearly 20 per cent of global emissions – were being used to dissuade the public from believing climate change was even a problem.

The *Australian*, the company's broadsheet flagship in Murdoch's home country, has consistently cast doubt on the scientific case for reducing greenhouse gas emissions. As Robert

Manne noted in his *Quarterly Essay, Bad News*, while in the outside world sceptics are outnumbered ninety-nine to one by scientists who believe that urgent emission reductions are required, the *Australian*'s opinion page has favoured sceptics by about ten to one. Even if *news stories* are included, those opposed to action to reduce emissions outnumber those supporting it by a ratio of at least 3:1. The 'science is far from settled', says the *Australian*'s editor-in-chief, who draws a parallel between climate change and the Malthusian hysteria of days gone by. Then there are the columnists promoting climate denial and opposing emission cuts, who are syndicated across the nation. The most prominent example, Andrew Bolt, even gets his own blog on the News Limited website, which he uses to dismiss climate change as 'neo-pagan hysteria'. The mainstream scientists are part of a corrupted movement, he argues, while hinting their 'doom-preaching' helps them gain research funding. Economics commentator Terry McCrann dismisses calls for emission cuts, saying things like 'Australia's fundamental comparative advantage ... is the production of CO_2'. The *Australian* bolsters these views with celebratory news stories about new major coal mine proposals, without once mentioning the carbon dioxide they will add to the atmosphere. When Murdoch visited Australia in 2010 he openly ridiculed the Greens, the only significant political party calling for the rapid emissions reductions his company claims to support. 'Don't let the bloody Greens mess it up', says Murdoch, advocating nuclear energy rather than a 'rush into a lot of mad schemes, fouling up the country with windmills and other crackpot ideas'.

The inconsistency between what News Corp does with its own operational emissions and what its most prominent voices say about climate change leaves Murdoch hoisted on his own petard. Murdoch says it's healthy for some journalists to have sceptical views, but this is not a case of a few dissenting voices. The company's loudest voices are dominated by messages that deliberately distort the case for combating climate change and perpetuate business as usual. Under this weight, News Corp's carbon-neutral crusade collapses in a heap.

National Geographic falls into a similar trap. The magazine has provided a bridge between the public and the scientific community to inform readers about the dangers posed by climate change. And yet, it undoes at least some of this good work through the sponsorship it accepts. The magazine's editor may say, 'We ... clear away the agendas, the rhetoric and the politics', but *National Geographic*'s advertisers are a who's who of greenwashers: big box retailers, cruise lines, car manufacturers, oil companies, coal miners, airlines, consumer electronics and air freight companies. It's not simply that *National Geographic* lets these companies advertise – it's what letting them advertise enables them to hide, and how as a result, this advertising can conflict with the content of the magazine's articles. In 2008, for example, there was an issue devoted entirely to climate change. Chevrolet got space for an ad on its new hybrid Tahoe SUV and ConocoPhillips (one of the world's largest privately owned fossil fuel producers) was able to sell the message that it's helping to reduce emissions. That ConocoPhillips fuels pump over half a billion tonnes of carbon dioxide into the atmosphere annually didn't get in the way. Nor did it seem to matter that Chevrolet is selling a relative handful of hybrids and electric cars as the total carbon footprint of its vehicles keeps rising. Meanwhile, although Ford was selling nearly sixty gas-guzzling F-series trucks for every Escape Hybrid, that didn't prevent the latter being advertised in *National Geographic*. That BP was busy chasing deep sea oil, ultimately with disastrous consequences that would feature prominently in *National Geographic*'s coverage of the Horizon spill didn't get in the way of BP's ads in the magazine pretending it was 'Beyond Petroleum'.

If this was just a matter of a few ads, perhaps you could dismiss it, but the more extensive collaborations make that harder. *National Geographic* advertises partnerships with big electronics producers such as Panasonic, hotel chains such as InterContinental, cruise lines such as Cunard and oil companies such as Statoil – each of which has a growing carbon footprint. There's the collaboration with Brazilian mining giant Vale, which allows the company to promote itself as 'a global agent for sustainability' – not just in an ad, but in a twelve-page lift-out and as a sponsor of an 'Eye on Sustainability' photo competition. Nowhere is there a hint that Vale is ramping up coal production to 40 million tonnes a year in the face of climate change.

Perhaps the most blatant example is the collaboration with Shell, a prolific greenwasher. In early 2012, *National Geographic*'s website linked to a carbon calculator as part of 'The Great Energy Challenge – a formal *National Geographic* initiative in partnership with Shell'. The Great Energy Challenge page says the collaboration is designed to help readers understand issues such as tar sands, while featuring two more ads by Shell, which has a vested interest in tar sands extraction. As part of the collaboration, a Shell spin doctor gets to talk up carbon capture and storage on the *National Geographic*–branded website and there's a separate blog promoting Shell's Eco-marathon. *National Geographic* says lamely that while Shell sponsors the blog, *National Geographic* 'maintains autonomy over content'. *National Geographic* does produce good content, particularly on the issue of climate change, and the vast majority of what it produces *is* objective. It's just a shame that it allows so many company 'agendas, rhetoric and politics' to pollute its publication.

Like News Corp and *National Geographic*, CBS is undoubtedly doing some climate-friendly work. The company has an impressive and growing list of initiatives, from being the first media company to voluntarily report the emissions of its California operations to cutting energy use by 20 per cent at CBS Headquarters in New York and running a series of TV specials, featuring 'entertaining green makeovers of celebrity homes', called the *EcoZone Project*. Yet while CBS says, 'our success will be measured by our progress in (among other things) reducing our greenhouse gas emissions', it can't even tell us what its global emissions amount to and whether they're being reduced.

CBS's other greenwash problem is its use of 'EcoAds' as evidence of its commitment to reducing greenhouse gas emissions. The CBS subsidiary EcoMedia encourages advertisers to allow a slice of their bill to be donated to worthwhile environmental projects. The emissions saved are measured and verified by an independent source. Part of the concept's originality is that the ad does not need to relate to the environment to receive the EcoAd tagline. While it's nice that a giant car maker such as Chevrolet or a growing airline such as Jet Blue Airways wants to donate money to a solar project, the juxtaposition of EcoAd branding with emissions-intensive brands is jarring. CBS denies that it provides these companies with a green seal of approval, saying, 'EcoMedia does not in any way certify, endorse or make any representations about EcoAd advertisers, their products or services'. And yet CBS's EcoMedia *does* call its EcoAd clients 'leaders, innovators, and pioneers' who are 'directing dollars into environmental projects (that can) improve the environment – one EcoAd at a time'.

CBS stresses that the reductions achieved by the projects funded by EcoAds are absolutely assured. This misses the point.

For at least some of the EcoAdvertisers, the ads are not about the projects (if they were, the companies could simply donate to the project), but about making not-so-green *brands* look greener. This also goes for CBS, which promotes the EcoAd as evidence of its own climate friendliness, while acknowledging that its EcoAd concept is at least in part viewed as a way to attract more advertising business. The time to take CBS's green push seriously will be when it demonstrates a reduction in its carbon footprint, and when it stops allowing big polluters to use EcoAds to greenwash their brands.

News Corp, *National Geographic* and CBS could all credibly claim to be climate-friendly if they took a few small steps. News Corp could do without its sceptic bias and ranters just as easily as *National Geographic* could flourish without its collaborations with Shell and other emissions-intensive advertisers. CBS could easily apply higher standards to its EcoAds. What's telling is that small steps are proving so hard. Going green is an idea the media will happily embrace, it seems, but they're equally as happy greenwashing big polluters and peddling climate change denial if that brings money through the door or boosts ratings and sales.

online searching, shopping, socialising

Let's click through the usual process: find something you like, add it to your cart, check out, enter credit card details, keep a copy of your receipt. Some days later, something you could probably never find locally – certainly not at this price – let alone have home-delivered, arrives at your door. It's like magic, and it intuitively feels much more environmentally friendly than driving all over town. Online searching and socialising seems even less damaging to the planet. A stream of digital code taking us exactly where we want, giving us the information we're after or transmitting what we want conveyed in a few seconds via a stream of electrons. It all takes electricity, of course, and occasionally a stickler will chastise us for the grams of carbon dioxide we might expend on a Google search, Facebook post or Twitter tweet, but no-one takes them too seriously. It seems incomprehensible that this wondrous array of technology could compare with the environmental impact of all the paper, ink, envelopes and stamps we relied on not so long ago.

And yet, like magic, it's a bit of an illusion. After all, your online purchase isn't beamed to you, Star Trek–style. You click 'buy' and an unseen system swings into action. The order is processed in a humming data centre, then sent to a warehouse at which the product is located and packed, whence it starts a long journey. This will usually involve multiple trucks, planes and trains. We know nothing of the electricity used at the data centre, and even less about the fuel used by the freight companies. The carbon footprint hardly enters our head, and yet it's vastly bigger than most of us imagine.

The explosion in e-commerce is driving rapid expansion in the freight industries and the construction of energy-hungry data centres, clustered close by cheap coal-fired power providers. The companies involved know this, which explains why so many are reluctant to say much about their contributions to climate change. They cite trade secrecy to avoid disclosing detail on data centres and emissions, and they disown the long emissions tail generated on their behalf by freight and packaging companies. Yet the many online corporations that clam up about this sort of information are the same companies spending millions on marketing campaigns to persuade us that their e-commerce is eco-commerce.

EBay began as a tiny website trading PEZ dispensers and has since morphed into the world's biggest marketplace. There are now more than 100 million 'active users' doing business on eBay's site at least once a year. That means that every day, at least 275,000 people either buy or sell something on eBay that goes into a box and into the hands of a freight company, which fires up its engines to carry it somewhere else in the world. Knowing that its supply chain has significant environmental impacts, eBay accentuates the positives, particularly the idea that eBay is all about recycling products – its business is portrayed as one big garage sale. It calls itself 'the biggest engine for re-use on Earth'.

The company says that since 1998 more than $100 billion in used goods have been traded on eBay.

The main conduit for eBay's climate-friendly marketing is the eBay Green Team. It started a few years ago when around forty eBay staff got together over pizza and decided to start looking for ways to green up the business. What began as an in-house brainstorm was then transformed into a mass movement by opening it up to the public, soliciting ideas from eBay customers while feeding them a steady diet of PR on the company's environmental credentials. Today, eBay says of its Green Team, 'Now we are nearly 300,000 strong ... committed to buying, selling and thinking green every day'. There's a Green Team logo, a flashy website and ads featuring people enthusiastically hugging trees.

The eBay CEO expresses his strong desire to 'make eBay greener' in a corporate YouTube video: 'I wanted to make this a core part of who we are because it is so aligned with our core values'. The video says that the company has succeeded 'in small ways' (people in eBay Green Team garb shown planting seedlings and recycling), and 'in big ways' (an extensive array of solar panels shown atop eBay's LEED gold-certified data centres and campuses). We also learn about eBay's 'commitment to breakthrough renewable energy technology', and how one eBay complex features 3248 solar panels – as big as a football field and equivalent to 18 per cent of the building's electricity needs.

It's stirring stuff, as is the Green Team's passion about 'making re-use cool', which drives its 'Common Threads Initiative' collaboration with outdoor clothing company Patagonia, encouraging people to resell the brand's sturdy clothing once they're done with it. Then there's the new reusable eBay box – winner of the company's 'Big Green Idea' contest, which invites eBay customers to suggest ways to make the company more sustainable. According to eBay, the use of this 'simple little box', 'made from environmentally friendly materials and designed to be reused', protects 'nearly 4000 trees, and conserves enough energy to power forty-nine homes for a year'. Some 100,000 are now out in the eBay ecosystem. On the side of the new box, there's a small bird on a tree saying, 'Yay!'

What no-one seems to have told the excited little birdie is that eBay's carbon footprint is spiralling – up by nearly 70 per cent between 2007 and 2010. This could hardly be more at odds with the climate-friendly story the company tells publicly. EBay had a plan to reduce its total emissions by 15 per cent from 2008 levels by 2012, which is still promoted on its Green Team website because, 'We are committed to running our business in ways that have less impact on the planet'. Yet, with emissions rising as fast as they are, the company has next to no chance of reaching its target. Meanwhile, in spite of the CEO's green enthusiasm, the company's 140-page annual report mentions the Green Team in just one paragraph, and climate change not at all.

Why is there such a disconnect between the talk and reality? Here's a hint: an estimated '430,000 people in the United States make all or most of their living by selling on eBay'. Of these perhaps a handful have enough second-hand stuff to make a living off-loading it – most are selling new goods. In early 2012, the first fifty items coming up on eBay's home page are brand-new: books, frying pans, smart phones, CDs, cordless drills, PC screens, barbeques. The Green Team talks up re-use, and the second-hand stuff is there if you search, but this is a company whose default setting is to sell you something new. In its annual report, eBay tells the investment community that its main competition is companies selling new – not used – goods, such as

Walmart, Target, Costco and Amazon. It openly admits that its 'highest growth rates in gross merchandise volume (GMV) and sold items in recent periods have been in our fixed-price listing format, *primarily for new items* that are no longer in-season'. Over the past six years, while the company has been busy promoting re-use, the share of eBay's total volume coming from fixed price (largely new) items has risen from 36 to 64 per cent. In Australia, the company even boasts that '78% of all items available for sale on eBay.com.au are brand new'. The rapid growth in eBay's volume – up 12.5 per cent since 2009 – means that greenhouse pollution generated by eBay's own operations, primarily energy use at data centres, is growing fast, as is the carbon footprint of the freight required to deliver the goods.

E-commerce isn't always about having stuff shipped to us – the booming online travel industry is all about shipping ourselves somewhere at the click of a mouse. In spite of the large carbon footprint that involves, online travel companies claim to be climate-friendly. Perhaps the best known is Travelocity, whose stated mission is 'making the world a better place one trip at a time'. A green pitch is a prominent part of the company's 'Travel for Good' program: there's a green logo and ads showing hands cupping seedlings. The company's best known marketing tool for nearly a decade – the roaming gnome with the voice of British comedian Harry Enfield – has also gone green. He used to be shown in various locations contrasting a pleasant trip booked through Travelocity with disastrous alternatives. More recently, he's been selling Travelocity's greenness, along with the company's 'Green Hotels Directory' (2300 properties around the world, with their own leafy green logo).

In 2011, Travelocity took him to New York City for a green scavenger hunt billed as 'the roaming gnome makes Earth Day sweet'. The gnome was quoted saying, 'Mother Earth is a dear old friend ... I can't wait to see all my marvelous friends in New York City lend her a helping hand'. Using Twitter updates hinting at the gnome's whereabouts, Travelocity generated 'flash mobs' of eager consumers at various locations, who were duly rewarded with organic cookies from a biodiesel-powered truck. A similar project ran in Las Vegas, where the gnome's 'followers' (presumably with time on their hands) deciphered clues about his whereabouts – as it turned out, underneath a statue's green toga at Caesars Palace. At a recent Sustainable Brands conference, a beaming Travelocity executive explained how cheap and effective such marketing is, especially if linked with an 'environmental holiday' like Earth Day: 'It was really clicking in consumers' minds – I get it, the roaming gnome is here, Travelocity is going green, it's Earth Week'.

For a more explicitly climate-friendly message, Travelocity uses its 'Eco-Bunnies'. In video commercials, two laid-back rabbits banter about the importance of offsetting one's carbon footprints. 'Zero it out by planting trees and stuff', explains one to the other. It ends with 'Help the Eco-Bunnies offset your travel with Travelocity's Travel for Good program'. The bunnies are clear that 'everyone is responsible for their own footprint', but the hint here and elsewhere is that Travelocity is dealing with its footprint. The company says, 'We are committed to minimizing the environmental impact of our global business operations', and since 2006, 'we've planted more than 23,000 trees that will trap an estimated 28,000 metric tonnes of carbon dioxide'. Under the heading 'Reducing our footprint', Travelocity talks up its LEED-certified company headquarters, its low energy fluorescent lighting, its 'industry leading Get There Green' carbon calculator, a hybrid car rental service and more.

It's all part of the Travel for Good mission, which is 'our way of conveying our sense of responsibility for the destinations we all love to visit and our commitment to minimizing the environmental impact of any journey'.

Presumably, the Mother Earth–loving roaming gnome and Eco-Bunnies would work only for a company whose carbon footprint is shrinking. Not so fast. Travelocity releases no information about the size of its carbon footprint, nor does its parent company Sabre Inc. Sabre used to release a short sustainability report, before it was privatised in 2006, but now there's just a two-page 'Social Responsibility Snapshot', at the head of which the company claims that 'Social responsibility is more than a business strategy at Sabre, it's our heart and soul'. It explains that 'people', 'profit' and 'planet' are the three pillars of the company's commitment. Yet, details on the company's carbon footprint, and any plans or timetable for reducing it are conspicuously absent from the 'planet' section.

Consider what Travelocity's green pitch glosses over: a company through which each year 'more than 300 million people purchase airline tickets'; that services over '350,000 travel professionals to more than 400 airlines, 93,000 hotels, 25 car rental brands, 50 rail providers, 13 cruise lines and other global travel suppliers'. The rough maths of the carbon footprint on the airline tickets alone – if 300 million fliers each generate, say, 0.55 tonnes (the equivalent of a one-way flight from Los Angeles to New York) – means flights booked by Travelocity might generate the equivalent of 165 million tonnes of carbon dioxide equivalent *annually*. Though these emissions are not by any means the sole responsibility of Travelocity, the 28,000 tonnes eventually saved by the trees planted by the company over five years seem positively diminutive by comparison. Based on the little Travelocity will tell us, it's reasonable to assume that the air travel facilitated by this company alone adds over 5000 times as much greenhouse pollution *each year* as will be saved in total through tree-planting. That's excluding the hotels, cruises, tours and much more.

No-one expects people to stop travelling and people are going to use the internet to book their holiday. It's not up to Travelocity to neutralise the carbon footprint of their millions of clients either. What brings Travelocity unstuck is the laughable pretence that its business and those it feeds the demand for are climate-friendly. Greenwashing is a conscious and unfortunate choice that they've made.

So what if we take all the stuff and the shipping out of the e-commerce equation, as with social networking – is it doing any better than online shopping? Facebook talks the talk, with its 'Green on Facebook' page, complete with a green logo. Until recently the logo incorporated the company's usual blue 'f' underneath a green tree; now the logo is something more like a green recycle symbol. The page promotes the company's collaboration with all manner of partners – the Audubon Society to count birds, the Natural Resources Defense Council to save energy, WWF to turn off lights. There's the obligatory carbon calculator to help Facebook users reduce their carbon footprints. And there is the affirmation that 'Green on Facebook' is 'liked' 100,000 times. The page also provides the company with the chance to roll out some rhetoric: 'With more than 800 million people around the world using Facebook, our greatest opportunity to effect environmental change is through the power and reach of our platform ... Since our founding we have been committed to operating Facebook in a way that minimizes our environmental footprint while ensuring our long-term sustainability'.

Facebook's reach is a wonderful tool for environmentalists, but they're not the only ones making the most of it to communicate and raise money – climate sceptics and the carbon lobby love Facebook too. Almost every big polluting company and climate sceptic organisation out there is taking advantage of Facebook's reach. Thousands of people have 'liked' climate sceptic pages such as that of Lord Monckton – a man famous for insights such as, 'The right response to the non-problem of global warming is to have the courage to do nothing'. Another good example is the 'Real agenda behind "anthropogenic global warming" fraud' Facebook page. It uses the platfrom to argue that 'Global warming is a fraud, cleverly designed to redistribute wealth and power to the global elite; whose main goal is to depopulate the world, and to establish a global dictatorship'. Facebook even hosts a Climate Sceptics Shop, which sells 'quality, branded merchandise with the profits going to climate sceptic websites'. With Facebook friends like these, the environment doesn't need too many enemies.

No-one expects Facebook to censor the platform, but the company can't pretend that its reach is inherently climate-friendly. Yet the main problem with the 'Green on Facebook' marketing is the company's own carbon footprint – for which there is no page. The company issues a media release when there's something climate-friendly to show-off, such as its hydro-powered and 'air cooled' data centre near the Arctic Circle in Sweden. When Facebook opened its 'first energy efficient data center in Prineville, Oregon', it created a fan page for the data centre itself (it's been 'liked' 36,000 times). Yet Facebook will not disclose any information detailing the extent of its carbon footprint, whether it is rising or falling, or whether it has a plan or timetable to reduce its emissions. For three years running,

Facebook has declined to participate in the Carbon Disclosure Project too.

Given that company founder Mark Zuckerberg has said that transparency is at the heart of Facebook, the lack of transparency on its environmental performance is hard to 'like'. What we do know is that Facebook is building new data centres in regions where coal is king. Recently, it spent some $450 million on a second such centre in North Carolina – a region with a power supply described as 'one of the dirtiest in the country, with only 4 per cent of electricity generation from renewable sources and the balance mostly from coal (61 per cent) and nuclear (30.8 per cent)'. Greenpeace consequently targeted Facebook for its carbon footprint, with an Unfriend Coal campaign calling on people to 'Help Facebook become 100 per cent renewable': 180,000 people 'liked' that. In late 2011, Facebook, in a joint announcement with Greenpeace, said that it had embraced the goal of clean and renewable energy. However, the commitment makes only vague mention of a preference for clean and renewable energy when finding sites for data centres. 'Facebook "friends" Greenpeace', says the company proudly on its website, but there is still no timetable for switching to renewables, let alone going 100 per cent renewable, and Facebook still hasn't publicly disclosed its carbon footprint or detailed how it plans to reduce it.

The other big online corporate going green is Google, with its logo, branding and graphics all promoting Google Green™. The Google Green website poses questions such as: 'Are we approaching a clean energy revolution?' to which the company answers, 'We believe we are, and here's how we at Google are contributing'. Its comments include, 'We look forward to the day we no longer need offsets because our operations are as efficient as possible and we rely exclusively on renewable energy'. When companies answer their own questions in this way and talk about renewable energy as a distant wish, it's hard not to be suspicious.

Conspicuous green advocacy from a company in an emissions-intensive business is also often a sign of something to hide. Google trots out a long list, 'including direct lobbying, funding policy research, organizing coalitions of leading companies and organizations, hosting "convenings"... blogging, speeches, and press outreach'. And it draws some long bows, such as arguing that Google Earth fights climate change by helping scientists track deforestation from space. From a company whose main contribution to climate change is vast energy-intensive data centres, it's hard to take seriously claims such as: 'we believe that bicycling directions in Google Maps will encourage some (small) percentage of users to bicycle to their destination rather than drive, thereby reducing users' carbon emissions'. It's difficult not to wonder about the coal miners, logging companies and Hummer drivers also merrily using Google's online tools. But two things make the Google Green story hard to dismiss.

The first is the scale of its investment in renewable energy. While it's commonplace for companies to have some conspicuous hybrid vehicles, and solar panels atop energy-efficient head offices – all of which Google has – what sets it apart is how much further it's gone beyond ticking these usual boxes. The company has invested some $915 million in renewable energy projects, which, according to the company, will generate enough power for 350,000 homes. Beyond the energy industry itself, few companies are investing in clean energy on this scale. Such investment helps to accelerate the pace at which renewable energy competes with fossil fuels and it's a great example of how a large company can go beyond managing its own carbon footprint to make a significant positive contribution. As well as taking equity stakes in renewable companies and projects, Google is also buying significant amounts of renewable electricity. In 2010 it got an estimated 25 per cent of its power from renewables, and wants to raise that level to 36 per cent by 2012.

The second thing that sets Google apart is that the company offsets *all* of its carbon footprint, something that very few large companies can say. Google's use of offsets is also more credible than most. While many companies do vague forest protection deals in distant lands with the emissions offset either very modest or unspecified, Google publicly details its carbon footprint and offsets 100 per cent of it relatively closer to home. The company could be more specific about its offsets rather than providing just a few examples and describing its approach to offset procurement. However, the overall impression is that its offsets – which seem to come mainly from landfill gas capture and agricultural methane capture in the United States – are more tangible and verifiable than most.

This isn't to suggest that Google is a saint. The amount of greenhouse pollution it produces annually (before offsetting) is still increasing. Google also acknowledges that the emissions beyond its operational control are increasing too. As Greenpeace noted in its recent *Dirty Data* report, Google 'generates more carbon dioxide than eighty-two countries'. The company is also building data centres in coal country – North Carolina, South Carolina and Oklahoma. And while its investments in renewable projects are large, they form a relatively tiny proportion of Google's $72 billion in assets. Even so, it's harder to see Google Green as greenwash. Google faces many of the same challenges as eBay (less the manufacturing and freight emissions) and

Facebook, but its operational emissions are far less out of control – rising by 6 per cent in 2010 (before offsets). Its intensity improvements and large-scale investments in renewables even suggest that significant absolute emissions cuts may soon be possible. It's the transparency so lacking at Facebook, eBay and Travelocity that gives Google credibility when it says that it looks forward to the day when it will rely exclusively on renewables. In all, it offers hope that e-commerce can be eco-commerce if a company is serious about it.

petrol

Maybe you're old enough to remember the Castrol engine oil ads featuring a nervous mechanic called Sol reporting to a Mafioso boss who showed up with the requisite dapper suit, hat and henchmen to check that his cars were being properly looked after. The ads usually included a moment in which Sol seemed headed for the bottom of the river with concrete shoes for not following orders. Invariably, though, the boss would end up chastising him with Castrol's slogan: 'Oils ain't oils'. Decades on, the Mafia-like grip of oil companies on the global energy industry is largely unchanged, but there's a new generation of advertising. These days, oil companies want us to believe they are something other than oil companies. Thanks to those pesky climate scientists, it's more like an 'Oil ain't oil' campaign now, with oil scarcely mentioned by the companies selling it. Chevron is apparently powered by human energy – not fossil fuel; Shell tells us, 'Grow our own fuels – Let's Go', as if they've opted for biofuels; while for the best part of a decade, BP told us that its initials stood for 'Beyond Petroleum™'.

Until its greenwash came tumbling down with the Deepwater Horizon oil spill in 2010, BP was the industry leader in pretending to be something other than an oil company.

Typically, the marketing would suggest that BP was deeply concerned about climate change, or that it was transforming into a company dominated by renewable energy. We'd see billboards saying, 'Oil + Gas + Wind + Solar + Biofuels = Energy Security' or that 'BP provides oil, gas, wind, solar, biofuels and options'. Then there were ads featuring smiling, whistling green petrol bowsers next to much larger images of wind turbines and the sun. These messages would come with the company's sunflower-patterned helios logo and the words 'Beyond Petroleum'. A steady stream of speeches by company executives urged governments to price carbon and reduce greenhouse gas emissions. There were even ads juxtaposing the message 'Beyond Petroleum' with the words, 'We always use 100 per cent fair trade certified coffee beans' as if selling sustainable coffee made an oil company green.

For many years, therefore, BP was the pin-up, born-again corporate greenie. The company entered into partnerships with environmental groups around the world, and every announcement sparked a chorus of applause: achieving its emissions reduction targets eight years early; investing over $5 billion in alternative energy since 2005; its voluntary offset program and other initiatives cutting emissions by 8 million tonnes between 2002 and 2010. The growth of natural gas within BP's portfolio was also smiled upon by many commentators as evidence that the company understood climate change and the need to shift to less emissions-intensive energy sources. But BP was anything but beyond petroleum: the company's overall carbon footprint was getting inexorably larger in spite of the marketing. It had met its emissions targets, but the 'reductions' targeted applied only to BP's internal operations, not to the actual use of its products – emissions that are over seven times greater. Notwithstanding the impressive-sounding $5 billion investment in alternative energy, fossil fuels still delivered some 98 per cent of BP's revenues; and although it claimed to have prevented 8 million tonnes of greenhouse pollution over eight years, emissions from the production and burning of BP products wipe that out every four and a half days.

Yet even after the Deepwater Horizon spill, BP's sustainability report still sports pictures of wind turbines as far as the eye can see and huge arrays of solar panels. It still waxes environmental, saying, 'Our focus is on low-carbon businesses and future growth options that we believe have the potential to be a material source of low-carbon energy and are aligned with BP's core capabilities'. By this, BP doesn't mean renewables, which remain a tiny part of its business; it means 'natural' gas. BP has toned down the greenwash but is still dining out on hitting its targets and its 8 million tonnes of cumulative savings. In its 2010 sustainability report, BP can't resist a graph showing its operational emissions falling, although the company was honest enough to acknowledge the role of the post–Deepwater Horizon sell-off of some of its business, so that 'After stripping out the effects of acquisitions and divestments in 2010, our emissions actually increased by about 1.2 [million tonnes] on a like-for-like basis'. That number would have been significantly larger had the company included the emissions generated by the massive clean-up in the Gulf of Mexico (which it left out, citing uncertainty). Had the company also included the emissions generated by the *use* of its products, which it quietly acknowledges are still rising, it probably wouldn't bother issuing a sustainability report at all.

At times, it seems as if Chevron has filled the gap left by BP after the oil spill. Given that oil-based mechanisation has made human energy redundant on a massive scale, Chevron's Human Energy™ marketing is as cheerily delusional as the 'Beyond

Petroleum' slogan. At the end of one TV commercial, Chevron flashes up its rejigged company logo featuring the words 'oil', 'geothermal', 'solar', 'natural gas', 'hydrogen' and 'conservation', followed by the claim, 'This is the power of human energy'. In the previous twenty-nine seconds, we've heard soothing piano notes and a silky deep voice accompanying expensive cinematography, motherhood statements and, more importantly, pictures of things you probably would never see in your neighbourhood, such as a Chevron hydrogen outlet. 'We need viable alternatives to oil', says Chevron on a website rattling off a long list of its solar projects. One involves eight different solar technologies being deployed on the site of an old Chevron oil refinery to work out which is the most cost-effective. Chevron says the project will 'enable us to build solar arrays 25–100 times this size'. The impression given is that Chevron is leaving oil behind.

The company's recent 'We Agree' campaign sends a similar signal, with ads saying: 'Protecting the planet is everyone's job – we agree'; 'Oil companies need to get real – we agree'; 'oil companies need to clean up their messes – we agree'; and, 'It's time oil companies get behind the development of renewable energy – we agree'. These statements are echoed on a split screen with members of the public on one side and Chevron employees on the other. In full-page newspaper and magazine ads, and in online advertising, the 'we agree' pledges are signed by the company's CEO, and sometimes co-signed by well-known public figures such as Australian naturalist Harry Butler. The campaign gives the impression that Chevron is making a major shift from fossil fuels to renewables in response to public concern about climate change and the harm caused by fossil fuels.

The evidence shows otherwise. Chevron produces the equivalent of over a billion barrels of oil annually – 2.2 per cent more in 2010 than the year before. The emissions generated to produce these fossil fuels fell slightly between 2008 and 2010. But that saving was wiped out fourteen times over by the rising emissions from the use of Chevron's products, which added around 404 million tonnes of greenhouse pollution in 2010, some 22 million tonnes more than two years prior. To put that into perspective, in the space of two years, brimming as it was with 'we agree' planet friendliness, Chevron's products added four times as much greenhouse pollution as the company claims to have saved in a decade through renewable energy and energy efficiency projects under its Chevron Energy Solutions initiative. Where was Chevron's 'Increasing emissions by 2 per cent a year is ok – we agree' commercial? This admission, and many more that few people would agree with, is hidden away in annual reports and Carbon Disclosure Project returns that few people seeing Chevron's marketing read. Perhaps for the disagreeable geeks who dig this deeply into the detail, Chevron has created a 'game' called Energyville, which gives players catch-22 choices between fossil fuel, renewable and efficiency options, to help them understand just how hard it is to stop using fossil fuels. 'Shameless greenwashing – we agree.'

But the award for most prolific oil industry greenwasher goes to Royal Dutch Shell, the world's biggest oil corporation. If you put the best pieces of climate-friendly greenwash on display, Shell ads would feature prominently on the top shelf. Where to begin? There are the Shell ads that show flowers, rather than pollution, billowing from refinery smokestacks, and which urge us not to throw anything away because 'there is no away'. There are the ads showing butterfly nets chasing carbon dioxide molecules, with Shell declaring wishfully that in the 'new energy future we need to think the impossible is possible'. An online version of the ad enables the public to use their cursors as butterfly nets to chase the carbon dioxide. Another ad shows an imaginary machine with brightly coloured dyes labelled 'energy security', 'CO2 management', 'energy efficiency' and 'energy diversity' being poured into one end. We're not told what the rainbow-coloured liquid emerging from the other end is precisely – presumably those who accept the idea of fighting climate change with butterfly nets will just go along with it. Although the ad explains that Shell is 'channelling our creative thinking to produce innovative solutions', it is possible that more creative thinking is going into the marketing.

Creative thinking is again cited by Shell in an ad declaring that 'In the new energy future, if it doesn't exist we'll have to invent it'. A human brain is depicted with various named segments – 'fuel from algae', 'fuel from straw', 'fuel from woodchips', 'hydrogen fuels', 'coal gasification' and 'gas to liquids'. More recently, Shell has even run a Let's Go campaign, which seems to suggest that it is a climate-friendly company being held up by everyone else's lack of enthusiasm. 'Let's make cleaner electricity – let's go', urges one of the ads with the last two words in bright red; 'Let's grow our own fuels – let's go', says another; 'Let's go yesterday – let's go'; and the pointed, 'Decisions, decisions, let's make some – let's go'. One ad shows an ultra-efficient one-off vehicle draped with a Shell logo and accompanied by the words: 'Let's go further on one litre of fuel'. It's one of hundreds of cars taking part in the 'Shell Eco-marathon®' run annually. Some are covered in solar panels, some run on hydrogen and all get pretty extraordinary mileage. These cars are duly promoted on Shell's website, in its sustainability report and elsewhere. That they are totally unlike 99.9 per cent of those vehicles actually using Shell's fuel seems not to matter.

The problem arises when you start looking at Shell's business. By 2014, the company expects to produce around one-sixth more oil and gas than it did in 2009, and it acknowledges that this will cause an increase in emissions. The company makes much of the $2 billion it has spent on alternative energy, but a large chunk of this is devoted to carbon capture and storage (CCS). Though CCS as a solution to coal-fired power is still a pipe dream, the oil industry's main interest in the technology isn't reducing emissions but enhancing oil and gas extraction with waste carbon dioxide. Alternative energy in Shell-speak means alternative uses of the same old fossil fuels, and even some such as tar sands, which have previously been considered too dirty and emissions-intensive to touch. The company's alternative energy investment is just over 3 per cent of the company's annual income. For all its talk of 'wind on the great plains' and 'sun wherever feasible', in the boardroom of Shell it's still 'fossil fuels rule'.

Last, but not least, are the algal biofuels companies that would have us believe they are set to replace oil with a renewable, emissions-free alternative – even though their business is predicated on the continued use of fossil fuels to provide them with a ready supply of 'waste' carbon dioxide. One obvious example, conspicuous for marketing its product as Green Crude™, is Sapphire Energy, a San Diego–based company which boasts support from an investment company owned by Bill Gates. Sapphire is one of many companies pushing the idea that algae-derived 'green gasoline' is the answer not only to American reliance on Middle Eastern oil, but also to rising greenhouse gas emissions. In 2009, it painted a Toyota Prius plug-in hybrid bright green, added a 'Powered by Algae' slogan and drove it across the United States – it was reportedly 'the world's first hybrid vehicle to cross the United States on algae-based renewable gasoline'. The company also ran a well-received publicity campaign based on trial flights with Japan Airlines and Continental Airlines using its refined Green Crude – the latter decked out in 'Eco-Skies' livery. According to the company's corporate video, with only sunlight and carbon dioxide, 'Sapphire Energy is turning algae into Green Crude that can be refined into gasoline, diesel and jet fuel'. Supportive US congressmen have been woven into the video spruik, saying that 'algae is the one technology that has proven that it can replace fossil fuels'. The company says it 'can actually produce 100% of our domestic requirements from this technology', and that the technology can be easily scaled up because it doesn't compete with food production or 'use natural resources that we're not using today'.

Here's where it gets interesting. By 'natural resources', Sapphire is referring mainly to coal, though you'd never know that from its marketing. It plans to re-use the very concentrated carbon dioxide from coal-fired power stations and other industrial facilities to turbo-charge its algae growth. As with almost every other algae fuel company in the world – with a few exceptions – Sapphire's business hinges primarily on access to carbon dioxide from fossil fuel use. To most people, coal is far from a renewable resource, and the carbon dioxide emitted from it is therefore anything but a renewable input, but Sapphire sees it differently: 'all of the energy we use, all of the energy we think about pulling out of the ground and burning' is really solar energy from 'ancient photosynthesis'. There we have it – all fossil fuels are 100 per cent renewable. What a relief.

Needless to say, Sapphire's people don't respond when you write questioning the 'fossil fuel equals renewable fuel' logic, and asking whether 'coal-fired algae' is perhaps a better description of their business model. After all, the emissions from the coal are still released into the atmosphere; they're just recycled for use in transport fuel first. The best that can be said for Sapphire and similar companies is that they can produce a petrol equivalent that displaces some foreign oil. However, in the process, companies such as Sapphire are giving coal and possibly other fossil fuels a grand new alibi. Already new algae pilot plants are popping up next to coal power stations and more are planned. Now a coal industry that has struggled to convince us that carbon capture and storage is workable will argue not only that its carbon dioxide is being recycled into gasoline, but that without coal there is no sustainable transport fuel solution.

For all of its efforts to change its image and change the subject, the oil industry is still the oil industry. Perhaps they should bring back the Castrol ad concept, only this time with a more enlightening punchline from the Mafia boss, like, say, 'Oils ain't renewable, Sol'.

pets

'This is your captain speaking. Welcome aboard this flight from New York to Los Angeles. We particularly welcome members of our frequent flyer program. Our crew looks forward to giving you the best possible service on your journey, and in a moment our flight attendants will be coming through to the cabin to prepare for take-off. In the seat pocket in front of you, you'll find our complimentary magazine with lots of great shopping ideas and information about our in-flight entertainment program. So, sit back, relax and enjoy the flight. We appreciate that you have a choice of carriers, and we thank you for choosing Pet Airways.'

OK, so the magazine and in-flight entertainment are invented, but everything else is true. This is a pets-only airline offering forty or so 'pawsengers' exclusive use of the climate-controlled main cabin and the regular attention of a 'qualified in-flight pet attendant'. There is a frequent flyer program, 'which offers members free flights along with big discounts on pet supplies from MyPAWS Pet Stores, discounts on pet-friendly hotels, pet health insurance' and other benefits. The airline offers the equivalent of first- and business-class sections: large and extra-large carriers in which wealthier pets can stretch out.

For more frugal pets, there are advance purchase deals and special offers. The company's website shows a cat at his laptop mulling over his travel plans. Perhaps he is surfing the airline's Travel Channel, which features 'TripAdvisor's Top 10 Properties for Jet-Set Pets'. Or maybe he's reading travel tips from fellow pets. A Pomeranian called 'Ginger' urges pets visiting New York to find some 'sexy and sassy clothes like mine' at 'Trixie and Peanut, my favorite pet boutique'.

Ventures such as Pet Airways encapsulate why we need to pay attention to carbon pawprints. Consider the numbers: there are currently around 1 billion pet cats and dogs worldwide (not to mention hundreds of millions of stray ones), and pet ownership rates are vastly higher in western countries. About 40 per cent of US households own at least one dog, compared with about 6 per cent of Chinese homes. However, the gap is closing fast, as the number of pets and the demand for food and other goodies in developing countries spiral. In India, dog ownership is growing annually at double digit rates, while in Vietnam and Thailand, the number of dog owners increased by around 50 per cent between 2004 and 2007. The ecological consequences of pets are significant when you consider the land needed to produce the energy and resources required for a large dog are equivalent to that of a four-wheel drive Land Rover; a medium dog is equivalent to a VW Golf. Or so say Brenda and Robert Vale, authors of the provocatively titled *Time to Eat the Dog*. Among many reasonable observations they note that we face real problems 'when everyone starts to have a big car, big house, big family and a big dog'. They also note that many pets in the west have larger ecological footprints than humans in some developing countries. So, while the rising population of pets is significant enough, the rising affluence of pets is also important.

The range of products and services hitting the market and encouraging pet owners to humanise their pets is staggering. There are dog houses with reverse-cycle air conditioning, some with flat screen TVs, and there are DVDs specifically catering to the tastes of different animals. From pet treadmills to electric blankets, a spiralling number of online stores and big box pet warehouses are selling aspirational pets an energy-intensive good life. Pet fashion is booming – hot-pink Swarovski diamante collars, Roberto Cavalli doggie tracksuits, Harley Davidson leather dog jackets. Hotels exclusively for pets are cropping up next to international airports. There's a pet diet industry, personal trainers for pets, and pet massage, manicure and aromatherapy. The aging pet is being sold plastic surgery, organ transplants and dye to hide grey hair – plus health insurance. Then there are lavish pet death services: pre-purchased funeral packages, luxuriously appointed 'poffins' (pet coffins) and marble tombstones.

As pet owners decide that 'what's good for me is good for my pet', they are creating a large, powerful and emissions-laden industry. In the United States alone, pet care is currently a $50 billion industry, having almost doubled in a decade. It is a microcosm of the same problem occurring with humans as developing countries become more affluent. Even as economic troubles around the world cause people to cut back on spending, the amount they are spending on their pets continues to spiral. At the heart of the decadence is the trend towards 'luxury' pet food, and the biggest beneficiaries are the four corporations that dominate the booming pet care industry and control 80 per cent of its largest component – the global pet food market.

With pet faeces reportedly making up 4 per cent of waste to landfill in some cities, clearly a great deal of pet food is being made. The food itself requires hundreds of millions of tonnes of meat and grain, as well as vast amounts of energy, most of it drawn from fossil fuels. It then has to be tinned, bagged and transported to all points of the planet. Who are the companies encouraging us to humanise our pets with their luxury pet food? Surprising as it sounds, think chocolate, toothpaste and cleaning products: the largest pet food manufacturers are Nestlé, Mars, Procter & Gamble and Colgate (no, they don't sell doggie toothpaste, but they do market a 'clinically proven' oral care product that 'works like a toothbrush to scrub tartar from teeth during meals and freshen breath'). Each of these companies would like us to believe that their booming pet care businesses are climate-friendly, but it's mostly spin behind the earnest-sounding pitches.

Nestlé invites us all to 'make the world a better place one pet at a time'. In Denver, Nestlé Purina launched what it billed as 'the nation's first major pet food plant to pilot a solar energy array'. The vice-president of the company said this would offset 'over 16 million pounds of greenhouse gases, equivalent to planting more than 40,000 trees' and that 'utilizing renewable energy at our manufacturing facilities is just one part of our overall company plan to create shared value for society'. Nestlé Purina claims that this is no isolated instance: 'We have a long history of being a sustainable brand'. Amid footage of solar panels, a corporate video explains how Nestlé Purina is 'Going Green from the Ground Up'. One Purina website for Friskies cat food shows a kitten jumping over a seedling, the picture overlaid with green paw prints and the line, 'By introducing smaller packaging, we're eliminating wasteful packaging by 600 tonnes per year'. The ad explains how 20,000 tonnes of material, including old phone books, have been recycled into a sustainable cat litter product called 'Yesterday's News'. The company also boasts: 'In recognition of our improved environmental performance, Nestlé was ranked second in the consumer goods sector in the (Carbon Disclosure Project's) Leadership Index 2010'.

If all you did was look at the company's marketing, press statements and glossy reports, you'd think Nestlé was making massive emissions-reducing strides. The company reports that in spite of a large increase in production volumes, in 2010 there was no increase in direct emissions – those generated by its hundreds of factories – and only a negligible increase in what Nestlé calls its 'indirect emissions'. What it doesn't say in its annual report or other PR is that *other* 'indirect' emissions – those from its supply chain, for which Nestlé doesn't take responsibility – are vastly greater. These are the greenhouse gases generated by growing the mountain of ingredients essential to its products and transporting them into Nestlé's hands – everything from cocoa and coffee to grain, palm oil and dairy cows. These and other supply chain emissions make the carbon footprint of Nestlé's products more than eight times what the company claims as its own – almost 60 million tonnes in all. Nestlé admits the non-manufacturing emissions are vast, but says they grew by only 2 per cent in 2010. That is a pretty good result compared with other large multinationals with long supply chains, but it's still equivalent to adding a quarter of a million cars to the road annually. With pet care accounting for roughly 15 per cent of Nestlé's manufacturing emissions, the total carbon footprint of its pet offerings are probably around 9 million tonnes a year – that's around 1.5 million Land Rovers, or 2.5 million Volkswagen Golfs.

So, although it's faring better than some competitors, greater production volumes and relatively modest steps make it hard to call Nestlé or its pet care division climate-friendly. To date, the company has focused on improving energy efficiency, such as optimising transport by using larger trucks and more direct routes. Nestlé has switched to less resource-intensive and more recyclable packaging to reduce the emissions of product use and disposal. But there's no sign yet that the company can keep increasing sales at the current pace and make deep cuts in the overall emissions of its products. That would require a large-scale switch from fossil fuels to renewables and a much greater focus on supply chain emissions, and there's little sign of either. The company acknowledges that the solar panels at the pet food plant in Denver are a small step; it points to a New York factory sourcing two-thirds of its power from renewables and one in Iowa that uses 10 per cent renewable energy. Nestlé says it plans to install more solar power at plants in California and Arizona. Nonetheless, the vast majority of Nestlé's energy (and emissions) still comes from fossil fuels.

Over at Mars – which makes Pedigree and Whiskas – the stated mission is to 'make a difference for people and the planet through our performance', which indicates a strong emphasis on saving the environment. Once again, there are the well-promoted but isolated examples of the company using green power to make its pet food, such as wind turbines in Yorkshire adjacent to a Mars pet care factory. Nestlé may have the world's first solar array at a pet food factory, but Mars has the 'first sustainable pet food manufacturing facility in the world'. The company points to emissions cuts due to a host of energy efficiency, recycling and packaging improvements, and its website features pictures of solar panels being installed at Mars Chocolate headquarters in New Jersey. The company says its operations generate around 15 million tonnes of greenhouse pollution, about 4 per cent less than in 2007. It has much grander plans for the future: a 'Sustainable in a Generation (SiG) program'. The company says it is 'committed to achieving zero fossil fuel energy use and zero greenhouse-gas emissions by 2040'. The distant timeline may be squint-inducing, but it sounds impressive enough – until you read the fine print. The commitment applies only to the company's *direct* emissions. Like Nestlé, most of the Mars carbon footprint lies elsewhere: supply chain emissions make up 87 per cent. The company admits that 'sourcing our raw materials leads to greater impacts than our factories and offices' – something many companies skate over – and it plans to 'develop similarly robust programs for each element of our value chain'. Until it does, however, we are left with a company nonsensically determined to cut its emissions to zero so long as the emissions tied up in producing its rice, beef, meat, dairy, corn, wheat and the rest of the supply chain are excluded. What is crystal clear, though, is that Mars, Nestlé and the other 'Big Pet Care' corporations are expanding into developing countries at a rapid rate, and enthusiastically pushing 'luxury' petfood brands intended to 'humanise' pets.

None of this is to suggest that pets are an emissions-intensive extravagance that must be forsaken in the fight against climate change. They are an important and very beneficial part of our lives – on average pet owners have lower blood pressure and fewer mental health issues, spend less time in hospital and ultimately live longer. But we shouldn't exempt pets from our efforts to tackle climate change, and companies that cater to pets shouldn't greenwash the contribution to climate change of the products, services and pet lifestyle they promote.

The American Pet Products Association's publication of 2011 trends in the pet care industry captures the current situation beautifully. The number-one industry trend is 'Reducing Your Pet's Carbon PAW print': 'Around the world people are making conscious efforts to help our planet Earth, and the pet industry is no exception. From natural litters to toys, accessories and organic food options, Earth-friendly pet products are sprouting up everywhere'. True enough, but what are the other pet care trends cited by the Association? Designer shampoos and fashion; hotel accommodation; electric toothbrushes and self-flushing litterboxes; automatic doors and touch-activated toys; toy gyms, spas and massagers; self-warming pet mats; not to mention faux mink coats, hipster lumberjack vests, designer plaid jackets, matching jewelled collar and leash sets ...

You can just picture advertisements for these products in the pages of the Pet Airways in-flight magazine, being enjoyed en route from Beijing, Rio or Mumbai, 'making the world a better place one pet at a time'.

phones, computers and office electronics

See if you can name this machine. It's made by Japanese office equipment company Ricoh and is a whopping fourteen metres high and thirty-eight metres long. It uses as much electricity as most homes, but runs on 100 per cent 'natural energy'. It can't print double-sided – heck, it can't print at all, and you can't make photocopies with it, scan a document, capture or store a digital image. It has enough battery power to last up to four days, but should it grind to a halt, don't expect any help from Ricoh's service division, as the company says if it stops working, 'that's OK'. In spite of its clunkiness, unreliability and almost total lack of utility, Ricoh promotes this machine worldwide with TV commercials, full-page magazine ads and YouTube videos. Give up? Say hello to Ricoh's giant greenwasher – otherwise known as the Eco-Board – a billboard powered with 100 per cent renewable energy.

Some companies dim billboards for Earth Hour, and others incorporate carbon dioxide–loving plants into 'living billboards', but Ricoh's Eco-Board takes things to a whole new level. In the past two years Ricoh has erected three Eco-Boards in prime locations: Times Square, New York; the M4 motorway between London and Heathrow Airport; and North Sydney, near the Sydney Harbour Bridge. Sydney's Eco-Board is powered exclusively by ninety-six solar panels, while the other two rely on a mix of solar and wind power; the one in Times Square has swanky vertical wind turbines; five more conventional windmills sit on top of the London billboard. All three enjoy plentiful back-up energy from Ricoh's marketing department. Video commercials for the New York Eco-Board end with a green light shining up into the Manhattan night sky, a green throwback to the Twin Towers' floodlights. 'Ricoh – Proud To Depend Solely on Sunlight; Billboard Reduces Carbon Emissions', declared the press release when it was launched by Mayor Michael Bloomberg, amid soft lighting and green tablecloths. The '100 per cent sustainable' London Eco-Board is 'demonstrating Ricoh's commitment to sustainable innovation', says another infomercial. A full-page magazine ad about Ricoh's '100 per cent sustainable, solar powered sign' in Sydney is drolly declared to be 'a solar powered print ad'.

Ricoh says the Eco-Boards are part of an environmental commitment that was made 'over 30 years ago'. Perhaps anticipating the obvious criticisms, there is even a video that tells us why the billboards matter. It explains that if all billboard advertisers followed Ricoh's Eco-Board lead, the carbon dioxide saved would equate to keeping all the world's cars off the road for a whole day. Ricoh sees this as 'Moving ideas forward'. What the video doesn't say is how far Ricoh is willing to move this idea forward. We're supposed to credit the company for the preposterously remote possibility that its three Eco-Boards might inspire the owners of 2 million billboards worldwide to go renewable, but there's no word on whether Ricoh will power all of its billboards with renewables. Nor is there any mention that Ricoh's own operations produce 10,000 times as much carbon dioxide annually as the forty tonnes that the Eco-Boards collectively save. But, of course, it's all about symbolism: 'Although the eco billboards have only a small direct effect on reducing our environmental impact', says Ricoh, 'we hope that the messages communicated through the billboards will help [make] more people aware of environmental issues and lead to a greater movement toward the creation of a sustainable society'.

It's lucky that Ricoh admits the billboards are only symbolic, because Ricoh itself gets over 98 per cent of its energy from non-renewable sources. What's more, its carbon footprint is increasing, contrary to the company's claim that 'the Ricoh Group is proactively reducing its environmental impact'. And the fact that its operational emissions are rising is only part of the story, because most of the carbon footprint of Ricoh products is tied up in the materials used to make them, and the use and disposal of them.

This isn't to say Ricoh hasn't made great strides in improving the efficiency of its manufacturing processes and the products it sells. Its latest printers can snap out of energy saving mode in less than ten seconds, cutting power consumption by over 80 per cent. However, the implications of Ricoh's Eco-Board marketing – that this is a company whose carbon footprint is shrinking, and which is leading the world in switching to renewable energy – are utter nonsense. When Ricoh's senior executives say the Eco-Boards are 'a visible demonstration of what we stand for, really', it's inadvertently true – Ricoh stands for using isolated greenwashing stunts to disguise the growing carbon footprint of its products.

What greenwashing stunt does computer company Dell have in common with the World Coal Institute (WCI)? Answer:

both run constantly updated 'carbon counters' through which each claims to have saved the atmosphere around 60 million tonnes of carbon dioxide. The WCI's claim is made to give you confidence that 'clean coal' is real and already safely capturing lots of pollution. It doesn't mention that it's taken ten years to capture the 60 million tonnes, that the carbon captured comes from oil and gas (not coal), or that coal burning without carbon capture adds almost this much carbon dioxide to the atmosphere *every day*. So, when Dell started using a WCI-style carbon counter on its website too, the greenwash detector crackled loudly.

Dell was already on the radar for the coverage it received about computers with an eco-friendly bamboo casing and its 'panda-safe' bamboo packaging. Another greenwash alert was the company's blog, which encouraged consumers to discuss the uncontroversial idea that climate change is a bad thing. Companies love getting consumers talking among themselves – it shifts the focus off company actions while generating green kudos for merely hosting the discussion. Then there was the 'Dell Go Green Challenge' in India, which rewarded people for coming up with great 'green' ideas. 'Got an idea for gadgets to go green? Submit it. Get votes. Win a laptop', it said. Another substance-free ad campaign in Canada also looked suspect. Against a green backdrop with a 'Dell Earth' logo, which looks like a windmill combined with the recycling symbol, the campaign simply declared, 'It's easy being green'. Sometimes the Dell Earth logo is run next to a picture of snowcapped mountains and wilderness. One ad featured a green tree inside an incandescent light bulb saying, 'Earth Day April 22, 2010. Go Green with Dell'. It looked as if someone was ticking the boxes in a greenwash handbook: 'green holiday' promotion – check; green logo – check; green slogans – check.

The biggest red flag, however, was Dell's marketing campaign with Southern Company, the second-largest electricity utility in the United States. In 2009, Southern bought some new servers from Dell, which improved the energy efficiency of its operations. Since then, Dell and Southern have held an ongoing environmental love-in via corporate videos, brochures and websites. On its blog, Dell describes Southern as 'no stranger to the "green" limelight'. One co-badged video describes Southern as one of largest energy generators in the country (cue collage of US southern states covered with energy-efficient light bulbs) that 'strives to do so with minimal impact on the environment' (cue cascading waterfalls) and is 'investing in capabilities such as solar, biomass and geothermal' (cue solar panels). A brochure available on Dell's website quotes a Southern spokesperson as saying, 'We've eliminated over 1340 tons of carbon dioxide emissions, which have a significant impact on the environment. That's a pretty big deal'. The marketing includes the catchcry, 'Partnering to power success'.

At no point is it mentioned that Dell is partnering to power the fourth-largest carbon emitting power company in the world. You'd never know that Southern gets a mere 2 per cent of its electricity from renewable sources or that, even with Dell servers, Southern's greenhouse emissions are up by more than 13 per cent in the last decade. Of course, Dell can't help that Southern wants to use its servers, but to run a co-branded green marketing campaign and promote Southern as a green company shows either extreme naivety or gall.

That Dell is comfortable in helping Southern greenwash its brand is especially counter-intuitive for a company that trumpets its green reputation. In Dell's 2011 fiscal year review, CEO Michael Dell notes proudly, 'Our environmental leadership earned us the *Newsweek* ranking of "Greenest Company in America" in 2011. We continue to innovate to reduce our own carbon footprint, and are more focused than ever on making "green" more practical and convenient for our customers'. The company has some of the most ambitious emission reduction targets, too: 'reduce worldwide facilities' [greenhouse gas] emissions by 40 per cent by 2015' and 'reduce global greenhouse gas (GHG) emissions per dollar of revenue by 15 per cent from 2007 to 2012'. As the deadlines loom, the corporate social responsibility report speaks guardedly of its progress – 'needs improvement' – and well it might.

In spite of the rhetoric, Dell's total emissions are still rising, and emissions intensity – the tonnes of greenhouse pollution per million dollars of revenue – was 7 per cent higher in 2011 than in 2009. Dell also acknowledges that emissions beyond its operational control are increasing. It doesn't say how much carbon is generated by the use of its products, a somewhat surprising omission since product use is at the heart of Dell's carbon-counter claim that it has saved 60 million tonnes of greenhouse pollution. While it's happy to calculate and publicise how much carbon has been *avoided* by more energy-efficient machines, does Dell deploy its carbon-counting talent to tell us how much greenhouse pollution is *generated* by its product use? Not on your life.

The greenwash detector first clocked IBM when it trademarked the term 'Stop Talking Start Doing' to show its seriousness about climate change. A magazine ad explained that IBM had surveyed over 1000 businesses and found 74 per cent of CEOs in Australia and New Zealand planned to invest more in corporate social responsibility. Who but a seriously green company would run such material in a full-page ad? For good measure there's a pristine forest backdrop, clear blue sky, and – you probably guessed – wind turbines, whose relevance is not explained. Happily, most climate-friendly IBM marketing is more fun, like Green Data Centre Man – a TV ad in which a mild-mannered CEO saves his company from spiralling energy costs and greenhouse pollution by buying IBM gear to optimise energy management and 'save the trees'. Another commercial features a boss responding dismissively to his employee's eco idea. 'I've been looking over your green proposal', the boss says, 'Should go over real well with the tree huggers ... but, you see, the people I report to don't eat granola ... why should I sign this?' The underling says bluntly, 'because it could save us 40 per cent on our energy costs'. There's a sudden 'Where do I sign?' conversion, music, splashes of green colour, butterflies and birds, and an 'IBM Go Green' Logo.

Given IBM's nickname, 'Big Blue', inevitably some bright spark made the leap to 'Big Green'. Infomercials promoting 'Project Big Green' explain that data centre energy use is doubling every five years, and IBM's 'Big Green' innovations can cut energy use by 40 per cent. The same sort of message comes through in a series of densely detailed 'Smarter Planet' advertisements, from which the average reader emerges fatigued but with a vague impression that IBM is more planet-friendly than they previously realised. The overall sense is that IBM is empowering a host of green superheroes across the corporate world.

So, you might expect spellbinding results – especially with the company winning the Climate Leadership Awards and gold medals for corporate achievement in sustainable development. Yet IBM's operational emissions are rising, having increased by around 200,000 tonnes between 2005 and 2010. IBM has the good grace to mention that the emissions from the use of its products are roughly equivalent to its own emissions, although this estimate covers only products sold in the latest year, not the 'power use and associated emissions of the entirety of our exist-ing product installed base.' The figures also exclude its supply chain, and transport and distribution of its equipment. To IBM's credit, it says openly what no-one else in this industry seems willing to – that it doesn't think it should bear any responsibility for these emissions: 'we believe real results in [greenhouse gas] emissions reduction are directly achieved when each enterprise takes responsibility to address its own emissions and improve its energy efficiency'. Asking companies to calculate all the emissions of products sold by their brand 'across an enterprise's value chain ... is misguided', says IBM. This suggests that 'Big Green' knows its own 'value chain' maths doesn't add up to something climate-friendly. If IBM is right in saying that data centre energy use is doubling every five years, then a 40 per cent improvement in energy efficiency is quickly wiped out.

Of all the companies in this sector, the maths of a shrink-ing carbon footprint are most overwhelmingly stacked against Apple. Yet it still puts up a greenwashed front, running commer-cials using a bright green Apple logo and claiming that its MacBooks are 'the world's greenest family of notebooks' – so efficient that 'it runs on one-quarter of the power of a single light bulb'. There's fine print behind the claim, of course. The laptop is assumed to be idle, unlike the virtually antique 60-watt incandescent light bulb with which it is compared. This is not the main problem, however. The MacBooks may well be 'the world's greenest family of notebooks', but as with any family, no matter how green the behaviour of individuals, the size of the family is all important when it comes to determining the overall environmental impact. In Apple's case, the 'greenest family' is getting inexorably bigger.

Consider the ubiquitous iPhone. Apple sold 20 million in 2009; nearly 40 million in 2010; then in early 2012, Apple reported it had sold over 37 million in just one quarter. At this rate, it could soon sell over 140 million a year. Stack that many iPhones on top of one another and you have a pile about 150 times as high as Mount Everest. Collectively, they have a large and growing carbon footprint. For a while, new iPhone models became more energy-efficient – the iPhone 4 was 18 per cent more efficient than its predecessor (and, to its credit, Apple publishes clear cradle-to-grave information on the carbon footprint of each product over its anticipated life). However, that trend has been reversed with the newer model iPhone 4S, for which the carbon footprint blew out by 55 per cent. This means that iPhones alone could soon be generating over 10 million tonnes of greenhouse pollution annually – the equivalent of 2.2 million cars or a couple of 1000-megawatt coal-fired power stations. Though some of the increase in iPhone sales is due to phones superseding other products such as the iPod, across *all* of Apple's product lines – iPods, iPads, iPhones, desktops and that green family of notebooks – the number sold is up by 92 per cent since 2009. With the total carbon footprint of its products more than doubling in the last couple of years, Apple has stopped lodging returns with the Carbon Disclosure Project. The company may still claim that it 'seeks to minimize greenhouse gas emissions', but minimised or not, its carbon footprint is still growing rapidly. Perhaps Apple should replace its 'Better Products. Smaller Impact' slogan with something closer to the truth, like 'More Products. Bigger Impact'. That goes for all the companies canvassed here.

professional services

See if you can guess what an accounting firm's most carbon-intensive activity is. No, it's not all of those air miles racked up going to conferences, team-building and professional development courses. It's not the hundreds of computers in the office, the high-rise elevators yo-yoing all day long, or the lights humming all night. It's not the forests logged to produce the reams of paper used or the printers churning endlessly. It's not the take-away cappuccinos either. Lest you devote too much mental energy to imagining life as an accountant, here's a hint – an accounting firm's biggest contribution is also the biggest contribution that a law firm makes to climate change. The same goes for management consultants, engineering consultants and many others. Still can't work it out?

Let's look for some pointers in the advertising of one of the 'big four' accounting firms. Companies publicly claiming to have cut their emissions will surely have dealt with their *biggest* contribution to climate change, right? In 2007, KPMG launched its Living Green™ campaign, stating in no uncertain terms that KPMG would 'be a driving force in environmental responsibility' and committing to 'reduce our carbon footprint by 25 per cent of 2007 emissions by 2010'. In 2010 the company announced that it had met its Living Green targets a few years early. Bold words, and it would seem they accomplished it by focusing on the little things. As a glossy Living Green brochure records: 'we can make a difference and play a role in creating a sustainable future ... Switch off the light in the office during the day ... Switch off your computer when you leave the office ... Think before you print ... Consider using video or audio conferencing ... practice "fuel-efficient driving"'. Yet, unfortunately, none of this deals with the biggest contribution that an accounting firm such as KPMG makes to climate change.

Perhaps we'll work it out at PricewaterhouseCoopers (PwC), another big four firm that enthusiastically markets itself as climate-friendly. The company maintains that 'corporate responsibility is about being a leader and doing the right thing', so it committed to cutting its carbon footprint by 20 per cent by 2012. In some jurisdictions, the company has even said it is going carbon-neutral. The PwC plan is pretty similar to KPMG's, involving everything from reducing waste-to-landfill, to videoconferencing and more energy-efficient data centres. And no, its biggest contribution is not those energy-intensive data centres.

Maybe we'll find the answer at a law firm. Some of the best known legal names have joined the fight against climate change, including one of the world's largest law firms, UK-based Clifford Chance. Clifford Chance says it has corporate responsibility 'in its genes'. It promotes itself as climate-friendly and has pledged to become carbon-neutral worldwide. The company doesn't seem to say how much greenhouse pollution it will be offsetting – or how – but it has committed to deriving 10 per cent of its energy from renewable sources where that option is available. Somewhat paltry, perhaps, but there are also energy-efficient improvements flowing from the internal push to make its offices more climate-friendly. In its Amsterdam office, Clifford Chance has cut its emissions by a third in spite of a more than 20 per cent increase in the number of employees. Here again, the posters on the office walls were encouraging employees to run a blank screensaver and think twice before printing documents. We still don't seem any closer to discovering the biggest ticket item, though, do we?

Let's try another law firm keen to be seen as climate-friendly: Baker & McKenzie. Unlike the other firms we've looked at, this one doesn't promote itself as carbon-neutral, and if there is a list of in-house green tips, it's kept in-house. Letting us in a little, the firm says: 'Naturally, the lights at Baker & McKenzie's office went dark when Earth Hour came', which the event's organisers duly promoted. Furthermore, 'The lights came back on as planned, but our offices' energy consumption remained in permanent decline'. There's not much detail on how this was achieved, but the difference between the 'think before you print' firms and Baker & McKenzie is that it doesn't make much of the in-house stuff. It's taken a different approach.

The firm is seen as relatively climate-friendly partly because it has carved out a niche in the climate law and policy sphere. As the company puts it, 'When Kyoto was signed, one of our partners in Sydney recognized that an entirely new area of law was about to emerge. Hardly anybody else in the legal profession took notice. Our executive committee said to run with it'. As a result, Baker & McKenzie can now spruik a long list of awards as proof that it is the best law firm for all things carbon-related. Arguably the main reason the firm is perceived as climate-friendly is through its associations. The firm is the founding sponsor of a Centre for Climate Law and Policy at the Australian National University, it sponsors numerous climate policy and carbon-trading conferences, and has even taken out corporate membership of renewable energy associations. It also provides pro bono advice to youth climate-activist organisations. Its most prominent association by far, however, has been with Earth Hour, and it is primarily through its pro bono work for that event that Baker & McKenzie claims to be 'inspiring commitment and change'. From helping WWF to trademark the term 'Earth Hour' in China to providing judges of WWF's Earth Hour awards, Baker & McKenzie's work for WWF and its other associations enables the firm to appear climate-friendly without spending money on green advertising campaigns. The appearance is a self-satisfying mix of pro bono and quid pro quo.

And with that, we are finally getting warm in our search for the biggest contribution that professional service firms make to climate change. No, it's nothing to do with WWF or Earth Hour, or any of the pro bono clients. Rather, it concerns the paying clients taken on by the big accounting, legal and other firms. As KPMG puts it, 'many of the decisions we make every day shape our planet's future'. In choosing which work to accept, many big professional services firms marketing themselves as climate-friendly are making climate-unfriendly decisions every day that indeed help to shape the planet's future.

Let's take another look at KPMG. While it's meeting its emissions targets years early, it's also raking in millions auditing the books of coal companies, whose core business contributes more to climate change than any other industry. KPMG's list of coal clients is star-studded: Coal India (the world's largest coal miner), China Shenhua Energy (China's largest coal miner), Peabody (the world's largest privately owned coal miner), BHP Billiton, Rio Tinto, Xstrata and Anglo American (the world's four major multinational coal traders), and Alpha Natural

Resources (the largest mountain-top removal coal miner in the United States). The KPMG staff involved with these accounts probably telecommute or carpool every day and are assiduously 'using coffee mugs instead of paper or styrofoam cups', in keeping with the Living Green manifesto. But that's more or less beside the point.

If KPMG was merely getting the books of coal companies ready for tax time, that would be hypocritical enough, but its work goes far beyond this. KPMG helps new coal companies get listed on stock exchanges, and not so long ago it took a job advising Coal India on how best to increase output and maximise profits. So while KPMG is bragging about cutting its emissions globally by 2 per cent (roughly 5000 tonnes of carbon dioxide), this saving is erased by the expanded production of just one of its clients – Coal India – every half an hour. 'When you walk into a KPMG office', croon the Living Green ads, 'you will walk on rugs made from recycled materials'. It's what's swept under the rug that you need to worry about – the emissions from fossil fuel companies whose expansion KPMG enthusiastically supports.

The KPMG Global Energy Institute even issues papers with coal seams on the front cover, inside which the firm's partners express their faith that 'clean coal' technology can 'enable the continued exploitation of vast coal reserves for the production of "clean" energy', and that 'the focus must be on reducing emissions, not on reducing the use of coal'. It's all music to the ears of an industry yet to supply a commercial-scale 'clean' coal-fired power station. Then there's the problem that while KPMG was declaring climate change one of the biggest problems facing the world, one of its best known executives, Bernard Salt, was writing newspaper columns equating climate change with public hysteria about martian invasions and the Y2K bug. 'Like Y2K', he said, 'climate change also relies on experts to decode the future and to issue dire warnings of peril, lest we heed their advice and fund their programs'. Yet, a firm so deeply complicit with the world's most polluting industries still has the nerve to publish articles on 'How to Avoid Greenwash'.

Over at PwC, the story is much the same: the company is cutting its in-house emissions and studiously ignoring those generated by clients. PwC is the accountant of choice to the world's top three oil companies – Exxon, Shell and PetroChina – and it's similarly reliant on the patronage of coal companies. One of PwC's green initiatives is a Facebook application called Carbon Bigfoot, which enables individuals to calculate and manage *their* carbon footprint. It asks pointedly: 'Are you a Carbon Bigfoot?' As the numbers are plugged in and the user's emissions mount, a yeti-like animation increases in size. PwC gently chastises you, provides a few tips on how to cut your carbon footprint and encourages you to compare your Carbon Bigfoot results with your friends'. But what about the corporate Carbon Bigfeet served by PwC? Few Carbon Bigfoot users get the slightest inkling that PwC unquestioningly accepts that coal will continue to be a major part of the global energy mix for some time. Whether it's cashing in on the good times by working for coal companies in takeover bids, such as Felix Resources' acquisition by Yancoal, or cleaning up as receivers when things go bad, as it did for Pike River Coal Ltd after its mine disaster in New Zealand, PwC is always there for the coal industry. It just happens behind a climate-friendly veneer.

What about those carbon-neutral lawyers at Clifford Chance? The firm's annual corporate responsibility report explains how it is helping clients finance solar and wind power projects and how its community initiatives are helping people recover from extreme weather events, 'many of which are linked to global warming'. There's less emphasis on its work with Canadian and Chinese firms on new coal-fired power stations in Botswana and with French companies to build a mega coal-fired power station in Morocco. While the climate-friendly drive back in the Amsterdam office cut annual emissions by 685 tonnes a year, a Brazilian power plant that the firm helped to finance adds around 3 million tonnes a year. In Asia, the firm was 'delighted' to help a Thai energy utility buy stakes in Filipino coal-fired power stations. In Europe, Clifford Chance recently helped twenty-three municipal utilities with a plan to build a large coal-fired power station in Germany; and it has helped Siberian steel and coking coal company Koks in its efforts to list on the London Stock Exchange. The firm also writes the contracts used by Global Coal, one of the largest coal trading platforms in the world. While Clifford Chance has been making its services as carbon-neutral as possible, it's also been happily providing those services to big greenhouse polluters the world over.

Meanwhile, as Baker & McKenzie was doing all that pro bono work to enmesh itself in Earth Hour, buying green sponsorships and shaving its office emissions ever lower, it too was busy helping coal companies. In Europe, it helped Ukrainian coal companies list on the Polish Stock Exchange; in China, it helped Shenhua list to fuel its expansion with more private investors. When Yanzhou Coal wanted to buy Felix Resources, Baker & McKenzie had no qualms about helping a company whose new mines in Australia will generate more carbon dioxide annually than has been saved by all the hybrid vehicles so far sold worldwide. It said it felt 'privileged' to help Japan's ITOCHU Corporation buy a big slice of the Maules Creek coal-mining project in Australia. The profits from this sale helped to turn former coal mine electrician Nathan Tinkler into Australia's richest man under forty. (Ernst & Young does his accounting, incidentally.) In 2009, as it was helping WWF to get Earth Hour up and running, Baker & McKenzie was running seminars in Mumbai for Indian companies on taking advantage of the 'new opportunities' to expand coal mining in Indonesia. A month before the 2011 Earth Hour kicked off, the firm was advising Cascade Coal shareholders to sell some mines to White Energy, which Baker & McKenzie described as a 'company focusing on cleaner coal technology'. In fact, White Energy aims to make briquettes from low-grade coals in various countries, which will exacerbate global emissions. For a climate-friendly law firm, Baker & McKenzie is surprisingly enmeshed in emissions-intensive activity.

It's easy to overlook the carbon lobby's hired help, and most of us tend to. It's easy also for these accountants, lawyers and consultants to disown responsibility for their clients' activities. The certified accountant might argue that the widely accepted approach to greenhouse accounting is to take responsibility only for the emissions for which a company is *directly* responsible. 'What, should doctors refuse to treat coal bosses; should hair-dressers knock back coal miners?' they might argue. The difference is that, unlike doctors and hairdressers, professional service firms are playing a crucial role in floating, financing or defending the world's biggest polluting industries. As such, they should not pretend to be 'carbon-neutral', 'living green' or 'inspiring commitment'. In choosing to service the companies most responsible for climate change, in sustaining industries they know to be unsustainable, firms cannot so easily absolve themselves from ethical responsibility for the environmental consequences.

real estate

For most of us, buying a home is not only the largest purchase we'll make in our lives, it will also have the greatest influence on our carbon footprint. It's not just the house itself, but where we choose to live, what appliances we fill it with, and how far it is from school, shops, friends, family and work. And no matter how we travel to and from work, our workplaces themselves make a major contribution to global greenhouse pollution. It's estimated that a third of global emissions come from the built environment. Materials and construction are part of it, but around 80 per cent is from the operation of buildings, particularly heating and cooling. Thanks in part to government-mandated standards, especially in developed countries, buildings are becoming more energy-efficient, and real estate seems to be getting greener.

We've all seen green home gurus – the crusading architect or green activist whose off-the-grid rammed-earth-floor home is featured in a book, magazine or lifestyle show. Inspiring as they are, the reality for most of us involves a real estate agent selling us a home or leasing us an office in whose design we had no input. Perhaps this is why few real estate agents trade on their environmental credentials. Sure, those poets who write the real estate advertising blurbs will do their darndest to highlight the eco-friendly sounding features of properties – 'natural breezes' (might mean no air conditioning); 'original timber' (could be extensive termite damage); 'waterwise garden' (maybe a concreted backyard). However, finding realtors that deal exclusively – or even mainly – in green homes will take dogged Googling. What you will find a lot more easily are real estate agents claiming to be reducing their greenhouse emissions and going carbon-neutral.

Babingtons Real Estate in Sydney is a typical example. It prides itself on being 'an ethical, sustainable and environmentally friendly organisation'. It's offsetting its own emissions, switching to recycled products, upgrading office lighting, reducing waste and offering telecommuting for staff. There's a monthly magazine with tips for communities to become more environmentally friendly. Click on the 'Babingtons Difference' tab, and the *only* thing the business nominates as setting it apart from the competition is its carbon neutrality. What this business has done is creditable enough, but it needs to be seen in context. By far the greatest impact that a real estate agency has on the environment is the houses it sells. The emissions generated by Babingtons itself amount to only thirty tonnes annually, while most single new homes embody at least fifty tonnes of carbon dioxide before they are sold and then, depending partly on the eco-friendliness of the house design and fit-out, another ten to fifteen tonnes each year afterwards when people have moved in. Yet if you check Babingtons' property list, you'll find no marked specialisation in climate-friendly properties. For perhaps A\$600 a year, it has merely bought a few offsets so that it can declare itself a certified 'No CO_2' business. Global real estate companies such as CB Richard Ellis are doing the same thing only on a much larger scale. It went carbon-neutral in 2011, but with 50,000 tonnes of emissions offset instead of thirty.

If climate-friendly real estate agencies are not making their core products any greener, how about the building companies? They get more say in the design of residences and offices, and in whether the heating, cooling, built-in appliances and lighting used are energy-efficient. When the topics of pricing carbon or mandatory energy-efficiency ratings are raised, the building sector is generally in the thick of lobbying against it. But, perhaps deciding that governments will win out in these environmental battles, some companies are looking to get ahead of the curve.

KB Home, one of the large players in the US housing market, is by far the most conspicuously climate-friendly marketer. The recession knocked KB Home around – it's now building around 10,000 homes a year rather than 30,000 – but if one of America's top five homebuilders is going green it is nonetheless significant. KB Home has the typical trademarked slogan – 'My Home, My Earth' – and the company's logo has had the standard green makeover. Its sustainability report showcases a Solar Demonstration House in California, but the biggest attention-grabber is the prototype GreenHouse™. Billed as an 'idea home created with Martha Stewart', it was launched at the 2011 International Builders' Show in Orlando. Strange as it may sound to enlist Stewart, who was jailed for lying, to reassure the public that KB Home is going green, her endorsement certainly guaranteed widespread media coverage. Beyond the pilot projects, however, KB Home is recognised by many as the greenest large builder in the United States, and with some justification. It's built 55,000 homes that have earned the internationally recognised energy-efficient label 'Energy Star', and it now exclusively uses Energy Star appliances in its homes. These are impressive steps forward, and the icing on the cake is the claim that KB Home cut its carbon footprint between 2008 and 2010 by over 60 per cent.

Even so, while KB Home has been among those announcing the death of McMansions, this doesn't mean it's designing smaller homes. Instead it's in the thick of a shift to the less fancy but just as large 'big box' homes, which often have over 5000 square feet of floor space – more than twice the US average. The second concern is that much of the impressive 60 per cent emissions reduction appears to have come as a result of building fewer homes – the number of houses built in that period dropped by 40 per cent. Factoring in the downturn, the numbers are still reasonably impressive until, that is, you stop and ask what exactly KB Home includes in its carbon footprint – not a question KB Home would answer when asked.

What we are left with is a company claiming to build around 7500 thousand homes with a carbon footprint of just 17,000 tonnes. That's just two and a half tonnes per house when we know that around fifty tonnes is normally embodied in most houses (largely from the production of housing materials). What seems likely is that KB Home is counting its operational emissions – corporate administration and some energy use on construction sites – but takes no responsibility for the emissions embodied in materials used to build the home, the emissions generated to transport those materials to building sites, or the ten to fifteen tonnes of annual emissions generated by the use of the home once people move in. There's no denying that the Energy Star commitment is helpful in minimising the carbon footprints of houses, but by disowning so much of the carbon footprint of its houses, and disclosing so little about what it does count, KB Home's claimed emissions improvement is pretty meaningless.

Factor in all the emissions not being counted and it's much less clear that the footprint of the new houses sold by KB Home is falling, let alone by 60 per cent. Add in the hundreds of thousands of existing KB Homes out there, each still generating emissions, and you're talking about a growing carbon footprint rather than a shrinking one.

Other developers have taken a different tack. Take Grocon, a large Australian company that has had a huge impact on the Australian skyline, building high rises such as Melbourne's 88-level Eureka Tower. It's also fashioned a public image as the country's greenest major building company, relying heavily on what you might call built advertisements or billboard offices. Built on the site of an old Foster's brewery, the Pixel Building has received the highest ever Green Star rating in Australia, a perfect score of 100. It could hardly be more conspicuous, covered in brightly rainbow-coloured panels that admit or block the sun depending on the season, but attract year-round publicity. The Pixel Building has hosted various grip-n-grin press events that enable politicians to laud the wind turbines, solar panels and 'living roof' and announce some green initiative of their own. This political praise amplifies Grocon's climate-friendly image. And the eco-friendly aspects of the building itself are undeniable: it's carbon-neutral due to renewable energy generated on site. Next door to Pixel, Grocon will soon construct an equally impressive triple-glazed wooden apartment complex, to be called Delta. Beyond promoting these buildings as evidence of its green commitment and leadership, Grocon expresses much welcome concern about climate change. But ultimately, while Pixel and Delta are groundbreaking buildings, they're not Grocon's core business – huge concrete-and-steel high rises are. For all the great PR, there's little evidence to suggest that the company's carbon footprint is shrinking. Grocon is using some aspects of its green buildings elsewhere and its recycling rates have increased, and it has pioneered the use of 'green concrete' (60 per cent less cement and 100 per cent recycled aggregate). But that doesn't overcome the problem that the company doesn't seem to publicly disclose its emissions. There are vague references to setting a challenge 'to meet LEED and equivalent standards in all our construction projects', but no hard evidence of how Grocon is progressing in that challenge. There is plenty of hard evidence, however, of the plethora of Grocon emissions-intensive projects – some rising over half a kilometre into the sky, such as the 122-level Pentominium apartment building in oil-rich Dubai (soon to be the world's tallest residential tower). These projects generate vastly more greenhouse pollution than the two green prototypes save, and, counterintuitively for such a green brand, its new projects involve some pretty carbon-intensive clientele. In Abu Dhabi, Grocon worked on Etihad Towers, developed by a member of the oil-rich nation's royal family. The development is one of eight that the company has helped to build in the United Arab Emirates. Somehow, building conventional high rises in nations built on money from oil seems a little at odds with the climate friendliness being claimed.

What about the landlords? Surely green-minded building owners are coming together to push the industry in a more climate-friendly direction? The Greenprint Foundation, which started in the United States, makes that claim. Since 2008, this network of property investors and developers has become the go-to voice for the high-rise industry when it comes to media events involving green building pledges – appearing with the Clinton Global Initiative, at the White House among much more. Greenprint has a logo of green bricks and the slogan, 'Reducing Carbon. Building Value'. Its mission is to lead the real estate industry in support of 'global greenhouse gas stabilization by 2030'. Greenprint releases an annual document called the Performance Report (previously known as the Carbon Index). In this it says it measures the carbon footprint of the 'Greenprint portfolio', which implies that it has measured the carbon footprint of its members' buildings. The numbers give the pretty clear impression that these emissions are falling, with the CEO citing a 0.6 per cent decrease in emissions between 2009 and 2010 in the report's foreword. The numbers aren't mind-boggling, but any annual decline in 'absolute emissions' is a glimmer of hope to be taken seriously. The CEO says he envisages the report as 'the global real estate industry's diary of our journey to dramatically lower our adverse impact on the global environment'.

Look more closely at the fine print, however, and you find that the report does not record a lowering of the real estate industry's impact at all. It does not measure the carbon footprint of all Greenprint members, either. It's the carbon footprint of a *sample* of its members' portfolios, and in 2011 it covered around 1600 properties, which turns out to be less than 10 per cent of the total. And the choice of which properties to be measured is left entirely to each member. Imagine how pointless and misleading a 'performance report' on a shares 'portfolio' would be if you only included the best 10 per cent of investments; or how good a wine collection could look if you only displayed the best bottle in every ten. Whether the Greenprint portfolio's emissions performance is representative of the industry is anyone's guess. What is clear is that Greenprint reluctantly acknowledges that it cannot say whether the collective footprint of its membership is falling, and that's a truer measure of performance.

sex

'Finally, they were alone. The summer grass danced in the breeze like massaging fingers, and a thousand voyeur cicadas screeched an excited chorus. As the couple melted into one another in broad daylight, Sarah felt deliciously naughty. Was anyone watching? They'd only just met and yet it was if they'd been physically attuned for years. How could a total stranger know her so well? She felt another climax welling up. Then, as a cloud went over them, it all came to a grinding halt. "Damn these solar &%&$ vibrators!" yelled Sarah.'

Yes, folks, some companies out there would have us believe that fighting climate change can be sexy. Sex is big business, and it's emissions-intensive in more ways than one. About one in every twenty-five websites is for porn and there are more than 280 million pages currently out there with millions more being added every month. That's a lot of material being downloaded. So while data centres may not have 'XXX' painted on the side of their buildings, a good chunk of the energy being used is sex-related. Pornography is estimated to be worth more than $30 billion worldwide, and the sex toy industry on its own could be worth $65 billion by 2020. This would mean some 400 million new vibrators each year plus a great deal else, one suspects – lots of plastic, lots of batteries and a growing carbon footprint. By some estimates there are over 40 million prostitutes working worldwide, many in brothels. That number means a lot of laundry and mood lighting. Then there's the well over 10 billion condoms sold annually, plus personal lubricant, lingerie and Viagra. The production of these goods, and in many cases their use, generates a significant carbon footprint, and as a growth industry it deserves our attention.

Although climate change is not on the radar of large sex-related companies – such as Larry Flynt Publications, which owns *Hustler* magazine, and the Barcelona-based porn empire Private Media Group – there *are* companies marketing climate-friendly sex. Let's start where that solar vibrator so rudely cut out. It turns out that there are quite a few solar models on the market (though no-one appears to have yet come up with one that runs on mini-hydro or a little wind turbine). The solar contrivance that's won most of the attention to date, which bills itself as the world's first solar vibrator, is the 'Micro-Kitty'. Supposedly, it can last two and a half fun-filled hours without needing a charge. For even more guilt-free enjoyment, it's recyclable and made of phthalate-free silicone.

The Micro-Kitty is marketed with a shoulders-up picture of a woman lying in the sun with a blissful expression. In competition with the Micro-Kitty are various 'solar bullet' models. One sold by a company called Libida is similarly promoted: 'Fancy tanning yourself out under the sun? Why not have some quiet personal time in the privacy of your own backyard with this solar-powered bullet vibrator ...? Should you feel shy about baring your bits in full view of anyone with a good pair of binoculars or telescopes, there is always the option to use it indoors ... This eco-friendly device retails for $29.95 a pop'. Another model even comes in green, leaf-covered packaging that is certified by the Forest Stewardship Council, enabling buyers to 'support healthy forests'. It doesn't scream 'greenwash', but these products form a negligible part of most sex toy businesses, and after the initial excitement some manufacturers have given up making them. So, as inspiring as it may be to imagine people the world over fighting climate change one solar vibrator at a time, they're not, and the companies selling them are not too serious about it either.

If solar vibrators aren't your thing, there are plenty more eco-sexy options on offer. One company proudly promoting an Ecorotic® sex toys collection is Good Vibrations, a collection of sex shops that are an institution in the San Francisco area. There's an impressive range of products available, including rechargeable vibrators. They even have an antique vibrator museum, where it's tempting to imagine a cumbersome and smokey coal-fired model rightly condemned to antiquity. Good Vibrations also offers 'anal toys' and 'g-spot dildos' hand-crafted from 'sustainably harvested' timber. Some man-made materials such as metal, silicone and glass get used, but while these may not be natural, Good Vibrations stresses that they're made to last a lifetime.

The environmental commitment of Good Vibrations goes further. As well as donating to worthy causes including the San Francisco Bicycle Coalition, it's set up an ecorotic rating system for sex toys. The system grades products on various aspects – whether they are animal free, naturally based, local etc. The company acknowledges that, 'While we wish that all sex toys were environmentally friendly, not all of our products receive an ecorotic® rating ... We believe that as awareness grows, more manufacturers will go ecorotic®, making ever more Earth- and body-friendly options available. In the meantime, we believe in giving you as many choices as possible'. The company concedes that it hasn't yet taken the step of switching to green power or offsetting its carbon footprint, but when it says it's 'proud of our role as leaders in helping our industry begin to question and change its practices regarding materials, packaging, and other issues impacting sustainability', it's hard to quibble.

Another company taking a slightly different green angle is Scarlet Girl, based in Portland, Oregon. It's so keen to save the environment that it's taken out the domain name Sextainable. org, trademarked the term 'Sextainable' and designed a green logo urging consumers to 'Love yourself and the earth'. Rather than selling green sex toys or rating environmental performance, Scarlet Girl is in the precarious business of recycling them. It offers customers a $10 discount on their next purchase in exchange for their 'broken or unwanted' sex toy. 'Did your Bullet lose its firepower?' asks the website, 'Cleaning out the ol' toy box after a breakup? Is a broken Jackrabbit just taking up space in your sock drawer?' Scarlet Girl can take the old toy off your hands and recycle the lot – even the electrical components. 'But', pleads the website, clearly from experience, 'please don't send anything wet or dirty! If it's too gross to handle we won't be able to process your shipment, and will have to return to sender'. Somewhat wearily it goes on, 'This offer only applies to actual sex toys; sending us empty lipstick tubes or a length of old garden hose doesn't count'. The recycling is, of course, positive, but it's hard not to wonder whether there might be more than this to being Sextainable™.

So what of the condom industry? In its brief but exciting lifetime, a condom saves a very significant amount of carbon dioxide by preventing conception. Contraception currently prevents around 300 million unintended pregnancies worldwide annually. As a recent UN report notes, 'Each birth results not only in the emissions attributable to that person in his or her lifetime, but also the emissions of all his or her descendants'. However, according to one manufacturer each condom generates up to 100 grams of carbon dioxide. With the market growing rapidly, what's being done to rein in the condom carbon footprint? Reckitt Benckiser is the owner of Durex, the world's top-selling brand. It produces glossy reports claiming to be on track to reducing its products' average carbon footprint by 20 per cent by 2020. While the 20 per cent reduction target is 'per dose', to the company's credit it is open in its PR about the supply chain emissions associated with its products. With this taken into account, the total carbon footprint of the company's products rose by 2.2 million tonnes between 2007 and 2011. The company says that by planting 5.4 million trees in British Columbia it is effectively offsetting its 2006–11 manufacturing emissions completely. However, the trees will take 80–100 years to store that carbon, and they won't begin to offset the supply chain emissions, which Reckitt Benckiser acknowledges are rising. Since the company sells so many other products, we can't see specifically what's happening with the carbon footprint of the Durex condom, but the signs aren't promising.

Catering to the top end of the market is the Original Condom Company from, of all places, Condom, France. Its 'luxury condoms' are carbon-neutral for that extra peace of mind, packaged in shiny, gold-embossed black boxes. According to the company, all of the emissions associated with the product are offset, and not just the company's operation but the entire life-cycle emissions of each sheath and its packaging. 'Unlike an ordinary condom', as the company says, these 'eco-aware'

condoms serve to protect our planet by offsetting emissions
through tree planting. There's a nice diagram of the whole supply chain showing how much greenhouse gas is generated at
each step in the process, per million condoms, and the Original
Condom Company says that all of the offsets have been verified
by PricewaterhouseCoopers. It should be a clear-cut good news
story, except that as soon as you start asking questions about the
total carbon footprint of the condoms, the company gets
extremely defensive: 'we do not communicate the numbers of
our production, it is strictly confidential'. How about some
detail on the offsets – can we see the PwC audit? Turns out, 'The
audit was made by PwC for us and is confidential too'. Then the
defence turns cultural: 'It's a shame to see how people of certain
countries think that they are allowed to access confidential
informations', says the company spokeswoman. 'Here in France,
we have laws that protects professional information. On the
contrary of the Anglo-Saxon countries, we respect the private
informations'. When it's pointed out that non-Anglo companies
routinely publish production numbers, the communications
stop altogether. It's probably not greenwash, but without transparency who can say?

Sometimes the opposite is true – something looks like
greenwash but turns out to be better than expected. Gel Works
is such an example – the Sydney-based company markets 'Wet
Stuff Naturally' as the first lubricant to be carbon-neutral from
cradle to grave. There's the usual green logo and for a company
selling over a billion lube 'uses' in seven years via dozens of
products, to carbon-neutralise just one product initially seems
greenwash of a pretty slippery order. However, when you look
more closely you find a small company doing more than most of
the multinationals with which it competes. To its credit, Gel

Works is upfront about the carbon-neutral claim only relating to the one lube, and there's no worry here about backing up the claims with production numbers. Currently, it's offseting Wet Stuff Naturally by buying renewable energy certificates from solar power (something it's been buying since the mid-1990s) and the company has offset four tonnes of emissions – enough to cover the first tonne of Wet Stuff Naturally. Mindful of warnings from climate scientists that we can't tree-plant our way out of climate change, the company is piloting a biochar plant, and the plan is to use it to offset the entire Gel Works range. So far it's made twenty kilograms of biochar from garden waste, which returns the waste to the soil, enriching it while locking up carbon for the long term. Twenty kilograms is not much, but according to the company it more than covers the propane used in manufacturing the first batch of its carbon-neutral product.

It's not only about offsets either – burning propane to sanitise the process water used in the lubricant is the main source of production emissions and Gel Works says improvements in burning in the past year have halved the amount of propane used per tonne of water boiled. The company is also keen to get to the bottom of its supply chain emissions in order to offset them as well. Says one company director of the carbon footprint of lube ingredients such as glycerin, hydroxyl ethyl cellulose and propylene glycol, 'My suppliers have no idea. I did ask. They were surprised and stumped!' If he can find out he says, 'I'd seriously consider offsetting that too'. No, there's no detailed emissions data, no Carbon Disclosure Project return, no PwC audit. And yes, Gel Works faces the same supply chain emissions problem as its larger rivals, especially if its sales are growing rapidly. But there is transparency here, rather than concealment, and enough information to feel confident that emissions are headed in the right direction.

OK, we've got our solar sex toys, our carbon-neutral lube and condoms. What about climate-friendly brothels? Heidi Fleiss's grand plan to run a 100 per cent wind-powered brothel for women in the Nevada desert would have been the ideal place to begin, but unfortunately it never left the realm of fantasy. It was to have been called the Stud Farm. Fleiss said it was meant for women 'who want a manicure, a pedicure, and a shag' (and presumably a warm inner green glow). Instead, it's in Europe that climate-friendly prostitution is advertised. Breaking new ground in 2009, one Berlin brothel started marketing 'green discounts' to customers who arrived either by bicycle or public transport. Citing a lack of car parking as a blow to business, the owner said that customers would get €5 off the price if they showed their bike helmet and lock key or their public transport ticket. An estimated 10 per cent of customers took up the offer, though how many kept their helmet and key in the car and drove in as usual is anyone's guess.

Another contribution comes from the online escorts directory in Birmingham, UK. Amid promotions for dirty phone sex covering an impressively diverse range of interests (from the relatively quaint categories of 'sympathetic girls', 'posh girls', 'big boobs' and 'knicker lovers' through to the more ominous-sounding 'spanking', 'corporal punishment' and 'pure humiliation'), the editors have the marvellous presence of mind to say, 'If you are visiting an escort in Erdington, then be a green carbon-neutral punter and travel by public transport'. Pimping local, but thinking global. Less impressive was the Melbourne-based Pink Palace brothel, which in 2007 launched a deal offering its clients a thirty cents per litre discount on petrol purchases as part of its Pump & Save campaign. Billboards promoting the offer were towed around stadiums before major football games. In its defence, the brothel did say it would consider offering a matching discount to public transport users.

We've covered some obvious categories here, but the market for sex-related eco-accoutrements is exploding. You'll find books on how to become an 'ecosexual', with tips on creating the ultimate eco-love nest – bamboo sheets with a high thread count; comforters and pillows full of Kapok tree fibres; mattresses full of wool or cotton; bed frames made of reclaimed timber or bamboo; soft energy-efficient lighting; soy candles for the right mood. To get a red-blooded greenie in the mood, an 'eco-friendly seductress' can now find carbon-neutral lingerie. There are waist cinchers, garter belts and stockings made from 'organic bamboo', 'hemp silk, vintage lace and even tree bark'. Even Marks & Spencer is selling carbon-neutral bras, produced at a plant in Sri Lanka which now sports solar panels. The company plants 6000 trees locally to offset the carbon bra-print.

With all this stuff presumably in great demand, and the 'Big Sex' corporations ignoring their responsibility and opportunity to become more climate-friendly, there is clearly a gap to be filled – especially in the porn business. Enter the small Norwegian outfit unsubtly called 'Fuck for Forest – Ecoporn' (FFF). It's a registered environmental non-profit organisation producing hardcore porn to raise money, which it then donates to worthy projects. 'Saving the planet is sexy', says FFF, which encourages people to 'pimp your karma' and 'become an erotic activist' by weaving 'public sex and nudity' into protest actions. Or, for the shy but nonetheless committed, you're welcome to become a subscriber and watch explicit footage, knowing your subscription is helping to fund a seed project in Ecuador and a nature corridor re-establishment in the cloud forests of Costa Rica. According to FFF, the Norwegian government now regrets providing start-up finding for the group, whose members have had sex on stage at rock festivals and even prostituted themselves as a fundraiser to bail fellow activists from jail.

Granted, FFF's approach to 'create a greener and more sex positive planet' is unconventional, but the reaction is perhaps more telling. Various established environmental organisations such as WWF have refused to accept money raised by the group, and pressure has even been applied to environmental projects to reject FFF funding. But who's doing more harm here – some dreadlocked nymphomaniacs using forest protection as an excuse for screwing outdoors, or a multinational group such as WWF refusing their money but still taking $70 million a year from corporations, the carbon footprint of whose products are in many cases still growing? Somehow the latter seems much dirtier.

soft drink

If ever they hold a Greenwash Olympics, you can bet it will be sponsored by Coca-Cola. Let's begin with the way Coke marketed its sponsorship of the 2010 Winter Olympics as climate-friendly. Coke was a major sponsor of the Olympic torch, and the company decided this was the perfect opportunity to showcase its environmental credentials to the world. Through TV advertisements, it ran a Live Green, Live Active campaign, which invited Canadians to submit stories about what they do in their own lives to be active and green. Winners were offered a stint carrying the Olympic torch. To show that the company was serious about the environment, Coke left no stone unturned at Olympic venues. The soft drink was brought in on hybrid electric trucks, stored in coolers and vending machines sporting coolants other than emissions-intensive hydrofluorocarbons (HFCs), and served exclusively in Coke's patented plant-material bottles (which were launched for the event). Just about everything associated with the sponsorship was recycled, Coke's emissions were offset, and it even decked out the cafés in the Olympic Village with furniture made from salvaged trees ruined by extensive damage from pine beetles, a problem that some scientists believe is exacerbated by climate change. The accolades flooded in from governments, environmental groups and the International Olympic Committee. High fives all round at the Coca-Cola marketing department.

Coke is good at using big events to generate a green halo for itself. Arguably no other company takes more conspicuous advantage of Earth Hour. 'As the most recognized brand in the world, The Coca-Cola Company lends its weight to the most important issue facing our planet today', says one senior executive. An important part of Coke's global presence is its iconic neon signs in London's Piccadilly, New York's Broadway and Sydney's Kings Cross. Switching them off for an hour really gets noticed. So, in addition to flicking the switch at offices and bottling plants in over fifty countries, Coke turns off those landmark signs to aid the impression that the company is committed to fighting climate change. Coke has found other ways to create a climate-friendly image through billboards. In 2008, the company announced that its Times Square billboard would now be run on electricity purchased from wind farms. 'We're turning our red billboard green', said the press release, noting that on its own, 'Coca-Cola's pioneering move' would save 376 tonnes of carbon dioxide equivalent. More spectacularly, in 2011 the company unveiled an eighteen-metre square 'living billboard' in Manila. The sign featured 3600 pots made from recycled PET bottles – with a Fukien tea plant in each one. 'This billboard absorbs air pollutants', claimed the sign, and in case there was any doubt, it also read: 'Coca-Cola helps save the planet with WWF'. According to an expert quoted in the company's press statement, the sign would absorb 46,800 pounds of carbon dioxide annually.

When the climate change conference in Copenhagen rolled around in 2009, Coke created yet another whopping billboard, this time as part of the Hopenhagen campaign run by

Ogilvy – the ad agency that helped bring us the Beyond Petroleum campaign for BP. The ostensible aim was to deliver politicians a strong message calling for an ambitious global emissions reduction. However, the campaign's other aim was to make Hopenhagen's sponsors look climate-friendly, and it did that beautifully. Coke seized the moment, releasing a series of posters depicting man and nature living in harmony. Underneath the Hopenhagen heading and the utopian graphics of snow-capped mountains, forests, flowers and butterflies was a Coke bottle with the words 'a bottle of hope'. The tens of thousands of politicians, diplomats, bureaucrats, businesspeople, media, lobbyists and activists arriving at Copenhagen airport walked through doors with this poster on it. In case they missed the message, Coke posted other huge billboards at prominent spots in the city.

Beyond its advertising, the company takes every possible opportunity to make its stance clear: 'Climate change is real and the time to act on solutions is now'. By 2015, Coke says it wants to grow its business without growing its emissions and to cut the absolute level of its emissions by 5 per cent by 2020 (compared with 2004 levels). This talk is backed up by a long list of green initiatives. By the end of 2011, the company says it had put 7 billion of its plant-based bottles into the system, and that the plant bottle would save 100,000 tonnes of carbon dioxide in its first two years. Coke says it now has the largest fleet of hybrid trucks in North America with over 700 vehicles. The company's website offers consumers suggestions about how to cut emissions, from recycling bottles to not buying new clothes so often. And then there's the cuddly stuff: ads featuring polar bears swigging a bottle of Coke, a white Coke can with a mother polar bear and two cubs on the side and a code on the lid that enables consumers to text a donation – adding to the $2 million

Coke has donated – to, you guessed it, WWF's efforts to protect dwindling bear habitats.

Another big focus of Coke's climate-friendly marketing is the machines that keep its products frosty for consumers. In a world where corporations routinely disown the emissions not associated with their direct operations, Coke, to its credit, acknowledges that by far the biggest contribution of its products to climate change is the over 10 million coolers and vending machines it owns with its bottling partners. It has begun a well-promoted program to phase out HFCs from these machines. By mid-2011, the company said it had rolled out 400,000 HFC-free machines, and it says that eliminating HFCs in its coolers should cut emissions from its machines by an incredible 99 per cent – potentially saving 52 million tonnes of carbon over the life of the equipment. For a company whose own operations generate one-tenth of that at most, this sounds mighty impressive. So, when we see a Coke HFC-free cooler ad saying, 'Try me – I'm climate-friendly', it's easy to extend the same tag to the product, the brand and the company.

And yet, we must resist the urge to do so, for once we start peeling Coke's green veneer away we discover a supreme green-washer, whose claims to climate friendliness are riddled with fine print and half-truths. Yes, they've committed to cutting emissions by 5 per cent, but *only* from industrialised countries. In the developing world, which is where the vast majority of Coke's growth is occurring, the target is stabilisation. This might sound reasonable under the circumstances, but it's less reasonable once you appreciate that the target applies only to 'manufacturing emissions', which account for less than one-fifth of the emissions tied up in the product, and not to millions of those cooling machines either.

The company's PR might give you the impression that Coke has that cooler issue sorted. As Coca-Cola's sustainability report says: 'We are also making steady progress against our pledge to have 100 per cent of our cold-drink equipment HFC-free by 2015'. In actual fact, Coke's HFC-free pledge relates only to *new* equipment. So, far from being 100 per cent HFC-free by 2015, Coke is merely promising to stop installing *any more* new equipment with HFCs some time between now and that date. As for the 10 million coolers already out there, at the current replacement rate (around one-fiftieth of the fleet annually) it could take decades before all the HFC coolers are replaced. And if that day finally arrives, don't think for a minute that the HFC-free coolers will actually cut total emissions by 99 per cent. The 99 per cent cut relates only to *direct* emissions of coolers, not to the substantial *indirect* emissions generated from the electricity needed to run them. As for the 52 million tonnes of carbon dioxide that Coca-Cola says its HFC-free coolers will save, those savings are spread over the cooler's long life of ten to fifteen years. Currently Coke's overall cooler fleet is generating around 15 million tonnes of carbon annually, and it is growing because many of those new HFC-free machines are *adding to*, rather than replacing, old ones. Factor in the extra electricity needed to run the larger fleet and an overall increase in emissions is much more likely than a reduction.

Coke's apparent switch to renewables is similarly bogus. The company says vaguely, 'Some of our bottling partners are installing solar panels on their bottling facilities to help reduce energy use and greenhouse gas emissions', and, 'Additional investments are being made in biodiesel and wind power generation technologies, among other initiatives'. But there's scant detail on any of this. The only thing you'll find under the wind power section of Coke's website is that 'red sign going green' in Times Square. The 700 or so hybrid trucks sound great until you find out that the company has a global vehicle fleet of 200,000. The 7 billion plant bottles sound tremendous too, until you realise this is a tiny proportion of what the company sells annually (equivalent to 26.7 billion 24-can *cases*). Even with 7 billion plant bottles in the system, they account for less than one in fifty Coke beverages sold. As for that living billboard in Manila, the impressive-sounding 46,800 pounds of carbon dioxide it saves converts to just over twenty-one tonnes – or less than what two households produce in a year. Coke would need 250,000 such signs just to offset its operational emissions (and a great deal more if you factor in the coolers). Alternatively, it could build a 'living sign' 3750 metres high and twenty-two kilometres wide – as long as Manhattan and over eight times as high as the Empire State Building.

But why would Coke need to greenwash if it is 'committed to growing our business but not our carbon emissions'? Well, to be blunt, the first commitment trumps the second. In 2011, Coke *increased* sales by the equivalent of 28.8 billion cans – if stacked end to end, they would reach six times further than the moon. Coke says 'to measure our growth *potential*, we look to our per capita consumption' and notes that, worldwide, people currently average eighty-nine Coca-Cola branded beverages annually. In India it's currently eleven, and in China it's thirty-four. Imagine Coke's production volumes and emissions if consumption in China and India rises to the global average, let alone the US average of nearly 400 drinks per person? With volumes growing in China at over 40 per cent annually, it's not out of the question, nor is the company's aim to double the size of its business by 2020. However, when you start doing the maths on how Coke can both achieve that and cut its total carbon footprint, there's only one way the numbers stack up: if it carves out the 10 million coolers, focuses on 'manufacturing emissions', limits absolute reductions to developed countries ... oh, and engages in one of the most extensive greenwashing campaigns on Earth. By doing all of this, Coke is offering anything but 'a bottle full of hope'. What it could really do with is a bottle full of reality.

Sadly, Pepsi's not selling a bottle of reality either. As with tasting the difference between Coke and Pepsi, differentiating between Coke and Pepsi's greenwash is just possible, but you need to concentrate. Like Coke, Pepsi likes greening itself through big events – it installed thirty-five green vending machines in Miami to coincide with the Super Bowl. Like Coke, Pepsi disowns the emissions generated by millions of coolers around the world, saying 'PepsiCo provides refrigeration equipment, called coolers or beverage coolers, to our retail partners around the world. Although PepsiCo retains ownership of the cooler, the electricity use for the coolers is the responsibility of the retailer'. Like Coke, Pepsi has released an 'eco-bottle'. Like Coke, Pepsi has hybrid vehicles and isolated instances of renewable energy being used at bottling plants. And, like Coke, Pepsi has impressive-sounding targets with some dastardly fine print.

Pepsi's 25 per cent emissions reduction target, for example, applies only to its US operations and is an intensity target: 'carbon per metric tonne of product'. Like Coke, it has a commitment to lower absolute greenhouse gas emissions worldwide – though, amazingly, Pepsi does not give a year, or even a date range, for when it will achieve this. You'd think that a timeline for this reduction would be a fairly important detail to include in a corporate responsibility report, but Pepsi doesn't. It's not on its website either, not even in the 'Climate change: reduce the carbon foot-print of our operations' section.

Some of its green marketing is similarly brazen. You've prob-ably never heard of Pepsi Green – it's not listed on the company website among its brands, but is available in Thailand. No-one one can quite identify the flavour – perhaps a bit of kiwifruit, some say – but there is no mistaking the drink's bright green col-our or the claim in its advertising that this beverage is somehow climate-friendly. One TV spot shows a young gang with lots of attitude waiting impatiently at the traffic lights amid the groan of angry engines, all with Pepsi Green bottle in hand. The lights change, and the shot pans back to reveal that the gang are on pushbikes. The ad declares, 'Pepsi Green ... Make your green mark!' According to the company, Pepsi Green was marketed specifically to Thai youth because polling research found that over 90 per cent were concerned about environmental degrada-tion. Pepsi says the green branding helps them get closer to their customers and respond to their needs. The company said it expected the product to increase its sales in Thailand by 3 to 5 per cent. Yet, other than the colour, there is nothing 'greener' about Pepsi Green than the dozens of other PepsiCo beverages.

In North America, the greenwash is more sophisticated. At first, with its vague, feel-good 'every Pepsi refreshes the world' slogan, Pepsi Refresh ads look like just another campaign. Instead, they're a competition in which the company makes $20 million dollars available and asks the public to nominate and then vote on worthy projects in half a dozen or so categories, one of which is 'planet'. This enables the company to run ads featuring newly installed energy-efficient light bulbs and solar panels, followed by the words 'So, could a soda really help make the world a better place?' So far around thirty environmental projects have received a slice of the grants – everything from wind turbines at schools to recycling t-shirts into shopping bags. The genius of this approach is that Pepsi doesn't have to do much advertising – the grant applicants are on YouTube promoting their application, seeking the support of the Pepsi voting public and talking up the company. Since these spruiks are by real people rather than a big ad agency, they seem more credible too. What's more, the voting consumers feel empowered. The competition also keeps people focused on whether their favourite environmental project wins rather than on Pepsi's environmental performance.

Pepsi's reason for keeping the environmental focus away from its emissions performance is the same as Coca-Cola's. You won't hear Pepsi talk too loudly about it, but the company acknowledges that its operational emissions are still going up, as are its indirect emissions. In 2011, the company acknowledged that 4.6 million tonnes of emissions were generated by product cooling and vending machines. This estimate suggests that the 4 to 5 million Pepsi coolers reportedly out there generate emissions roughly equivalent to a 1000-megawatt coal-fired power station. And with Pepsi's beverage volumes growing by 10 and 15 per cent respectively in China and India, there are millions more coolers coming. As the company – already growing at 8 to 12 per cent annually – euphemistically puts it, there is 'runway on per capita consumption', meaning there's scope to dramatically raise consumption in developing countries. The open-ended commitment to grow the business without growing emissions masks a rising contribution to climate change, as do Pepsi's targets and its all-important fine print.

The soft drink industry talks as good a game as any on climate change. Compared with their competitors both Coca-Cola and Pepsi are making an effort. Coke is recognised by many prominent environmental organisations from WWF to Greenpeace as one of the most environmentally-friendly companies in the world, and by eco-rating organsations like the Dow Jones Sustainability Index and the FTSE4Good. And that's the great worry. In practice, 'leadership on climate change' doesn't necessarily mean reducing a company's current contribution to the problem – it means being noticeably greener than the competition and being *perceived* to be taking the big steps. It's not that Coke and Pepsi can't take the big steps, but that it makes better commercial sense not to until government policy forces their whole sector to move together. The role of greenwash is to stop these truths bubbling to the surface.

sports

While governments and corporations have been busy procrastinating, professional sport has been leading the way – going a very carbon-neutral shade of green at every opportunity: punching above its weight, batting above the average, knocking down the points, from all over the park ... When America switched on to watch the Super Bowl in 2012, the carbon footprint of the game was offset with renewable energy. Each Olympics once aspired to being declared the 'best games ever', now they're after the 'greenest games ever' tag. From the carbon-neutral X Games in Los Angeles to the carbon-neutral World Rafting Championships in Costa Rica, major sporting events the world over are going green. Some make more sense than others – a carbon-neutral surfing event on Australia's Sunshine Coast seems a pretty natural fit; as does a carbon-neutral marathon in Hartford, Connecticut. But there's seemingly no limit to the sporting world's determination to be climate-friendly. World Rally Championship events are offsetting their carbon footprint, as are Formula 1 racing teams, and IndyCar races. You'll even find Irish professional surfers buying up seedlings in Malaysian rainforests to offset the emissions from the jet-skis that tow them into the big waves.

These moves are positive if a little token and unrepresentative of the sports concerned, but occasionally the grating inconsistency goes beyond the pale: when car commercials dominate the half-time break of the carbon-neutral Super Bowl, when the Red Bull Air Race announces that it's carbon-neutral, or when the Wallabies rugby team goes carbon-neutral in partnership with Qantas and Lexus – just for the World Cup, mind you. What are we to think of the carbon-neutral football World Cup planned for 2022 in Qatar, a country whose economy is built on oil and gas production? This once-off event will save perhaps 2 million tonnes of greenhouse pollution. Meanwhile, Qatar has doubled oil and gas production in the last ten years or so, adding an extra 350 million tonnes of carbon dioxide annually. What should we make of the 2012 London Olympics offsetting its emissions with BP? Or of a BP executive in a slick corporate video, with clips of wind turbines and tree seedlings, explaining how this oil company is going to use the 'technologies of the future' to help green the 2012 games? All this deserves a closer look.

One of the early movers in climate-friendly professional sports was the Cincinnati Reds professional baseball team, which in 2007 held the world's first carbon-neutral major league baseball match. The team obtained carbon credits to cover the electricity and gas use associated with the game – some eighty-seven tonnes. 'The Cincinnati Reds [have] become the first professional sports team to go "carbon-neutral" ... the Reds are giving back to the environment', announced the press release. 'We are excited to participate in eco-friendly projects that expand our mission', said a senior Reds executive of the support that the offsets would provide to a new wind farm in India. The Cincinnati mayor was full of praise: 'Carbon-neutral baseball may not have an effect on the game on the field, but it is a huge step toward protecting our future'.

Whether the fans bought the idea that carbon-neutral baseball was that huge a step, many probably thought that carbon neutrality was about to become as routine as the seventh-innings stretch. However, the world's first carbon-neutral game wasn't really carbon-neutral, because none of the carbon credits associated with tens of thousands of fans coming to the game were offset. The Reds have held more carbon-neutral games occasionally. And to their credit, they've made lots of improvements to their carbon footprint – cutting their electricity use in half by retrofitting lights in everything from exit signs to the scoreboard, among much else. But here's the problem – the Reds' enthusiastic partner in sponsoring carbon-neutral games and giving away energy audits to fans is none other than Duke Energy, America's third-largest carbon dioxide emitter. Every day, Duke emits 2500 times as much as it helped the Reds save on opening day in 2007. And while the Reds are less upbeat about those eco-friendly projects these days, Duke is still out there trying to build new coal-fired power stations. 'This is a great opportunity for Duke Energy to help raise awareness of global climate change in the community', said the company's spokesperson at the time of the Reds' carbon-neutral game. A great opportunity for greenwashing was more like it.

Not to be outdone by baseball, the New Jersey Nets professional basketball team announced soon afterwards that they would become the first carbon-neutral NBA team. A YouTube video featured a perky Nets cheerleader explaining America's disproportionally high contribution to global greenhouse emissions. There was a new 'Nets Go Green' website, and fittingly, the team held the NBA's first ever carbon-neutral game.

The Nets broke new ground by offsetting all fan travel as well as the other emissions associated with the game. 'We have a social responsibility to do our part to combat climate change', said chief executive Brett Yormark, 'but it also makes smart business sense'. What made even smarter business sense was that the Nets weren't dipping into their own pockets to buy the offsets for the game – stepping up to do that was Barclays Bank. According to estimates by the company providing the offsets, the game produced around 407 tonnes of carbon dioxide. At the cost of $8–20 a tonne, carbon neutrality would have cost Barclays and the Nets less than $10,000, which was small beer compared to the $400 million paid by Barclays for naming rights at the Nets' new stadium. The press coverage in the *New York Times* and elsewhere was suitably positive, and the climate-friendly rhetoric from Barclays flowed freely. 'Barclays is aware that, as a global financial services organisation, it has a significant impact on the environment', said the company press release. 'The firm takes this issue seriously and its strategy for reducing this impact is integral to the way it conducts business.' Barclays said it had funded the offsets 'as part of our ongoing commitment to energy efficiency and reducing carbon dioxide emissions'.

What it didn't mention, however, was Barclays' huge stake in fossil fuel extraction. Through what was Barclays Global Investors (acquired in 2009 by BlackRock – the world's largest funds manager), Barclays has consistently invested billions of dollars in coal and oil companies. Barclays emerged from the 2009 deal with 19.7 per cent of BlackRock, which has large shares in ExxonMobil, BP and Chevron. It also owns around 6 per cent of the world's best known coal exporters BHP, Xstrata, Rio Tinto, Anglo and Peabody among many more. The thermal coal produced annually by these companies alone is already producing perhaps 1.6 million times as much carbon dioxide as was offset by the Nets' carbon-neutral game. ExxonMobil's daily oil production wipes out the benefit in just thirty-five seconds. Barclays recently signalled that it wants to sell out from BlackRock – not, mind you, for any environmental reason. Even so, the bank still has significant stakes in other fossil fuel companies, it still spends billions of dollars financing new coal mines and coal-fired power stations, and it still acts on behalf of state-owned coal companies in developing countries that are looking to expand production.

You'd expect that, sooner or later, someone would notice the absurdity of the Nets going green with one of the most carbon-friendly financial institutions in the world – especially if this was to be a long-term commitment to the environment. The Nets' 'Chief Environmental Officer' had, after all, stressed that the carbon-neutral game was no flash in the pan: 'I believe this will be our strategy for years to come ... This is part of who we are'. But no-one appears to have noticed – perhaps because the whole thing fizzled, just as it did in Cincinnati. The Nets kept up the cheerleader climate change video briefings through Green Week in 2009, but there does not appear to have been a single carbon-neutral game since. As of early 2012, the 'Nets Go Green' website is a shadow of its former self. The 'carbon-neutral' tab has gone, as have the 'greener travel' and 'conserving energy' tabs. There's a link to Amtrak and how it can help fans go green, but it looks to be a paid ad.

Aside from that, the sole sad remnant of the Barclays–Nets climate-friendly push appears to be a 'threes for trees' promotion. For every three-point field goal scored by a Nets player, a lawn company plants a tree. In early 2011, after the Nets made 459 three-pointers in that season, 459 maple trees were planted in Brooklyn with the requisite fanfare. Cheerleaders looked more at home with the tree-watering photo opportunity. Gone was the talk of 'reducing carbon dioxide emissions' – now it was all about beautifying the neighbourhood into which the Nets and Barclays were pushing the new stadium. All talk of carbon neutrality was gone, and the closest anyone came to mentioning it was local congressman Ed Towns, who said the initiative would 'go a long way in helping to reduce pollution in our environment'. Not compared to the Nets' overall carbon footprint it wouldn't, let alone that of Barclays and its investments.

The greening of Australian Rules football is another instructive example, involving as it does both the national sport and the greenest-looking major energy company in the country. In 2006, the Australian Football League (AFL) announced that it would become the first carbon-neutral sporting league in Australia and the world. The plan was to offset all of the emissions tied up with the pre-season competition, the regular season and the finals, as well as the greenhouse gases generated by the AFL's headquarters. It would take a few years to achieve, but was said to be equivalent to taking 25,000 cars off the road. The marketing blitz was impressive. Politicians launched the program to an eager press pack, even kicking specially made footballs with an Origin Energy 'Green for Footy' logo. The league set up a broader AFL Green campaign with tips for footy fans to go greener in their own lives. There were green competition rounds featuring green-shirted referees, and in 2010 there was another world-first unlikely to be repeated: a green grand final powered with 200 per cent renewable electricity (that is, the match run on green power was drawn and had to be replayed – a green marketer's dream). Various AFL clubs jumped on the bandwagon, promoting a deal with Origin Energy whereby fans

could get the green football and other goodies, such as free light
bulbs and water bottles. There was a catch, though: you needed
to become an Origin green electricity customer. To sweeten the
deal, the AFL and its teams offset about a tonne of carbon for
each person taking up the offer. A steady stream of media coverage, involving some of the game's biggest stars and most
respected coaches, led more than 35,000 football fans to switch
to Origin GreenPower.

Notwithstanding all the benefits generated by the AFL
going green, there's a legitimate reason to see this as greenwash,
at least from the point of view of Origin Energy. For all its
investments in renewables (it is the largest green energy retailer
in Australia), Origin is still essentially a big fossil fuel company
getting bigger as fast as possible. Nearly half of Origin's power-
generating capacity in Australia is coal-fired, and the company
runs a growing number of gas-fired power stations. Though natural gas–fired power generation is less emissions-intensive than
coal, the emission savings from Origin's gas and renewables are
dwarfed by plans to export coal seam gas as liquefied natural gas
(LNG). Origin has a 37.5 per cent share in the Australia Pacific
LNG project which is currently drilling 10,000 coal seam gas
wells in Queensland to export as much as 18 million tonnes of
LNG a year. Origin's share of the greenhouse pollution generated by this expansion would amount to 25.6 millon tonnes of
carbon dioxide annually. That's roughly eleven times the carbon
footprint of the products Origin currently sells, and each year it
would erase all the emissions saved by Origin's green power sales
since 1999 ten times over. So, although the company boasts more
than half a million GreenPower customers, the carbon footprint
of what Origin produces is still growing. That thousands of AFL
fans signed up for green power is of course a good thing. It's just

a shame that the environmental contribution of the green power they're buying is being erased by the very company selling it – something few of the fans merrily kicking 'Green for Footy' balls in their backyards would know.

The lesson here is not that the world of sport can't contribute in a meaningful way to the fight against climate change. Far from it. Professional sports has an extraordinary reach, and it is probable that athletes, celebrity coaches and even cheerleaders are taken more seriously by billions of people than are politicians or captains of industry. But the example set by professional sports needs to go beyond tokenistic carbon-neutral events; it needs to be about reducing emissions season in, season out; it must be about more than writing a cheque to plant a few trees. As a safe climate depends on reducing fossil fuel use and it also needs to involve credible partners and collaborations. With the right sort of game plan, professional sports can become a serious player.

sweet treats

If you have a sweet tooth, the increasing number of tasty treats being advertised as climate-friendly may present a problem. With carbon-neutral ice-cream makers Ben & Jerry's urging us to 'Lick climate change one scoop at a time', you may be tempted to sacrifice your waistline to save the planet.

Is there a more wholesome, politically correct and comforting brand than Ben & Jerry's? The Cinderella story of the two bearded amateurs from Vermont who turned their home-made ice-cream into a dairy industry icon is legend. From early on, Ben & Jerry's mixed progressive politics and philanthropy with ice-cream just as enthusiastically as it mixed in fudge brownies and cookie dough. From world peace to happy cows, seizing the opportunity to use business as a vehicle for social improvement became as synonymous with the brand as the kaleidoscope of colourful tub labels and flavour names. So it should come as no surprise that Ben & Jerry's seized on climate change with a Lick Global Warming campaign. As Jerry Greenfield put it, 'when we face a problem like global warming, and you understand that the biggest impacts on global warming come from business and industry, I think business needs to take a leading role. Business can be a source of progressive change'.

The brand has made many of the changes you might expect – from tracking its emissions performance to improving energy efficiency and installing renewable energy in its manufacturing plants. It teamed up with Greenpeace to announce a switch from HFC-powered coolers to the less emissions-intensive hydrocarbon coolants. It also neutralised its remaining emissions with 'gold standard' renewable energy offsets – those ticked off by WWF as being the most credible. 'Less wind, more wind-farms', it quipped, referring to its methane 'belchin' bovines' – offsetting all the greenhouse gases meant this wasn't just carbon-neutral, it was 'the world's first climate-neutral ice-cream'. In conjunction with WWF, it even established Ben & Jerry's Climate Change College. For three years, the college educated 'ambassadors' from all over the world on how to get across the need to combat climate change. At the college's UK launch, Greenfield told the *Guardian*, 'Remember these words from two old ice-cream guys: if it's melted, it's ruined'. A new 'Baked Alaska' flavour was released with the 'If it's melted, it's ruined' slogan, and some of the proceeds went to climate change campaigns. It's all been downright wholesome and good – just as you might expect from two home-made ice-cream makers.

Behind all that creamy greenness, however, stands a multinational corporation whose green credentials are not nearly as clear. In 2000, Ben & Jerry's became one of the many dozen brands owned by the massive Unilever corporation. Just like Mövenpick (owned by Nestlé) or Häagen Dazs (owned by General Mills), Ben & Jerry's is a victim of its own success. We might still think of the brand as a down-home, artisan outfit, but in Unilever's hands it is well on the way to becoming just another ubiquitous franchising opportunity, running its scoop-shops (with their emissions-intensive freezers) in dozens of countries around the world and enthusiastically expanding.

What about Unilever? It has no qualms about using Ben & Jerry's credentials to make its brand look more sustainable and ethical – from Forest Stewardship Council–certified ice-cream cups and Fairtrade-certified cocoa to pictures showcasing Ben & Jerry's HFC-free 'Cleaner Greener Freezers' in its glossy Sustainable Living Progress Report. However, while carbon-neutral Ben & Jerry's ice-cream is something Unilever is happy to support, it wouldn't dream of offsetting the rest of its business. And the emissions of Ben & Jerry's pale into insignificance by comparison. As the company boasts, every day 2 billion people – 30 per cent of us – use a Unilever product. The carbon footprint of producing everything from Hellmann's mayonnaise to Lynx deodorant is hefty, and the sales volume is rising fast at nearly 6 per cent a year. Unilever has also been one of the largest consumers of palm oil produced from land illegally cleared of rainforest. Yet the green claims flow freely under the banner of Unilever's 'Cleaner Planet Plan' and a new U-shaped logo made up of fish, birds, bees, flowers, recycle symbols and love-hearts, sometimes presented against a pristine rainforest backdrop.

Among Unilever's claims is an impressive 27 per cent cut in its carbon footprint between 2004 and 2010. The company also points to a 44 per cent *per tonne* fall in emissions between 1995 and 2010. What's given less prominence is that these numbers exclude all of the non-operational emissions associated with Unilever's products – such as destroying rainforests and peatlands in Borneo to produce palm oil, raising cattle and dairy cows, and producing eggs and all the other ingredients purchased to produce the wide range of Unilever products. The company says of its 27 per cent cut, 'this is approximately a 1 per cent reduction against scope 3 emissions [i.e. supply chain and other emissions beyond Unilever's operations]'. This implies that the operational improvements *result* in a 1 per cent reduction in the overall carbon footprint of Unilever products. What it really seems to mean is that the operational savings of nearly 1 million tonnes annually are about 1 per cent of what the supply chain emissions were back in 2004. At the moment the scale of these emissions is anyone's guess. The most recent data released by the company – relating to 2009 – suggested that non-operational emissions are more than *fifty* times operational ones at over 150 million tonnes a year; in 2008 the estimate was 110 million tonnes; in 2007 it was between 120–140 million. With the company's production growing faster than at any time in the past thirty years, it's hard not to wonder whether upstream emissions are rising by much more than the company's operational emissions are falling.

In its latest submission to the Carbon Disclosure Project, the company merely said, 'We don't have any emissions data', flagging an extensive peer review of its performance metrics (including for carbon dioxide), the results of which were to be released in mid-2011. As of mid-2012, the data available is provided in percentage terms or by individual product. There's a slick online product analyser that enables you to work out what percentage of emissions associated with a dose of hair conditioner sold in China come from raw materials, manufacturing and product use. What it doesn't reveal is the total carbon footprint of *all* of Unilever's products. Nor will Unilever reveal this when approached directly. Unilever was asked to clarify all this uncertainty, and its Global Corporate Media Relations Manager promised a response by early June 2012 at the latest – utimately none came. So next time you're tempted to 'Lick climate change one scoop at a time', just keep in mind that you may also be dressing Unilever's window in green one scoop at a time.

If you are so tempted, you may also be susceptible to Climate Change Chocolate. It hails from New Zealand, produced by a company called Bloomsberry whose casual marketing style might well have been modelled on Ben & Jerry's. Bloomsberry has decked out the Climate Change Chocolate website with green wind turbine graphics and the tempting claim that 'reducing your carbon footprint has never tasted so good!' There's a guarantee that each bar of Climate Change Chocolate comes with carbon offsets equivalent to the average person's emissions in one day. According to TerraPass, the company providing the offsets: 'It's a great way to treat yourself while washing away your sins'. And though there are probably healthier ways to achieve the same result, in theory you could erase your entire annual carbon footprint by eating 365 bars of Climate Change Chocolate.

If an environmentally-friendly chocolate bar from New Zealand brings to mind a homespun operation minimising food miles by using local milk from cows raised under snow-capped peaks in the Land of the Long White Cloud, stop right there – Climate Change Chocolate comes all the way from Switzerland. The company doesn't dwell on the food miles that involves – and probably just as well – but it's the least of the problems here. What most people unwrapping a bar of Climate Change Chocolate don't realise is that Bloomsberry makes a chocolate for any occasion. There is Emergency Chocolate for rapid relief of everything from anxiety to lovesickness and exam pressure. If you're worried about wrinkles or crows feet, there's Bochox, designed to look like a prescription drug; and if PMS has got you down, there's the Snappy chocolate bar, which looks like a box of tampons. Worried about global warming? Have some Climate Change Chocolate ... you gullible mug.

Bloomsberry simply uses whichever cause- or gag-related wrapper it thinks will sell more imported Swiss chocolate bars. And herein lies the greenwash: Climate Change Chocolate has helped to propel Bloomsberry's burgeoning expansion into the United States, Europe and a host of 'bizarre and exotic places', as they put it, where they are 'spreading like wildfire'. The green cause has certainly proven profitable for the company – media reports suggest that the company may have sold 80,000 bars of Climate Change Chocolate. But it seems to be the only Bloomsberry product being offset. The company releases no information on the size of its carbon footprint, whether it's rising or falling and what is being offset. When asked for this, Bloomsberry had nothing to say. So, while eating a bar of Climate Change Chocolate might offset some emissions, it inadvertently drives an overall increase by raising the profile of the broader Bloomsberry brand, which helps it to expand. Of course, if it was all a gag like most of Bloomsberry's other chocolate, that'd be fine – the problem is that Bloomsberry wants us to take its carbon offsets seriously. Don't.

At this point, some of you may be thinking that the answer is to hunt down a chocolate company that only does things the green way. That thinking has possibly already led you to the Green & Black's brand. As many chocoholics with an environmental conscience know, Green & Black's sells only organic chocolate; it was the first chocolate to win the Fairtrade badge. One public statement by the company's founder, Craig Sams, initially gives the impression that the chocolate is carbon-neutral too, but it turns out that his remarks were over-paraphrased – he'd been talking about his involvement with Whole Earth corn flakes. Sams confirms 'There is no formal plan for Green & Black's to be carbon-neutral'. Instead he calls the business 'carbon-conscious'. Green & Black's is working with an offsets company, 'planting trees that will, over a several decades time span, soak up the carbon that was emitted in a current year' – something that other companies would seize on to sell 'carbon-neutral chocolate'. But Sams is derisive, saying, 'My view of this approach is that it is like eating breakfast today and then paying for it in forty years' time. Prevention is better than cure'. Hence the focus on being carbon-conscious, by which he means a reduced carbon footprint through organic production: no nitrate fertilisers means less nitrous oxide emissions, no herbicides, fungicides or insecticides avoids the fossil fuel burnt to produce them, and a canopy of shade trees increases the carbon dioxide absorbed on cocoa farms. In Belize, rather than burning tree trimmings, the company is turning them into biochar. It all sounds delicious, but as with Ben & Jerry's ice-cream and Unilever, this independent 'born green' outfit was scoffed down in one gulp by Cadbury in 2005.

In 2007, having fought for years for exclusive rights to use the colour purple, Cadbury announced that it was going green, committing to a range of new climate-friendly initiatives and unveiling a new logo and slogan: 'Purple Goes Green'. Green & Black's fans were no doubt pleased to hear that Cadbury was committing to a 50 per cent reduction in its greenhouse gas emissions by 2020, and that Green & Black's would be run as a separate company. Then in 2010 Cadbury was itself gobbled up by Kraft. Now the cool, carbon-neutral Green & Black's is one tiny brand among 120 at the world's second-biggest food and beverage corporation. If you peruse the list of sweet treats on offer – from Oreos to Fig Newtons, Chocolate Oranges to Chips

Ahoy! cookies, graham crackers to Toblerones – there is much less talk of being 'carbon-conscious'. Still, Kraft has said it will honour Cadbury's pledge to cut emissions by 50 per cent against 2006 levels. It's also been showered in environmental accolades and one of the reasons it's been hailed as a green giant is its claim to have cut carbon dioxide emissions by 18 per cent. So is the multinational that ate the multinational that ate Green & Black's really being carbon-conscious? Or has poor old Green & Black's fallen into a vortex? Let's take a closer look.

As part of its Better World™ campaign, Kraft has a website featuring a rainforest stream, complete with twittering bird sounds, and the claim that 'for more than twenty-five years the company has been addressing sustainability initiatives that help Kraft leave a better world behind'. The words 'Better World' are, naturally, highlighted in green. The company says it's measuring its performance globally to 'see how we're progressing on ... reducing energy-related carbon dioxide emissions'. With the company saying it's 'shown steady progress', it sounds as if these are being reduced. Kraft's return to the Carbon Disclosure Project even claims a small decrease in absolute emissions in 2008–09. It's proof, says Kraft, that it can curb emissions while continuing to grow. Kraft makes it sound so simple: 'we're exploring different ways to save energy generated from fossil fuels ... Some factories are using coffee grounds to generate energy ... We're experimenting with wind turbines on factory roofs ... And we're simply remembering to turn off the lights'.

But it's not so simple at all. In its PR, Kraft makes the blanket claim that, 'we've cut greenhouse gas emissions and energy use ... ↓18 per cent' since 2005. It's not quite what it seems. The company's emissions have in fact risen in recent years, largely because of the acquisition of Cadbury, among others. So the direct operational emissions for which Kraft is responsible are over 11 per cent higher than they were in 2005. Once you factor out these acquisitions, the company has indeed cut the operational emissions of its 'legacy businesses' since 2005 by 28 per cent, and that's a very good result relative to most multinationals. However, it doesn't necessarily mean that the greenhouse gas emissions or energy use associated with Kraft's products is falling. That's because Kraft's impressive claim relates only to the company's own operations. As the company notes, non-operational emissions associated with Kraft products, 'by far account for the largest share of our [carbon dioxide] footprint'.

As with Unilever, it's hard to know whether emissions are rising or falling. Kraft's latest estimate is that in 2010 the emissions of its supply chain, the use of its products and other sources beyond its operations were 37.2 million tonnes. The company claims that this figure has decreased by 5 per cent in a year – from around 39.2 million tonnes in 2009. However, there's justified caution since recent changes in how Kraft measures the emissions of purchased goods and services, transport and product usage also reduced the estimated figure by over 5 per cent, and the result was also influenced by the sale of frozen pizza businesses (think emissions from microwave oven use). There are two other big reasons for caution. First, Kraft's estimate of most non-operational emissions comes with a margin of error of plus or minus more than 30 per cent. Second, Kraft is a growing business whose revenues are rising at over 11 per cent a year and which is rapidly expanding into developing country markets. So, even if the company is making great strides in greening up its operations, the other 92 per cent of the carbon footprint – from growing cocoa to cashews to coffee, transporting it to and from factories, and its subsequent use – is going to be near impossible to rein in.

And yet there is cause for optimism here too. There's no denying the progress being made in-house at Kraft (and at Unilever, for that matter). Kraft *is* being transparent – measuring and sharing estimates of the overall carbon footprint of its products, and being careful to say that these are 'road-testing' estimates, recognising in advance that some large areas of uncertainty are very likely to persist. Best of all, though, Kraft is discussing the non-operational emissions of its products as if it owns them, saying its estimates are being done to help better understand 'our carbon footprint', and with those words in bold, what's more. In a world of big brands disavowing all responsibility for these emissions, that's a breath of fresh air.

All the same, it doesn't mean you can save the planet from climate change one scoop or block at a time – something every sweet tooth probably already knows deep down. You're better off buying one of those little plastic pigs that grunts every time you open the fridge door. Every time it guilts you into closing the door without removing a sweet treat you'll be doing yourself and the planet a favour.

conclusion

From climate-friendly cigarettes to washing powders that promise to help save orangutans, there's much I didn't have space for in *Greenwash*. Even so, we have covered a cross-section of the big companies conspicuously marketing themselves as climate-friendly, to get a picture of whether the green revolution being sold to consumers is genuine. Now that we have the picture, it is disturbingly clear that it isn't – not even close. And if we had space to include more companies, the picture would be the same, only in higher resolution.

After more than a decade of green marketing campaigns in response to public concern about climate change, we might reasonably expect impressive results. Yet almost no major company examined here can credibly say that its overall carbon footprint is getting smaller. For the footprint of a big brand to be shrinking, all the emissions associated with the products it sells need to be shrinking. That's what matters to the atmosphere. Yet as soon as we factor in the emissions that the companies disown, those from the supply chain and use of products, their claims to climate friendliness collapse. As we've seen, for many of the world's big brands – from Kraft to Levi's to Walmart – these emissions often account for 90 per cent or more of their total carbon footprint.

In response, many companies would argue that they should only be responsible for their operational emissions: if everyone takes responsibility for their share, and if everyone in the 'value chain' of a product faces pressure to reduce their carbon footprint, then overall emissions should fall. That's nice in theory, but in practice we see something very different. Typically, a western brand uses raw materials from developing countries, and processes and manufactures its products there too. It then excludes most of the emissions this generates from the carbon footprint it claims publicly. Meanwhile, in the developing countries themselves, few of the big brands' partners publicly claim their share of the emissions, and there's almost no pressure to rein them in.

Similarly, at the other end of the chain, scarcely any companies take responsibility for the emissions generated by product use. Together these disavowals create a misleading impression for consumers and a golden opportunity for corporations. It means they can dramatically expand production volumes to meet increased demand coming largely from the developing world, knowing that the rapidly increasing supply chain and product use emissions can be excluded from their carbon accounts. Better yet, by taking a few relatively small steps – solar panels at company headquarters, hybrid vehicles, light bulb switches or carbon offsets – they may even be able to claim modest reductions in what they define as their carbon footprint. Almost every large 'green' branding effort is based on this game plan. Yet even allowing for this narrow definition, just a handful of the companies examined in *Greenwash* seem likely to achieve overall emissions cuts in the next five years. If this is how badly the 'greenest brands' are performing, we can only assume that the laggards who can't be bothered with a green veneer are doing much worse.

So how do the big brands get away with their carbon scams? Well, the now-familiar tricks of the trade play an important part: slogans and logos, a few green products advertised heavily but made in very small numbers; impressive-sounding emissions intensity targets; boasts about saving tens of millions of tonnes of carbon dioxide versus what would have otherwise occurred (even where this still involves an overall increase); conspicuous renewable energy installations at company headquarters; vocal speeches by the CEO; a glossy sustainability report full of isolated instances of green success stories; enthusiastic participation in coalitions lobbying government to be greener; a voluntary carbon offset program for customers; switching off for Earth Hour.

These greenwashing tools don't run themselves, however. They require an army of carbon accountants, energy-efficiency consultants, polling companies, issues management experts, advertising agencies and PR flacks. Many careers have been built on meeting this demand, such that there is now a greenwash industry with a strong stake in representing its work as part of a genuine business push to combat climate change. Beyond the greenwashers there are many others with a stake: politicians arguing that business is leading the way so government should leave it to them; bureaucrats, investor groups and ratings agencies desperately looking for large green corporations; and environmental groups that have come to rely on the idea of a green revolution as a lucrative source of donations.

Regrettably, the profitable path of least resistance for almost everyone involved is to continue greenwashing. Yet if the science is right, this is a very dangerous path indeed, and now is not the time to delude ourselves that great progress is being achieved. Instead, it's time for a rethink, by all those

involved in what has become the greenwash industry, by governments and by consumers.

For the advertising industry and PR consultants, it's time
to ask whether the work that many of them believe is positive
for the planet is actually being used to greenwash brands.
Advertisers and PR firms cannot bask in the green glow they've
created for one brand, while expecting no-one to notice the
hypocrisy of their work for some of the world's dirtiest companies. Those in the business of ranking green companies also
need to reflect. Almost every 'climate-friendly' brand we found
to have increasing emissions has been ranked highly on the
Dow Jones Sustainability Index, the FTSE4Good, Climate
Counts or *Newsweek*'s green rankings. It's emblematic of the
current situation that BP was on both the FTSE4Good and
Dow Jones Sustainability indexes when the Horizon oil spill
occurred, and that since the spill, Halliburton – another core
participant in the disaster and one of the largest contractors to
the oil, gas and tar sands industries – has been declared a Dow
Jones Sustainability Index 'World Leader'. The awards themselves have become yet another greenwashing tool.

For environmental groups that coin slogans such as 'The
clean revolution is underway' and 'The (sustainable) revolution
will be branded', it's time to reconsider whether cheering on the
revolution, however fake, will somehow make it real. Many of
the worst offenders we've looked at have been lauded by or even
collaborated with WWF, Conservation International, the
Climate Group or other prominent environmental groups.
Often this relationship involves significant sums of money
changing hands, and, in a surprising number of cases, it also
involves senior corporate leaders sitting on the boards of the
environmental groups concerned.

So we see the Climate Group promoting the climate friendliness of partners such as Coca-Cola, Dell, Duke, HSBC, Origin and News Corp, and we see WWF calling IBM, Coca-Cola and Sony 'Climate Savers'. We see Walmart's chairman chairing the executive committee of Conservation International, and we see Unilever's CEO and the retired CEO of Starbucks on its board. What we don't see are the greenwashing problems of these companies being so much as raised by their environmental partners. A conspicuous collaboration with WWF, Conservation International and a few others has become one of the boxes to tick en route to a climate-friendly image. As the Conservation International whistleblower Christine MacDonald highlighted in *Green, Inc.*, groups like this are becoming satellite PR offices for their corporate donor base. It's something that needs to change.

For governments, it's time for a reality check. Faith in business leadership on climate change has become a convenient excuse for avoiding regulation. Yet, as *Greenwash* highlights, the reality is that companies will not step far ahead of the pack while their competitors can get away with standing still. So we are drifting towards a dangerous and expensive adaptation to the more extreme climate change impact scenarios with political hopes pinned on an advertised revolution that we now know is false and an agreement to negotiate a new global deal by 2015 that will begin in 2020. In short, governments worldwide are preparing to squander *the* decade during which, according to scientists, emissions would need to start falling to have any reasonable chance of limiting the worst effects of climate change. Over that same decade, coal use looks set to increase by one-third or more, with no prospect of carbon capture and storage on any meaningful scale, along with massive growth in other emissions-intensive fossil fuels such as tar sands. Renewable energy use is expanding impressively in percentage terms, energy efficiency continues to save emissions, and tree planting and other bio options offer many potential savings too, but the benefits pale in comparison to the continuing growth in fossil fuel use. Governments need to stop kidding themselves (and the public) that they are taking the big steps required to return the climate to safe territory, and start actually taking them.

It's obviously time for a rethink by the greenwashing companies themselves. Sooner or later companies will be held accountable for more of their supply chain and product use emissions. Scrutiny is coming not only in books such as this one, but from large investors looking to properly understand the carbon liabilities of large corporations. Hence, the increasing focus of the Carbon Disclosure Project on supply chains and other indirect emissions, much to the chagrin of many of the brands examined here. Eventually the greenwash veil will be lifted. Some big brands such as Kraft, Walmart and UPS, with their focus on supply chain emissions, or Panasonic, with its emphasis on product use emissions, are bravely dipping a toe in this water. It's cold and uncomfortable, but the longer companies hold out, the harder it gets.

Lastly, it's time for a rethink by consumers. We can't shop the planet green, no matter how much we might want to believe it. The savings from the relatively small number of green products being sold are swamped by production growth due to dramatic increases in sales volumes. As we've seen, while Toyota has sold 4 million hybrids over fifteen years, it sells 3.5 million more cars a year than it did back then, and its SUV and truck sales still outnumber hybrid sales by nearly three to one. This pattern is replicated in almost every industry. So, we won't make the world a 'better place' by buying Adidas shoes any more than we'll make it a 'better world' by buying Nike instead. We can't 'fight global warming one cup at a time', or one 'EcoAd', and we can't 'lick climate change' by buying ice-cream. We aren't making the world a better place 'one Subway sandwich at a time', nor 'one Pepsi at a time', nor 'one pet at a time', nor 'one trip at a time'. We're deluding ourselves if we think we are.

Most of us living in developed countries have only the vaguest idea of the size of our individual carbon footprint. Any idea we do have is likely based on per capita emissions in the country where we live (ranging from around eight to twenty-eight tonnes per year). In some cases, we might have gone to the trouble of using a carbon calculator to get a more accurate estimate. Yet, embedded in the measures we might use are the same tricks used by greenwashers. That is, a large chunk of these emissions are accrued not by us, and not by our countries, but by the developing countries where the products are commonly sourced, processed and manufactured.

From the cars we drive to the iPhones we use to tell people about the cars, from the food we eat to the appliances we use to keep it cool, a personal plume of invisible greenhouse pollution extends largely offshore, and is largely unclaimed by us. We are all using the developing world as a carbon waste dump much more than we acknowledge. And while rising population and affluence in these countries is driving emissions growth, so too is consumption in developed countries. None of this means that we should stop buying – or stop buying the greener product – but it does mean we need to be realistic about the brand behind the products, and about the impact that our purchases make.

It would be wrong to think that the companies whose greenwash dominates these pages are the least climate-friendly. As their long list of green awards suggests, many companies discussed here are among the better performers. Some have made real progress on a range of environmental fronts, and many are offering consumers products and services far less emissions-intensive than was the case a few years ago. What this progress hides, however, is the widening gap between what is occurring and what the global scientific community is telling us must be done. This is what *Greenwash* has highlighted – the gulf between the green revolution being advertised and the progress actually occurring

There's no easy fix here. I'm too realistic about the power of the inertia and the politics of stopping it to foist a grand manifesto or fairytale ending upon you. What is clear, though, is that we won't have a genuine clean energy revolution while a fake one is being so successfully sold. Comforting as it might be, the idea of a consumer-led revolution must be exposed for the pipe dream it is. Shopping the planet green will not get us where we need to go fast enough. What is more feasible is a consumer-led revolt against greenwash – one that demands much better from corporations while there is still time. We all have opportunities to help expose greenwash – whether it's speaking up at a shareholder meeting, supporting the work of culture-jamming activists, or using social media to call companies out for their hypocrisy. Even if we don't do these things personally, we can help those that do. We can also learn to look behind the marketing and contribute more effectively with our wallets, and if we tell those around us what we've learnt, we can magnify our impact. We must seize these opportunities and stand up to greenwash if we want a reality more like the revolution being advertised.

If I never see a greenwashed piece of marketing again, that'll be just great – but if having read *Greenwash* you fall for fewer of them, that'll be even better.

your pocket guide to greenwashing

Congratulations on winning your dream job as Global Head of Sustainability at _____ Corporation. Welcome to the dark side.

We love your passion about the environment. We're passionate about it too, in spite of what you may have heard or the recent controversies in which the company has been involved. We pride ourselves on being a sustainable company and we know climate change is the number one issue. We're absolutely committed to helping the world tackle this problem, and we're committed to providing consumers with climate-friendly alternatives. As we provide them, we intend to become an even more climate-friendly brand.

Now that you're on board, please don't waste time reinventing the wheel. Whatever business you're in, the template for running a climate-friendly brand is the same. What follows is the 18-step plan that many Fortune 500 companies swear by. At _____ Corporation it's fair to say we're playing catch-up, but follow this template and I look forward to us joining the top ranks of the global business leaders on

climate change very soon. Forget that bland official job description we gave you – this is the real one:

- Rejig the company logo: lots of green, a leaf or
  something sunny, a windmill, perhaps – and weave in
  the recycle symbol if you can. While you're waiting for
  the right logo, just paint the one we have green.

- Come up with a marketing slogan and take out a
  trademark. (This may take longer than you expect,
  since most using the word 'green' are already taken.)

- Get one of our senior executives on the board of a
  friendly 'independent' environment group. Flicking it
  some cash will help. Don't worry, we're not buying a
  green stamp of approval. We're merely joining their
  Leaders Program.

- Have me issue a new mission statement declaring in
  bold terms how the company is turning over a big
  new green leaf. If possible have this coincide with a
  launch of our greenest product and conscript a
  celebrity for the launch.

- Get some visible things happening on site – a few
  hybrid vehicles or solar panels, say – then publicise
  them well. But not too much detail – the ribbon-
  cutting ceremony pics will do nicely – as we don't
  want people overthinking things.

- Open a pilot store showcasing green technologies
  and get it LEED-certified. One store will do, so long
  as we issue enough press releases. Mention the
  'eco-store' as much as possible in corporate social
  responsibility reports, brochures, on the website, in
  interviews and my speeches.

- Make a corporate video on the eco-store and other green initiatives, and post it on YouTube or Vimeo. Include interviews with our suppliers, with grabs of them saying how our company 'gets the environment'. (They know what will happen if they refuse.)
- Introduce a voluntary scheme enabling our customers to offset their business with us – that way, we don't have to.
- Start a new green website and invite people to 'chat', to be part of a dialogue between the company and the public. Include a company blog so we can broadcast our side of the story, but be sure to run a competition that asks for ideas on how we can be a greener company – this will help us look really interested. Set up some accounting software to let members of the public calculate their carbon footprint. Include some tips to help them green up their lifestyles.
- Switch off for Earth Hour. Hold some well-publicised events in the dark, and try to get a quote from WWF patting us on the back.
- Set up a company 'Green Team' and have them set up a Facebook page. Make sure they keep it fresh – lots of upbeat talk about our environmental leadership. Looking spontaneous, voluntary and enthusiastic is mandatory.
- Give pro bono help to some environmental organisations. It must be visible enough that people think better of our company, but nothing likely to draw uncomfortable attention to our core business: stick to student groups, tree-planting charities and anti-litter campaigns etc.

- Now, the pointy end: emission targets and timetables. This is dangerous territory since the company is growing at a cracking pace. First, measure our emissions. Odds are that while they are rising overall, there has been an impressive fall in emissions per unit of output due to energy-efficiency improvements happening anyway. Promote this as proof that we are reducing our emissions.
- Next, set an ambitious-sounding emissions-intensity target – cutting emissions per unit of output by a percentage similar to the ones being demanded of governments – say, 20 to 30 per cent over the next decade. The business-as-usual improvements in energy efficiency will get us most of the way there, and a few other small changes should do the trick.
- If you must talk about total emissions, and commit to an absolute target, use 2007 as your baseline year. The economy was booming at the time, so it's likely our emissions were too. This buys us a few years of breathing space.
- Unless it helps, ignore emissions from the products and services we purchase, and the use and disposal of sold products. Repeat after me: they're someone else's problem, not ours.
- Collect as many environmental awards and stamps of approval as you can. Most don't require companies to be reducing their overall carbon footprint to win recognition. ISO environmental management standards, *Newsweek* green rankings, the Dow Jones Sustainability Index, FTSE4Good – you name it.

- Hire more consultants to assemble a thick collection of green good news stories from around the company.

If the whole thing sounds a bit inauthentic, don't worry – we can buy 'authentic' by making some hippie and their 'born green' brand an offer they can't refuse.

One last tip that may help you survive – it's only greenwash if you believe it is.

Don't blow it ...

Chief Executive,
Fortune 500 Company

acknowledgements

I want to begin by acknowledging Black Inc.'s Morry Schwartz for meaning it when he said: 'So, you're going to do your next book with us'. This was quite the tonic at the time. I'm very grateful to Chris Feik for commissioning *Greenwash*, and for his deft editing touch, astute questions and sensible advice. The same goes for his trusty and insightful offsider, Nikola Lusk. Thanks to Sophy Williams for guiding me toward the unfamiliar world of international publishing, and to Elisabeth Young (in advance) for the publicity side that I've predictably neglected until the last minute. My agent Tara Wynne believed in this book idea from early on – I'm grateful that she encouraged me to persevere.

Next I want to thank the University of Queensland for supporting my research via a fellowship at the Global Change Institute. Specifically I want to thank Professor Ove Hoegh-Guldberg, the Director of the GCI, for his unswerving commitment to an effective climate change response, and to intellectual freedom. Thanks to Graham Readfearn for parachuting in late to help me to negotiate the mountain of fact-checks. Best endeavours notwithstanding, a few errors have probably found their way into these pages. They're all mine, and hopefully all minor. I'll post any necessary corrections and clarifications in the book's online references, which will be at www.guypearse.com.

Without naming names, I want to acknowledge that senior staff at numerous companies covered here took the time to speak or correspond with me about the minutiae of their companies' carbon footprints. I appreciate their candour. I'm also grateful to the Carbon Disclosure Project for granting me access to corporate returns as required.

Last, I want to pay tribute to my family for their steadfast support. They repeatedly made unreasonably large sacrifices to accommodate this unreasonably ambitious venture. So they deserve much of any credit due, but none of the blame. As my dad thumbed through the final draft he sagely and fairly observed, 'Of course we all do partake in these things, you know'. Spot on, and hence the book.

index

index

index

index

index